A Celebration of Western New York

There's So Much To Love

Writing by Mark Donnelly, PhD.

Photography by Mark Donnelly & Friends

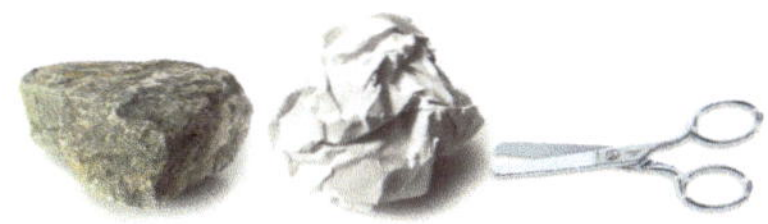

RPSS Publishing • Buffalo, New York
www.rpsspublishing.com

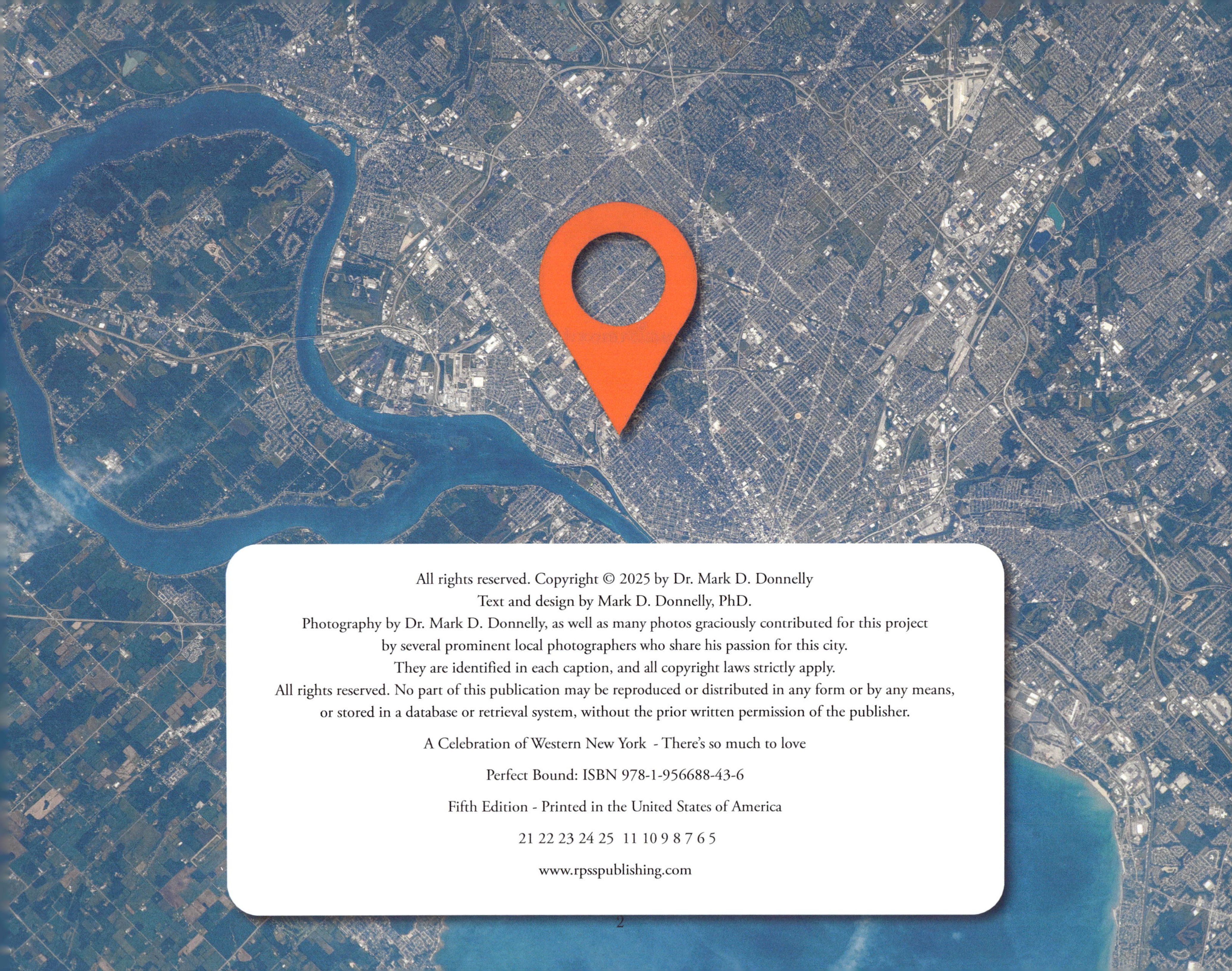

All rights reserved. Copyright © 2025 by Dr. Mark D. Donnelly

Text and design by Mark D. Donnelly, PhD.

Photography by Dr. Mark D. Donnelly, as well as many photos graciously contributed for this project by several prominent local photographers who share his passion for this city.

They are identified in each caption, and all copyright laws strictly apply.

All rights reserved. No part of this publication may be reproduced or distributed in any form or by any means, or stored in a database or retrieval system, without the prior written permission of the publisher.

A Celebration of Western New York - There's so much to love

Perfect Bound: ISBN 978-1-956688-43-6

Fifth Edition - Printed in the United States of America

21 22 23 24 25 11 10 9 8 7 6 5

www.rpsspublishing.com

Western New York is a place of endless discovery

On the cover:
View from Serendipty Labs, *Seneca One Tower, 29th Floor*

Opposite:
We are all right here, *waiting to give you a giant Western New York hug. If it were counted as a single area, the population of Western New York would number just over 2.6 million, and would rank as the 24th largest metropolitan area of the United States.*

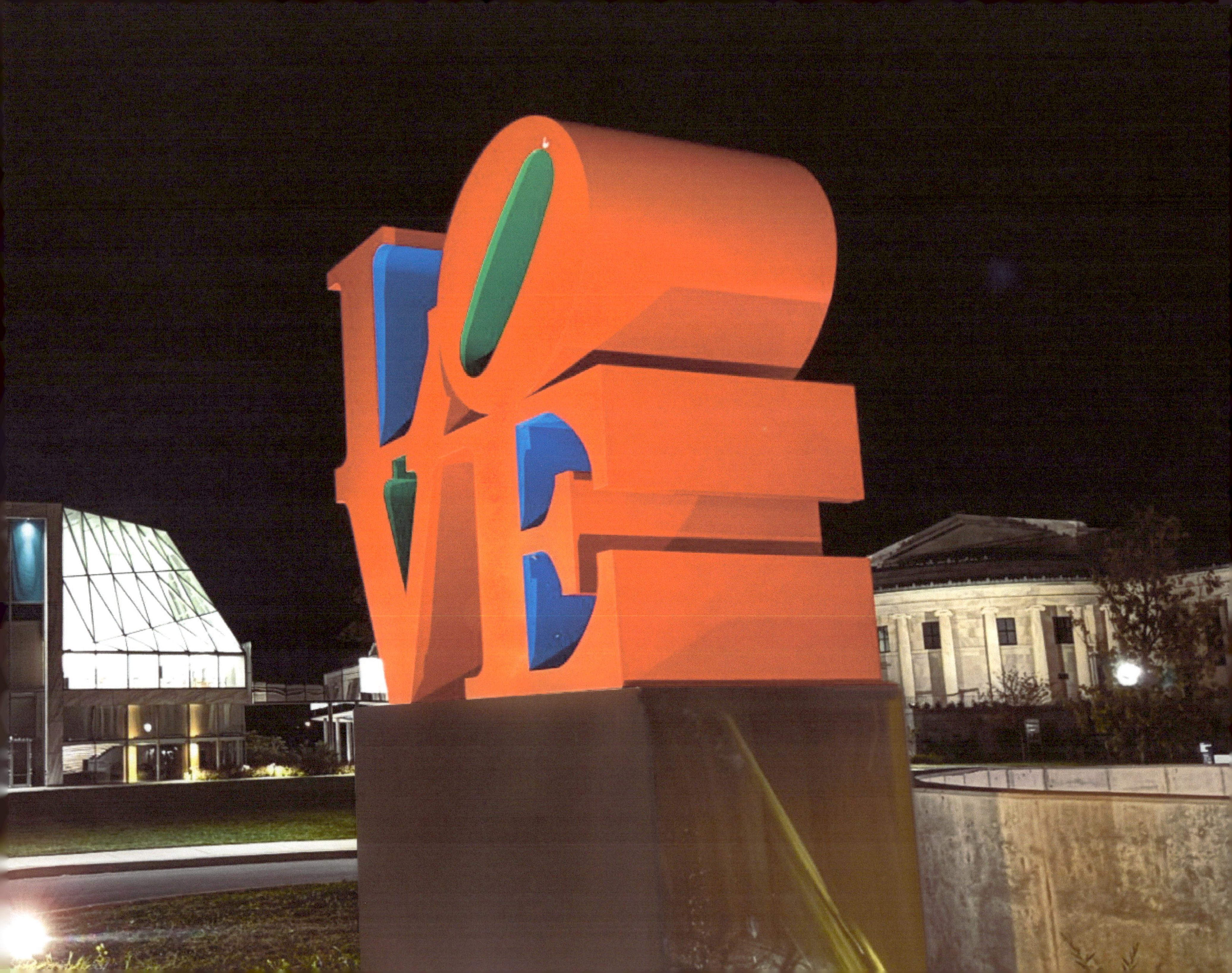
LO
VE

There's so much to love

"Western New York is a place of endless discovery. Right about the time you think you've grasped the abundance of joy this region has to give, something new unfolds and totally blows your mind."

Here in Western New York, it's hard to look around and not be awestruck by our vast wealth of arts, heritage, and special character of place. This region is home to a mind-boggling array of beautiful parks and gardens, cultural activities, a vibrant waterfront, architectural treasures, and dozens of remarkable neighborhoods, each with a unique pulse, spirit, and personality.

A walk down the street is often a walk through our rich history. And there is a sensory overload of fairs, festivals, galleries, concerts, sports, and other unique activities for everyone to get their heads and hearts around.

Please visit these places, frolic in our spectacular four seasons, and fall deeply in love with our city and region over and over again.

Opposite: Buffalo skyline.

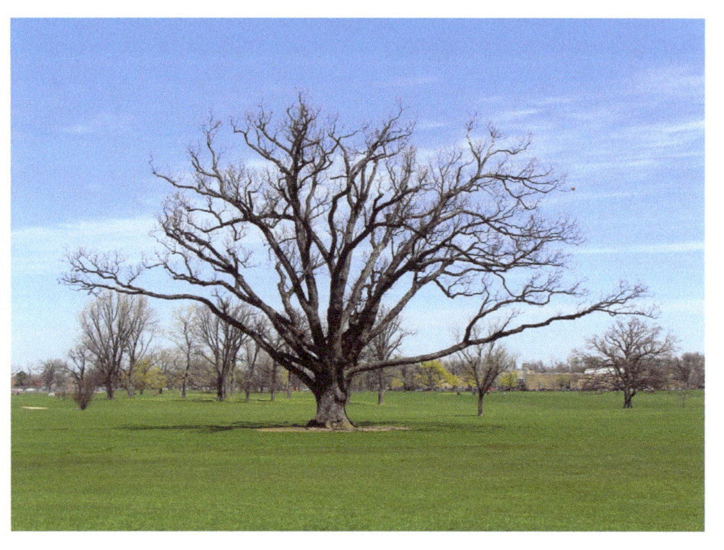
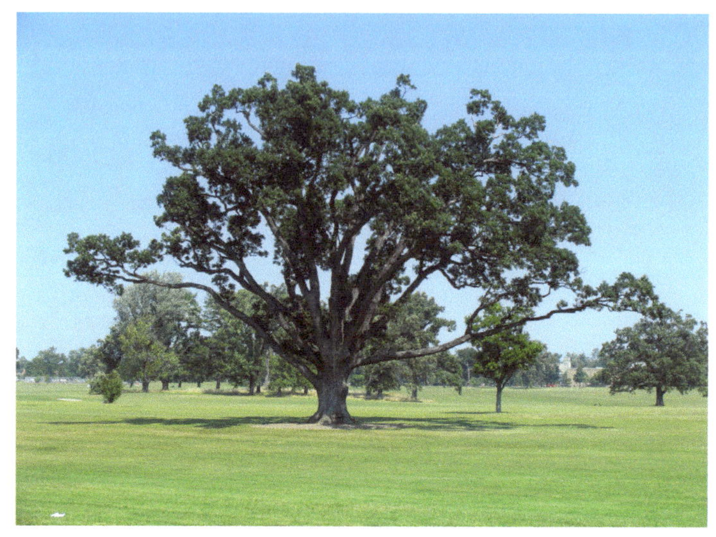
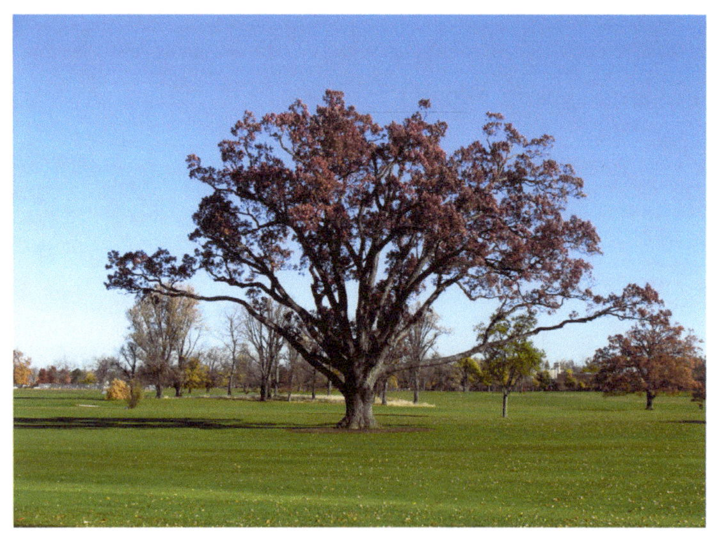
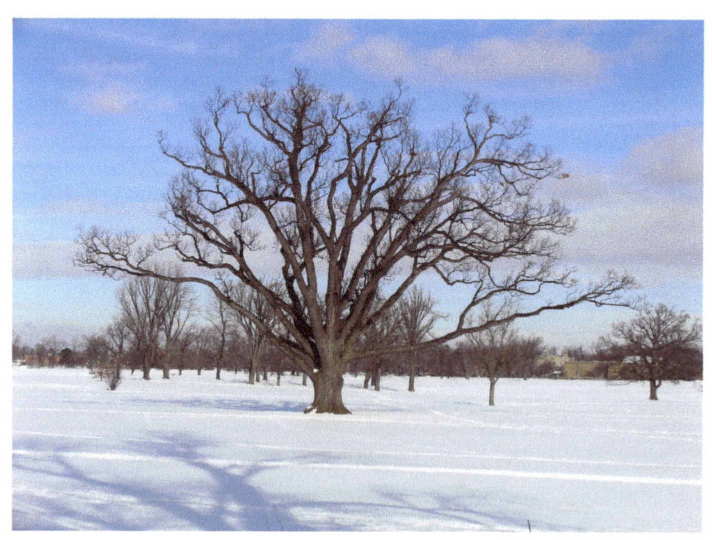

Blessed with Four Seasons

While Buffalo is famous for its snow, if you dig a little deeper you'll discover that our region enjoys four distinct seasons - Winter, Spring, Summer, and Football, each remarkable in its own right.

Here in Western New York, we enjoy four very spectacular seasons, each with a distinctive tone and character. Real estate professionals have an explanation for this – location, location, location.

Tucked in between two of the world's largest freshwater lakes, it's here that we grow the grapes that make our NY State wines so famous. It's also here that we maintain a full range of ways to frolic – in the sand, in the leaves, in the snow, and beside the tulips.

While our weather diversity may play havoc on your closet space by necessitating the storage of everything from flip-flops to ugly sweaters, it never truly reaches the extremes of many other cities. We lack days that exceed 99 degrees, tornadoes, mudslides, hurricanes, dust storms, and tsunamis, so at the end of the day, we always know where our houses are. According to the National Weather Service data, we are far from thesnowiest, blowiest, or coldest American city.

In fact, when even our worst weather disasters are finished, we get to play in them.

Opposite: A Great Oak stands in Delaware Park proudly showing off its love for the changing of our seasons, just like it has nearly 300 times before. © Photos by Jackie Albarella

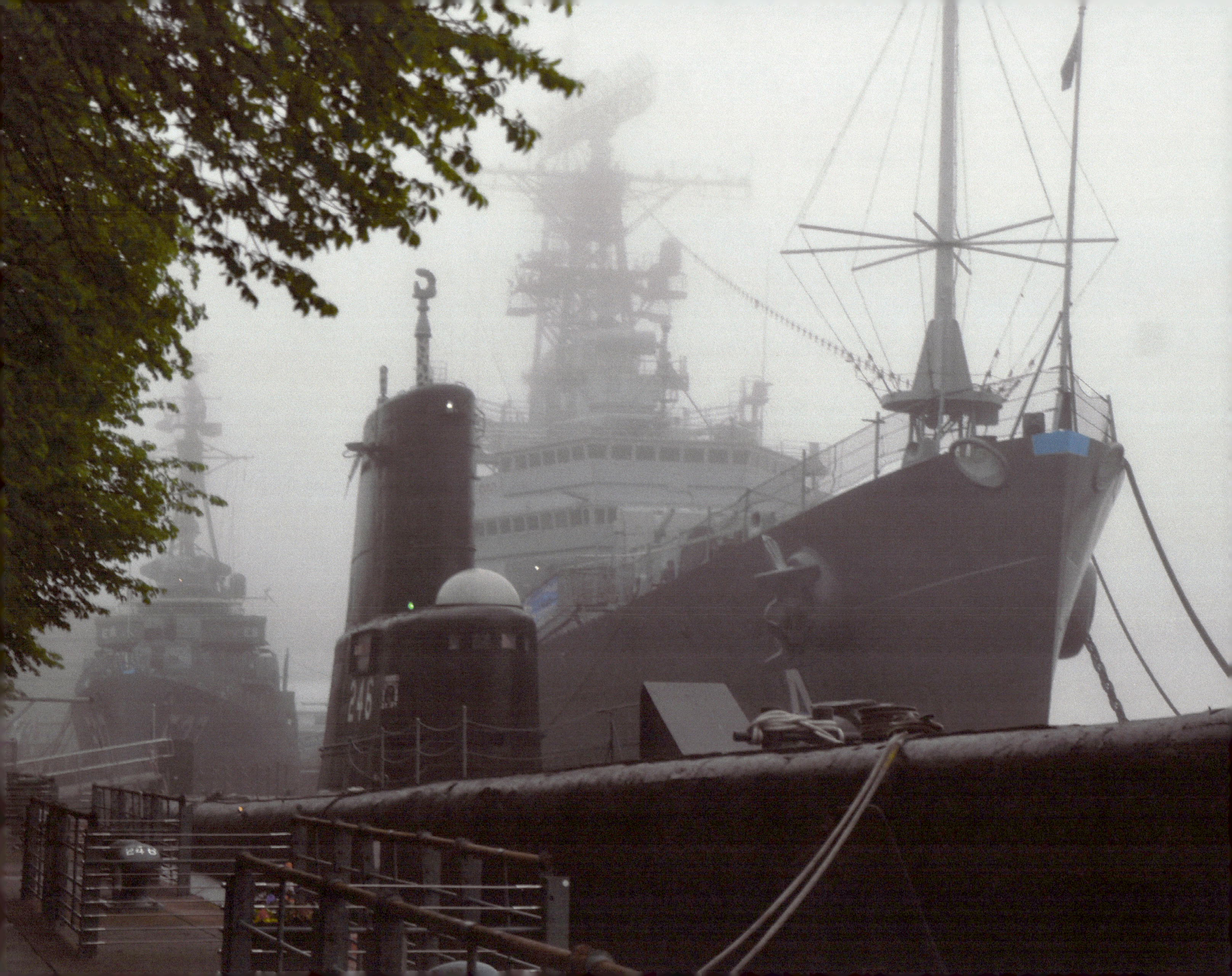
246

Our Rich History

"History, by connecting us to our past and to our community, helps us to understand our present, and provides us lessons to guide us towards our future."

In Western New York, history has never been a spectator sport. The narrative of the Underground Railroad, Women's Rights, the Chautauqua Movement, the Niagara Movement, the Arts and Crafts Movement, the War of 1812, a presidential assassination, and the development of modern architecture were all forged, in no small part, right here in our backyard.

Fortunes were made by William G. Fargo, founder of American Express and Wells Fargo. Jazz legends like Louis Armstrong jammed at our Colored Musicians Club. And American presidents lived, governed, died, and were buried here.

The city's position at the western terminus of the Erie Canal made us the "Gateway to the West" – the departure point for immigrants on their way to the heartland. Today, this area has been newly revived at Canalside.

Buffalo was also a gateway for runaway slaves seeking freedom on the Underground Railroad, then later fertile ground for the Civil Rights Movement.

In short, it's all too easy in Western New York to walk on the same ground where history vastly changed the world.

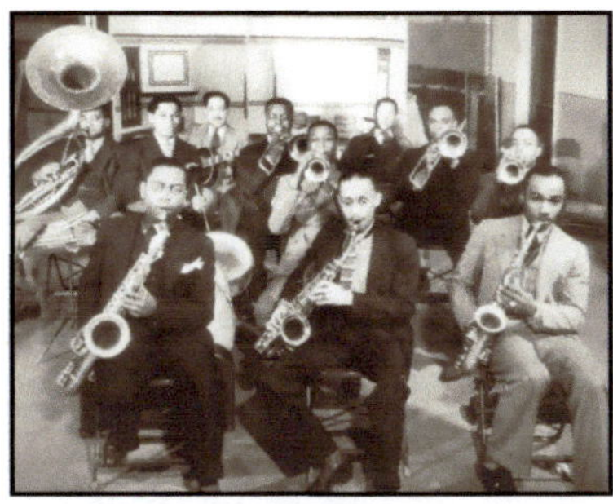

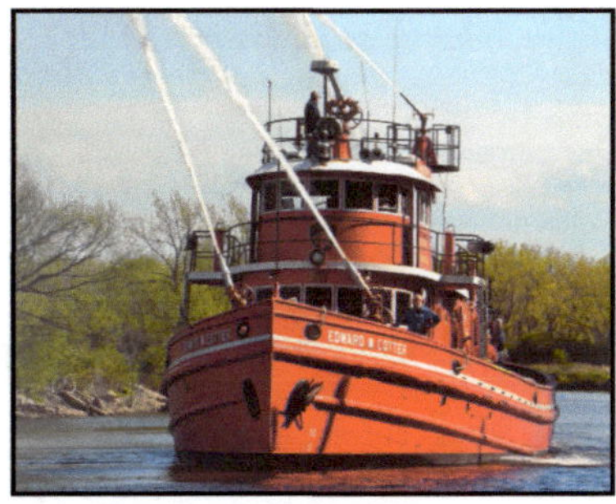

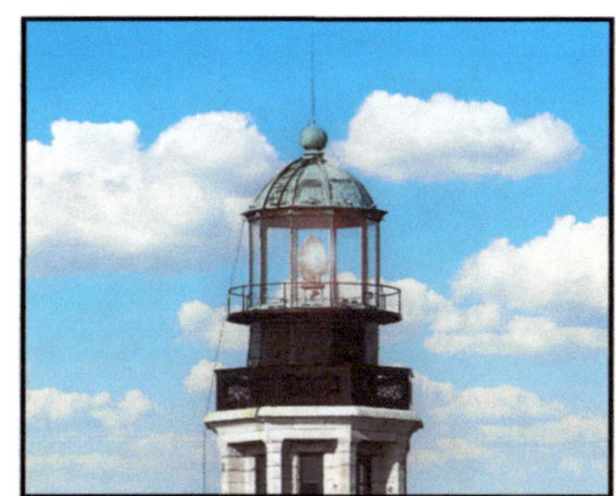

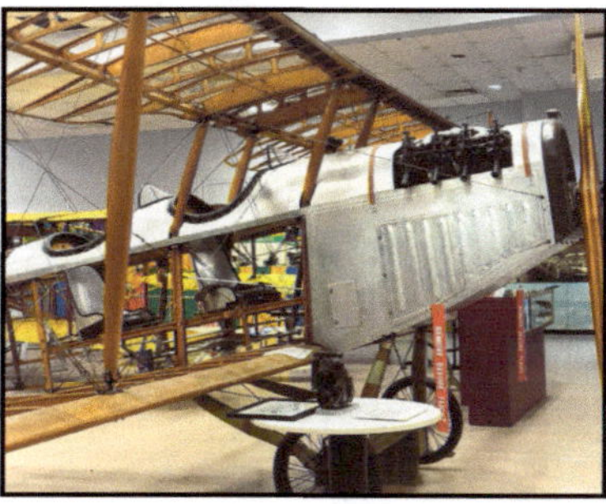

(Opposite:) The Buffalo and Erie County Naval & Military Park is home to several decommissioned US Naval vessels, including the Cleveland-class cruiser USS Little Rock, the Fletcher-class destroyer USS The Sullivans, and the submarine USS Croaker.

(Left to right:) The Colored Musicians Club. Over the last century, the Club has had many internationally known jazz greats walk through the door.
- Buffalo's historic Edward M. Cotter is the world's oldest working fireboat,
- The Buffalo Main Light, built in 1820. It is now part of an outdoor museum operated by the Buffalo Lighthouse Association.
- This 1910 Curtiss Pusher replica housed at the Niagara Aerospace Museum.

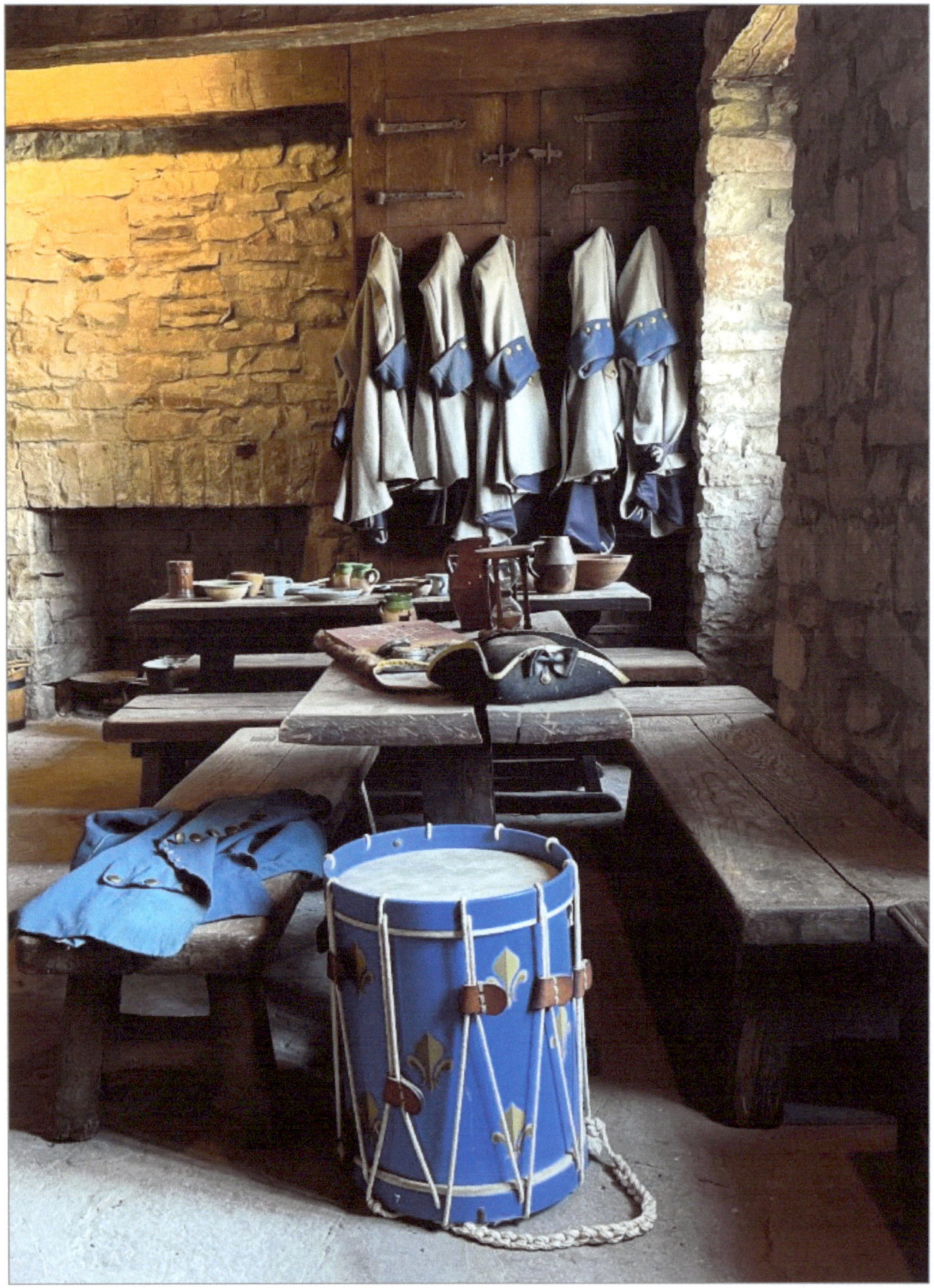

War of 1812 | Old Fort Niagara

The War of 1812 is a poignant reminder that war can happen as close as your backyard. Much of that fighting occurred right along the U.S. and Canadian border.

The history of Old Fort Niagara spans more than 300 years. During the colonial wars in North America, a fort at the mouth of the Niagara River was vital, for it controlled access to the Great Lakes and the westward route to the continent's heartland. With the completion of the Erie Canal in 1825, however, the strategic value of Fort Niagara diminished. It nonetheless remained an active military post well into the 20th century.

The fort has been occupied by France, Great Britain, and the United States. A visit to this historic and scenic site will transport you back in time as costumed interpreters and reenactors reveal the stories behind this legendary stronghold.

(Opposite:) Visitors to the fort will see the oldest buildings in the Great Lakes region, living history programs, exhibits, and special events. The French established the first post in 1679 and built the impressive "French Castle" in 1726.

(Below:) Reenactment of The Battle of Queenston Heights, the first major battle in the War of 1812.

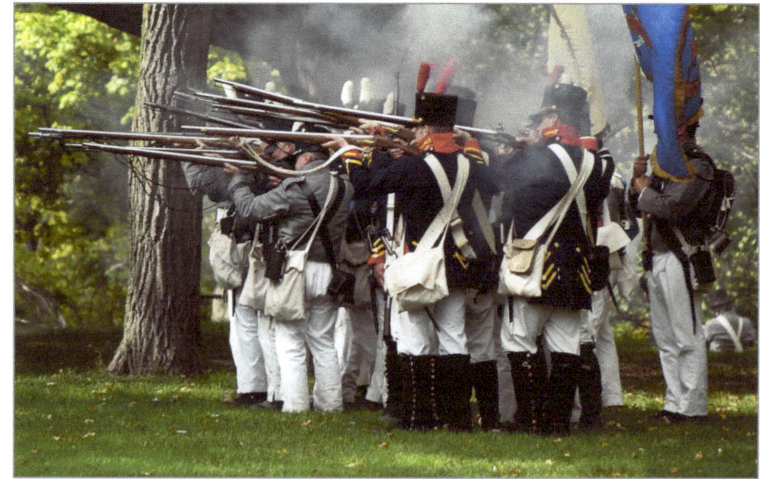

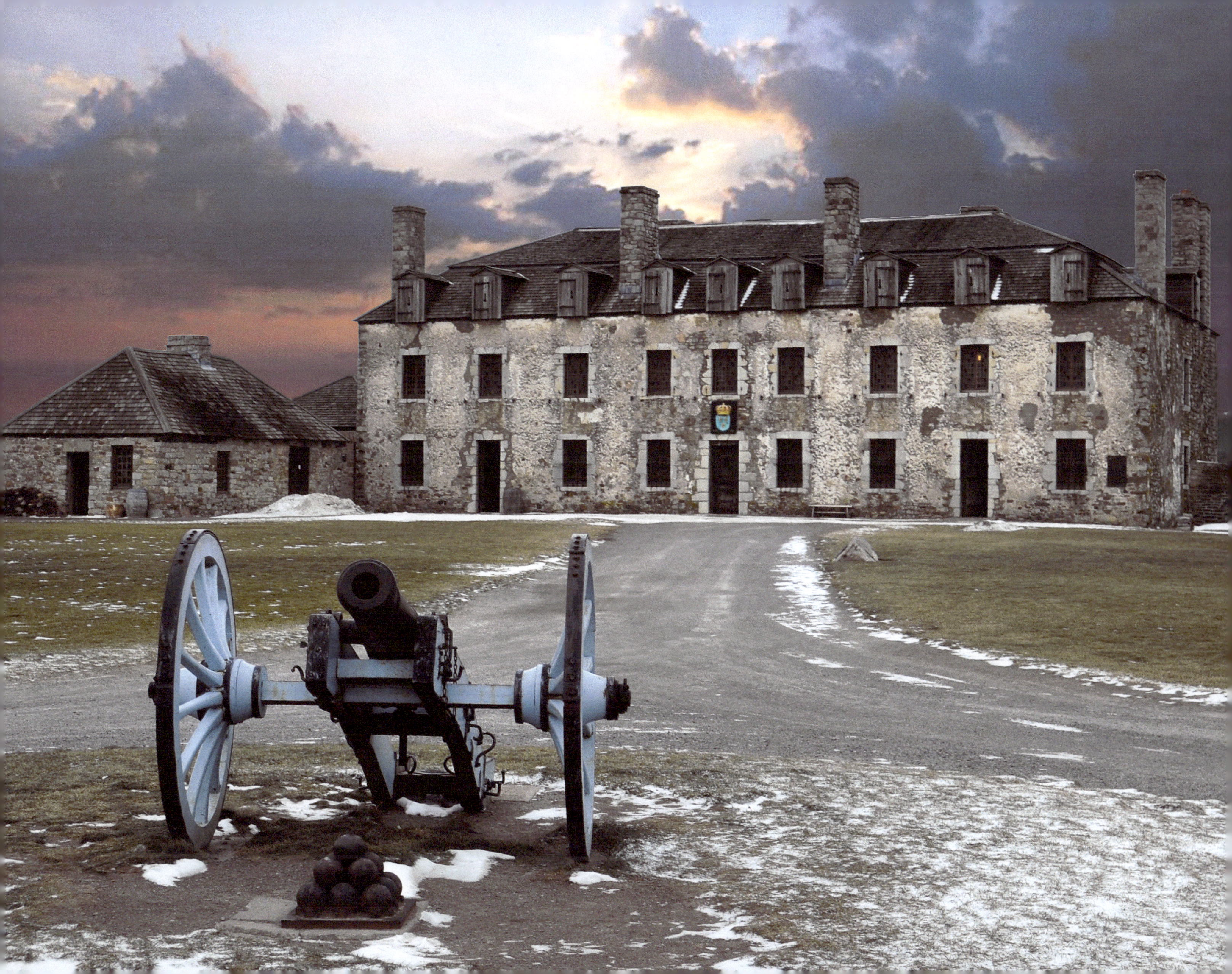

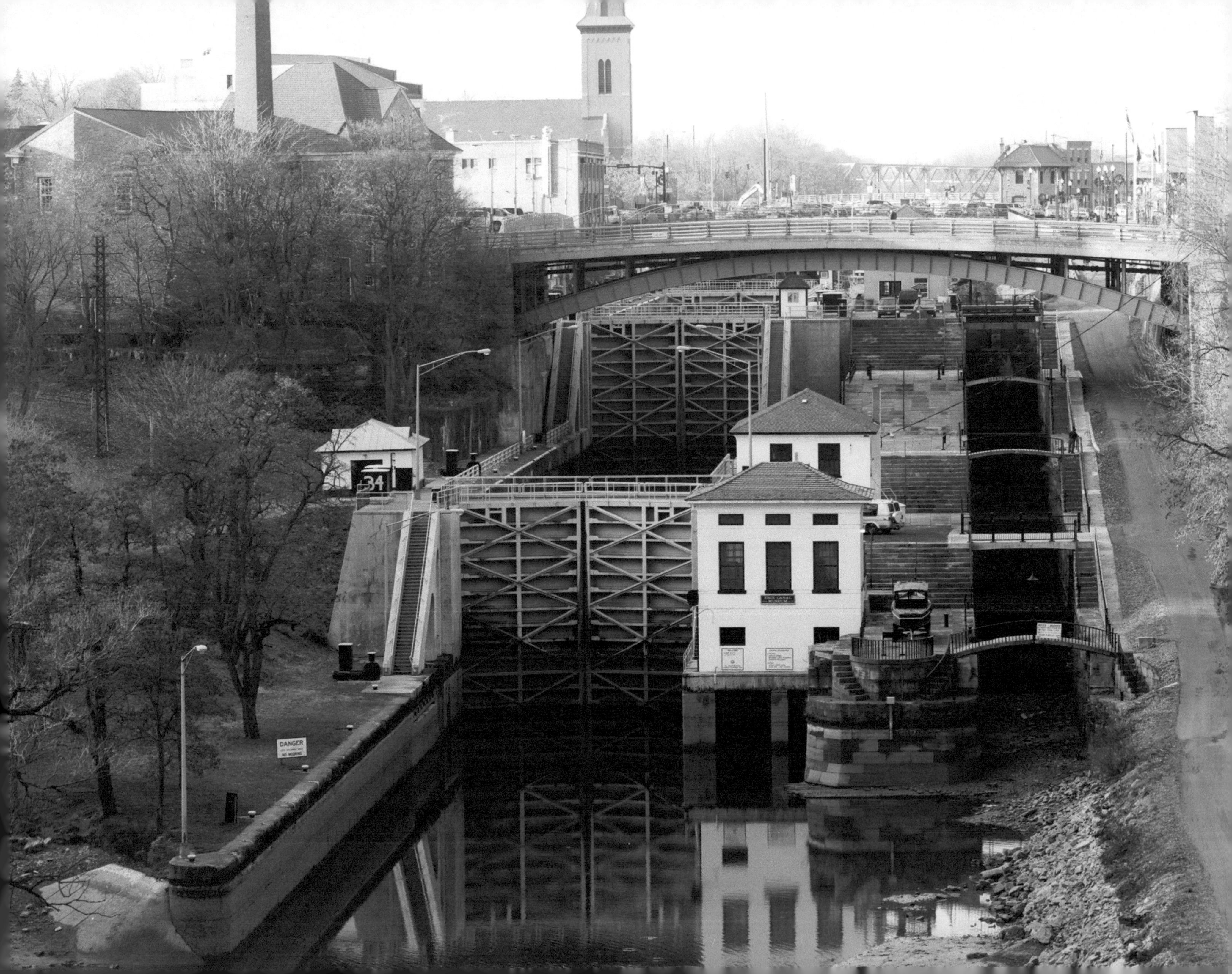
34
DANGER
NO MOORING
ERIE CANAL

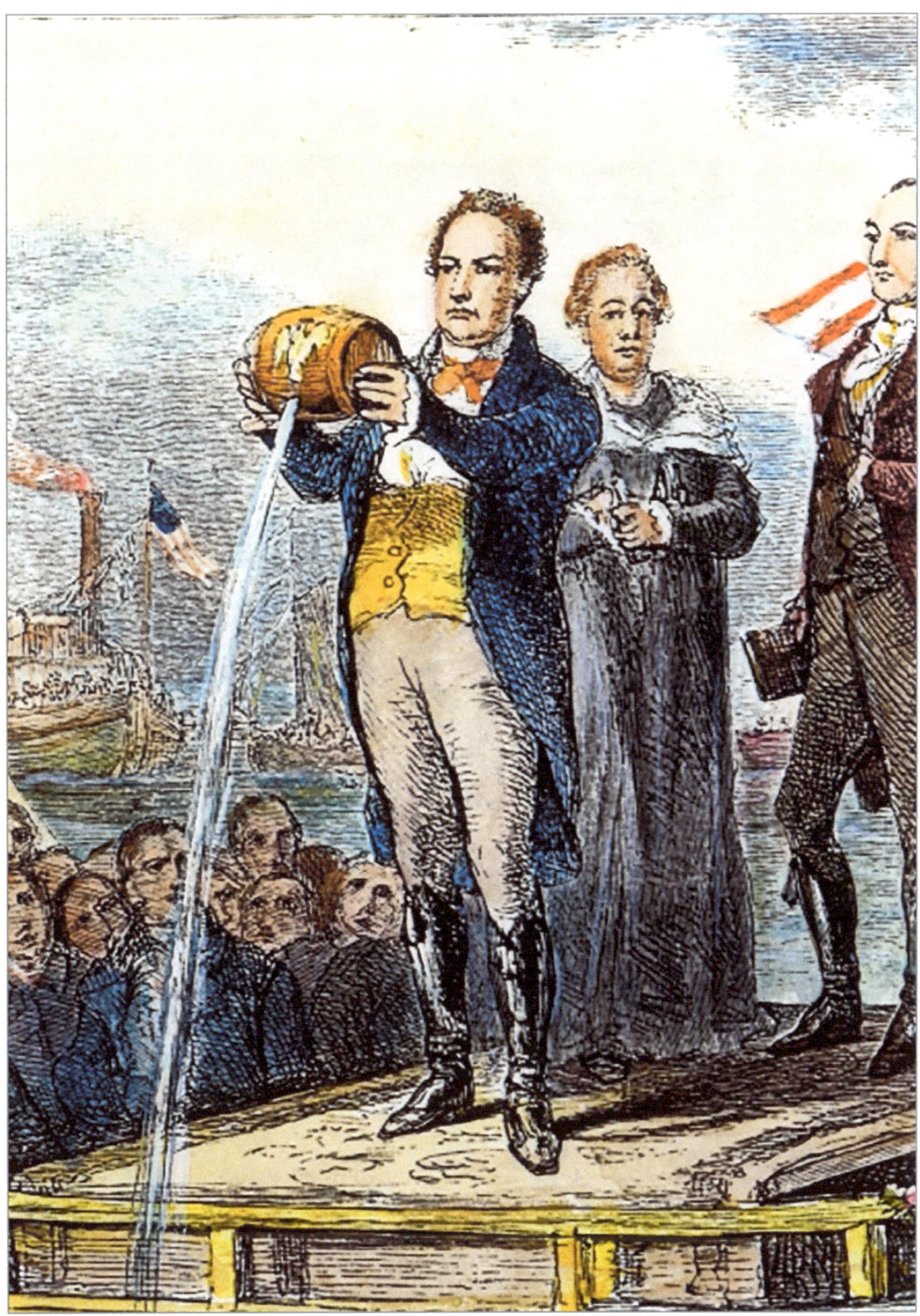

Erie Canal

The advent of the Erie Canal arguably made Buffalo the center of the known universe. It was the crossroads connecting the manufactured products from the East with the rich agricultural bounty of the West. The building of the Erie Canal became the principal driver behind Buffalo's explosive growth in the mid-to-late 19th and early 20th centuries.

In 1825, Buffalo became the focus of the most demanding engineering projects in the country. Built between 1817 and 1825, the original Erie Canal traversed 363 miles from Albany to Buffalo. Originally four feet deep and 40 feet wide, with removed soil piled on the downhill side to form a walkway known as a towpath. It cut through fields, forests, rocky cliffs, and swamps; crossed rivers on aqueducts; and overcame hills with 83 lift locks. Although its builders borrowed and adapted ideas and techniques from earlier European canals, they applied them with audacity on an unprecedented scale.

Despite the Canal Terminus's lofty role during its 1860s heyday, the waterfront was the polar opposite of paradise. It was chock-full of riots and fun, emancipation and war, booze, brothels, battles, and more, depicting a wild, wondrously wicked, absolutely ruddy hell of a place to romp and hope to survive.

Canalside is a growing regional destination and entertainment district. Viewing it today, it's hard to imagine this area was formerly known as "the Infected District," a hotbed for drunkenness and debauchery, especially among visiting sailors. At one count, there were 75 "houses of ill-fame" and over a hundred saloons, all within an eighth of a mile radius.

(Opposite:) Lockport Locks, E34 and E35. They comprise a rare 19th-century example of multiple locks directly connected into a flight and an in-situ example of once-common cut-stone lock construction. This flight is the most complete surviving artifact from the enlarged Erie Canal,

(Left:) On October 26, 1825, the Erie Canal was officially completed. Governor Dewitt Clinton made the 10-day journey down the canal from Buffalo to New York Harbor. At the harbor, he ceremoniously poured Lake Erie water into New York Harbor, officially "Wedding the Waters."

THE UNDERGROUND RAILROAD/ FREEDOM CROSSING

The Underground Railroad was a secret network for those escaping slavery run by people who assisted by providing money, food, clothing, and temporary shelter. Many fugitive slaves came through Western New York, crossing to freedom in Canada using the Suspension Bridge in Niagara Falls and the Niagara River at Broderick Park.

Right: The Niagara Falls Underground Railroad Heritage Area celebrates, interprets, and preserves an unparalleled density of historic resources, narratives, sites, and experiences associated with the City of Niagara Falls.

Below: The Michigan Street Baptist Church, erected in 1845, was a legendary Underground Railroad station. The building provided refuge for hundreds of freedom seekers before they crossed the border to Canada. Later, the church became a meeting place for abolitionists and anti-lynching activists like Frederick Douglass, William Wells Brown, W.E.B. Du Bois, and Booker T. Washington, each of whom graced its sanctuary.

Opposite: The "Freedom Crossing" monument in Lewiston by Susan Geissler depicts a slave mother, father, and child ready to be taken across the river in a rowboat by Tryon, a volunteer "station master."

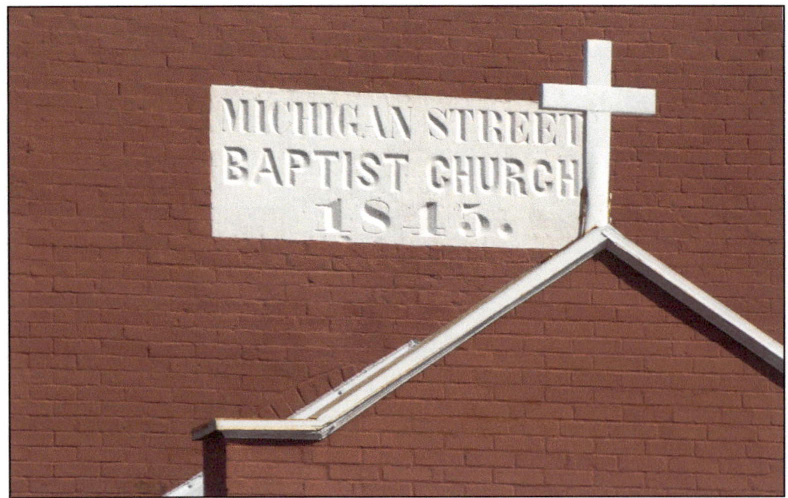

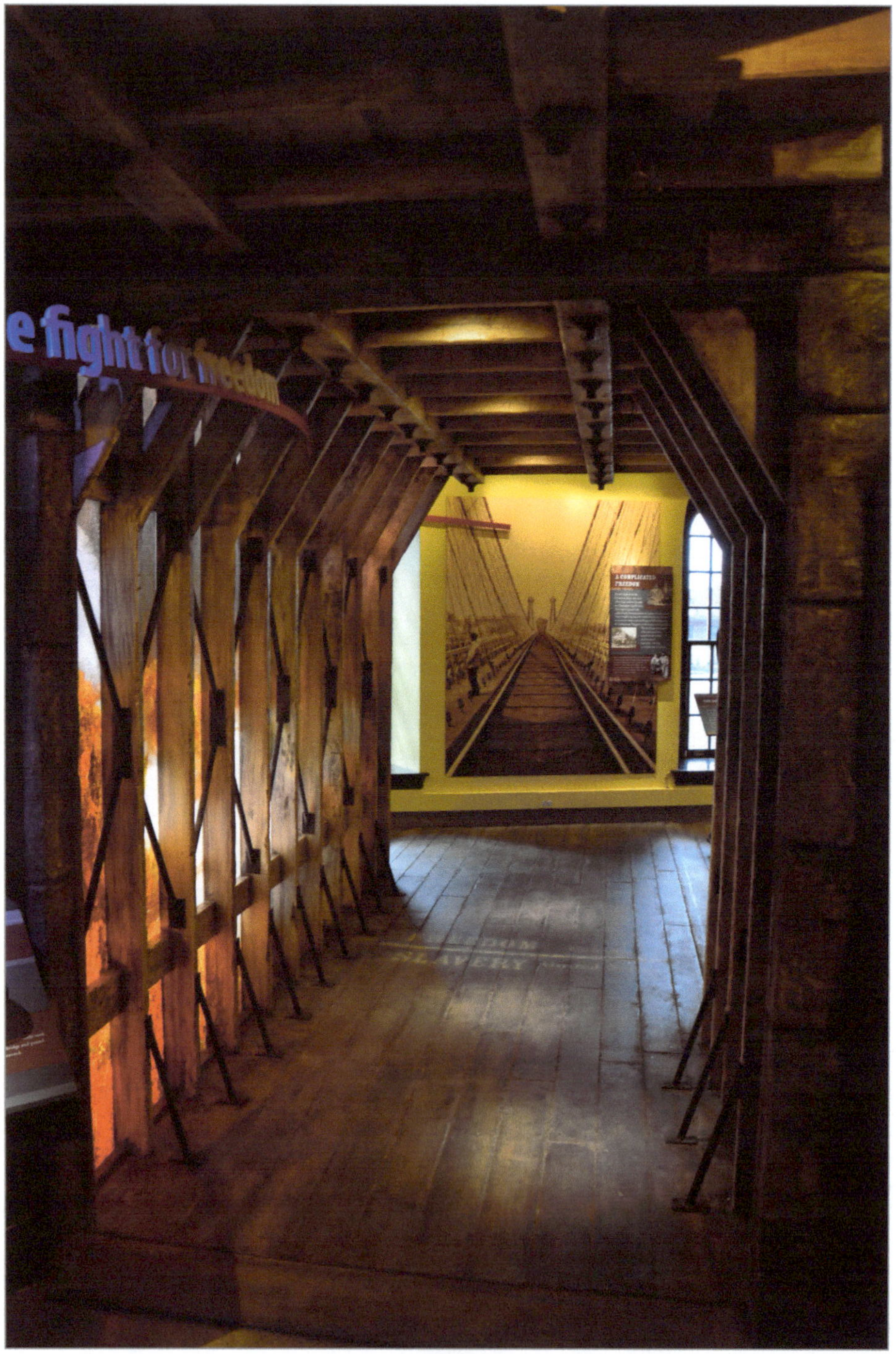

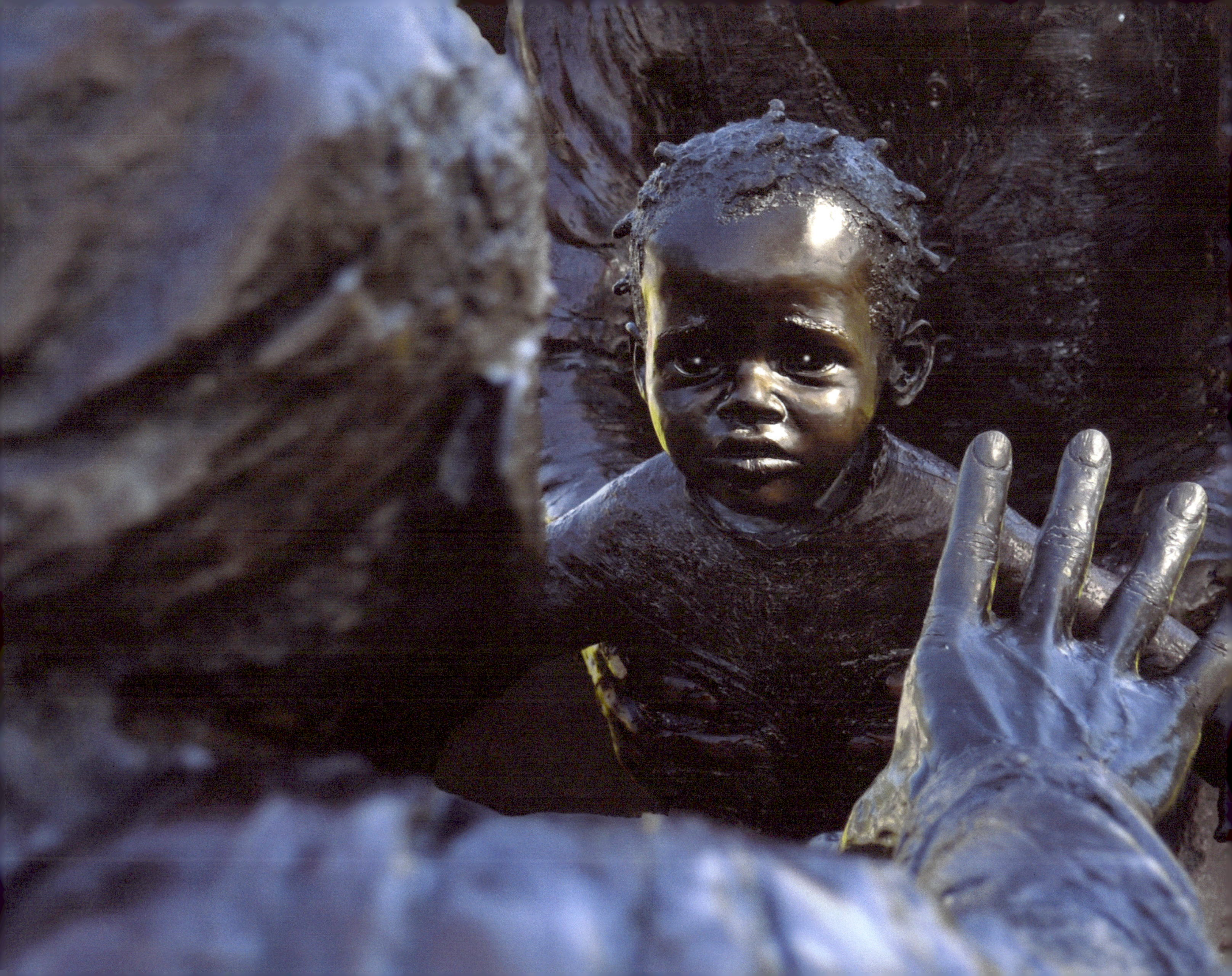

Grain Elevators

Buffalo's giant concrete castles serve as monuments to a bygone era when they filled the skyline and symbolized our industrial stature as the largest trans-shipment point of grain in the world.

In 1842, Buffalo's Joseph Dart, formerly a hat merchant, designed the first grain elevator. It was a tall, wooden structure for grain storage that employed steam power and an ingenious elevating mechanism called a "marine leg" that streamlined how grain was unloaded. This innovation not only had a profound impact on profitability and productivity, it radically changed the role of the working class and the trajectory of the city.

Highly flammable grain dust caused fires that were the demise of the early wooden elevators. Over the next 50 years, the wooden elevators evolved into massive concrete structures up to a quarter of a mile long.

Grain elevators influenced the development of modern architecture, especially skyscrapers. While many are still in active use, the remainder have sat quietly at the water's edge for years, waiting for those with the imagination to put them to creative reuses. Their patience is now being rewarded with their recent transformations to art and performance spaces, recreation areas, and even a brewery.

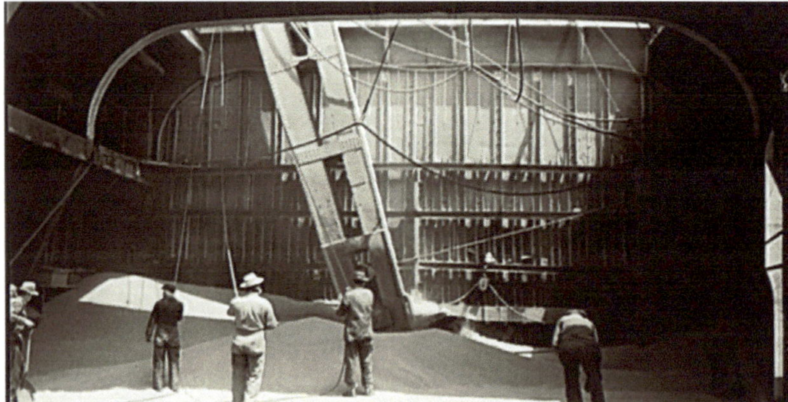

(Opposite:) Fog rolling in on the Buffalo River
(Right and above:) Inside the nearly-emptied hatch of a Duluth grain boat unloading wheat in a grain elevator on the Erie Canal. Men who work here are called scoopers. Here they are guiding the ropes of a shovel which scoops grain into the range of the "leg" which draws grain into the tower on an endless belt of buckets.

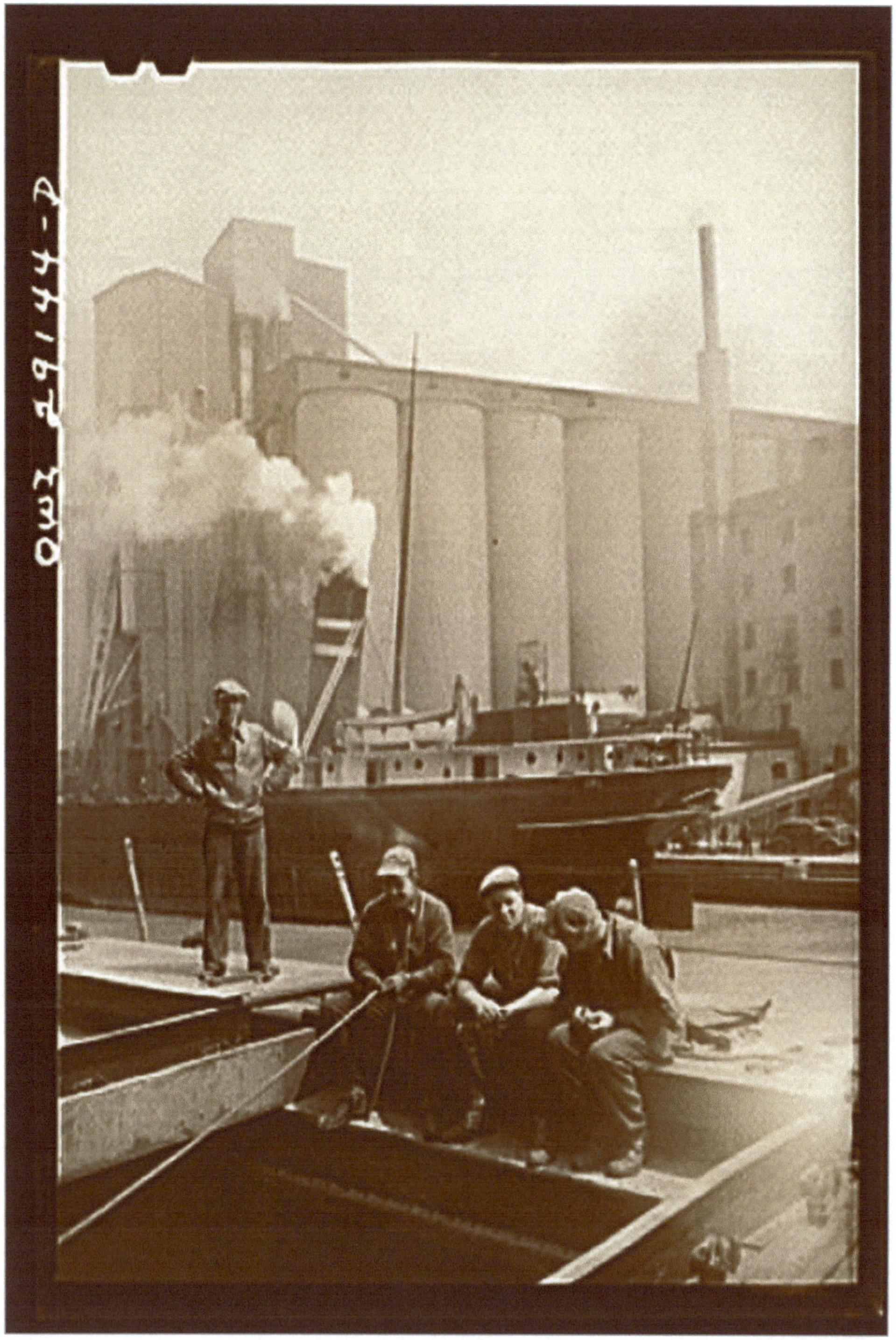

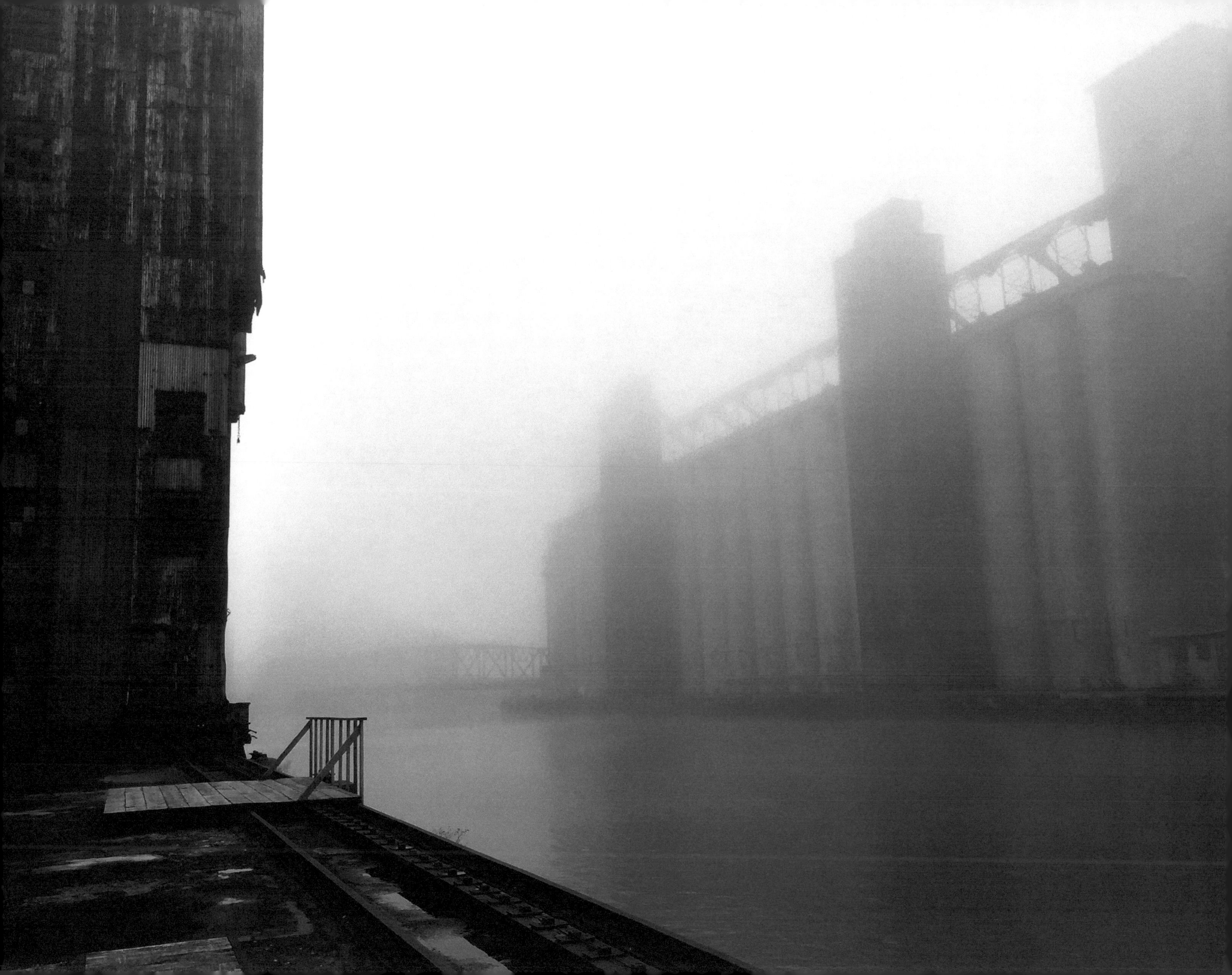

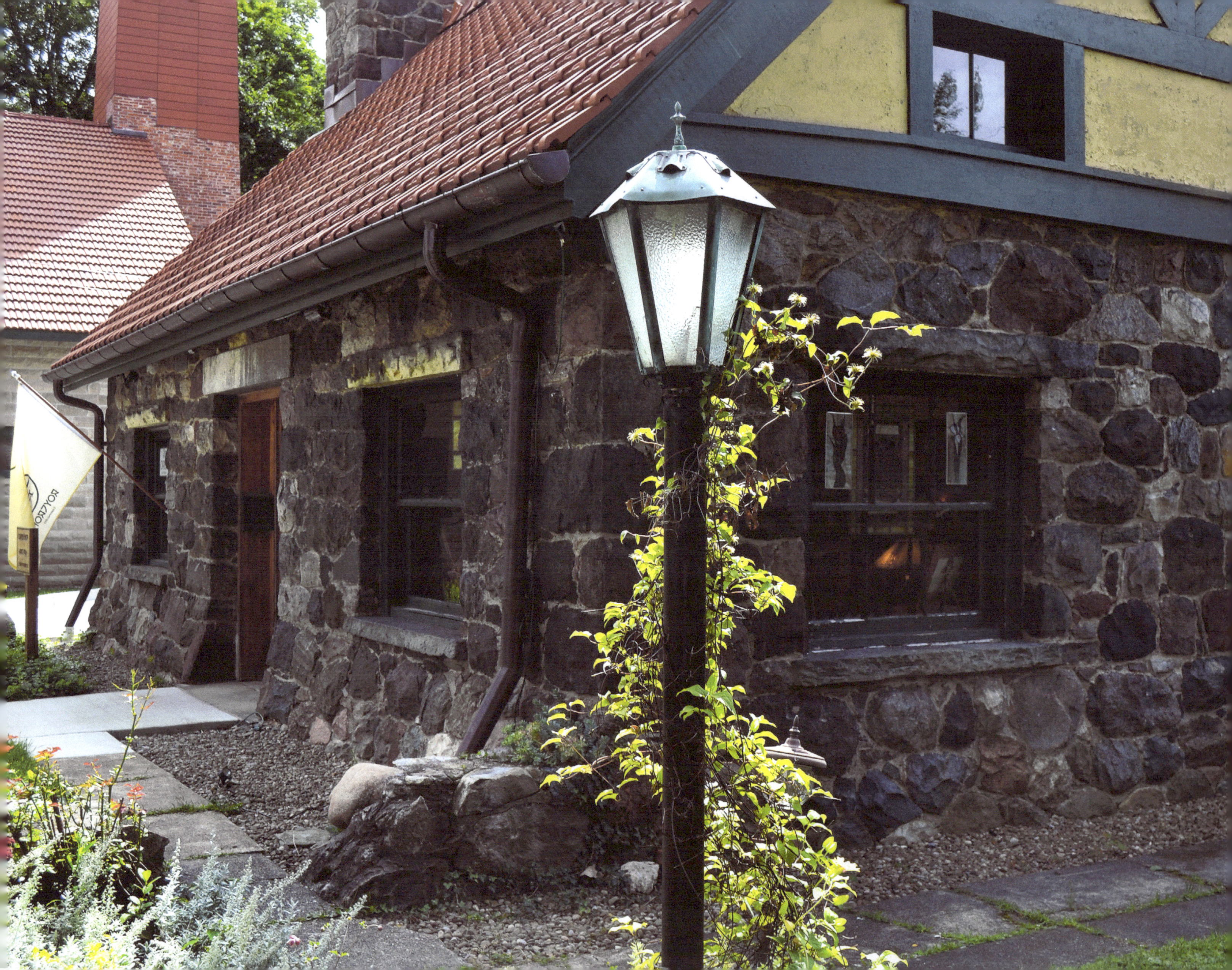

Roycroft Campus

The Roycroft Campus in East Aurora, NY, was home to a significant cultural movement that was a response to the mass production of the applied arts. Roycroft was a reformist community of craft workers and artists founded in 1895 by Elbert Hubbard, which formed part of the Arts and Crafts movement. His championing of the Arts and Crafts approach attracted many visiting craftspeople to East Aurora, and they created a community of printers, furniture makers, metalsmiths, leathersmiths, and bookbinders.

The Roycroft Campus is the best preserved and most complete complex of "guild" buildings remaining in the United States that evolved into centers of craftsmanship and philosophy. It was awarded National Historic Landmark status in 1986.

(Opposite:) The Copper Shop, constructed in 1902 in a small English cottage style, was used as a second blacksmith shop where they created hammered copper products and bottled East Aurora maple syrup and honey.

(Right:) Metalsmiths working at the Coppershop.

(Below:) Roycroft Chapel (not a religious building, but a guild hall)

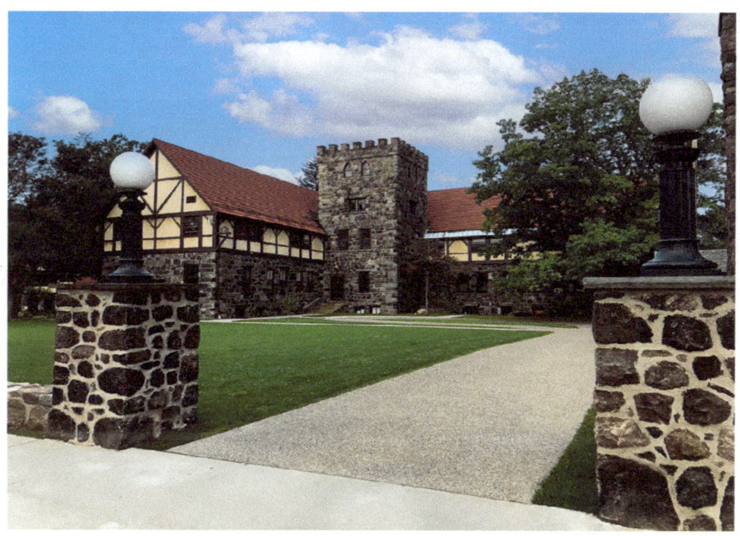

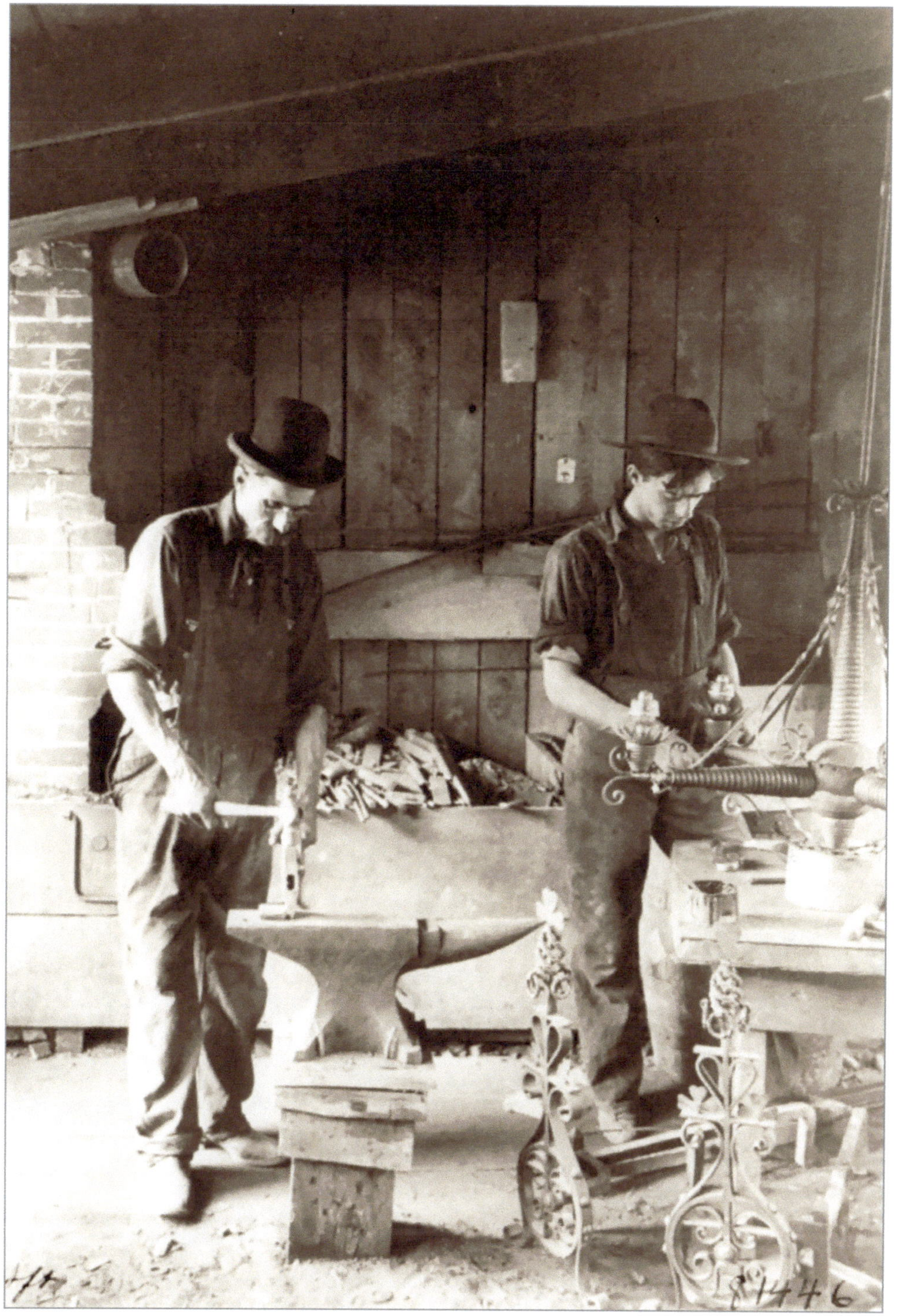

THEODORE ROOSEVELT INAUGURAL NATIONAL HISTORIC SITE

The Wilcox Mansion, also known as the Theodore Roosevelt Inaugural National Historic Site, is an early nineteenth-century Greek Revival mansion. Owned by the Ansley Wilcox family, it was here in the library that Teddy Roosevelt took the oath of office as our 26th President after the assassination of President William McKinley at the Pan-American Exposition. It is now a museum showcasing items related to the assassination and the inauguration in 1901.

(Opposite:) The exterior of the Wilcox Mansion. A 7½-foot bronze sculpture by Antonio Tobias "Toby" Mendez was installed on October 26, 2015, outside the Theodore Roosevelt Inaugural National Historic Site. It depicts the 26th president much as he looked on the day of his inauguration. His ascension to the presidency was so unexpected that he had to borrow clothes for the ceremony. Just hours before, he had been hiking high in the Adirondacks. Then, President McKinley, recovering from a gunshot wound sustained in an assassination attempt the week earlier, suddenly worsened and died. Fresh off Mount Marcy, Vice-President Roosevelt urgently needed something decent to wear. He scrambled to borrow a frock coat, striped trousers, a waistcoat, a four-in-hand tie, and patent leather shoes. He also didn't use a Bible when inaugurated in 1901 because there was no time to plan a ceremony.

(Below:) A stereoscope photo of the library where Theodore Roosevelt took the oath of office. A stereoscope is a device for viewing a pair of separate images, depicting left-eye and right-eye views of the same scene as a single three-dimensional image.

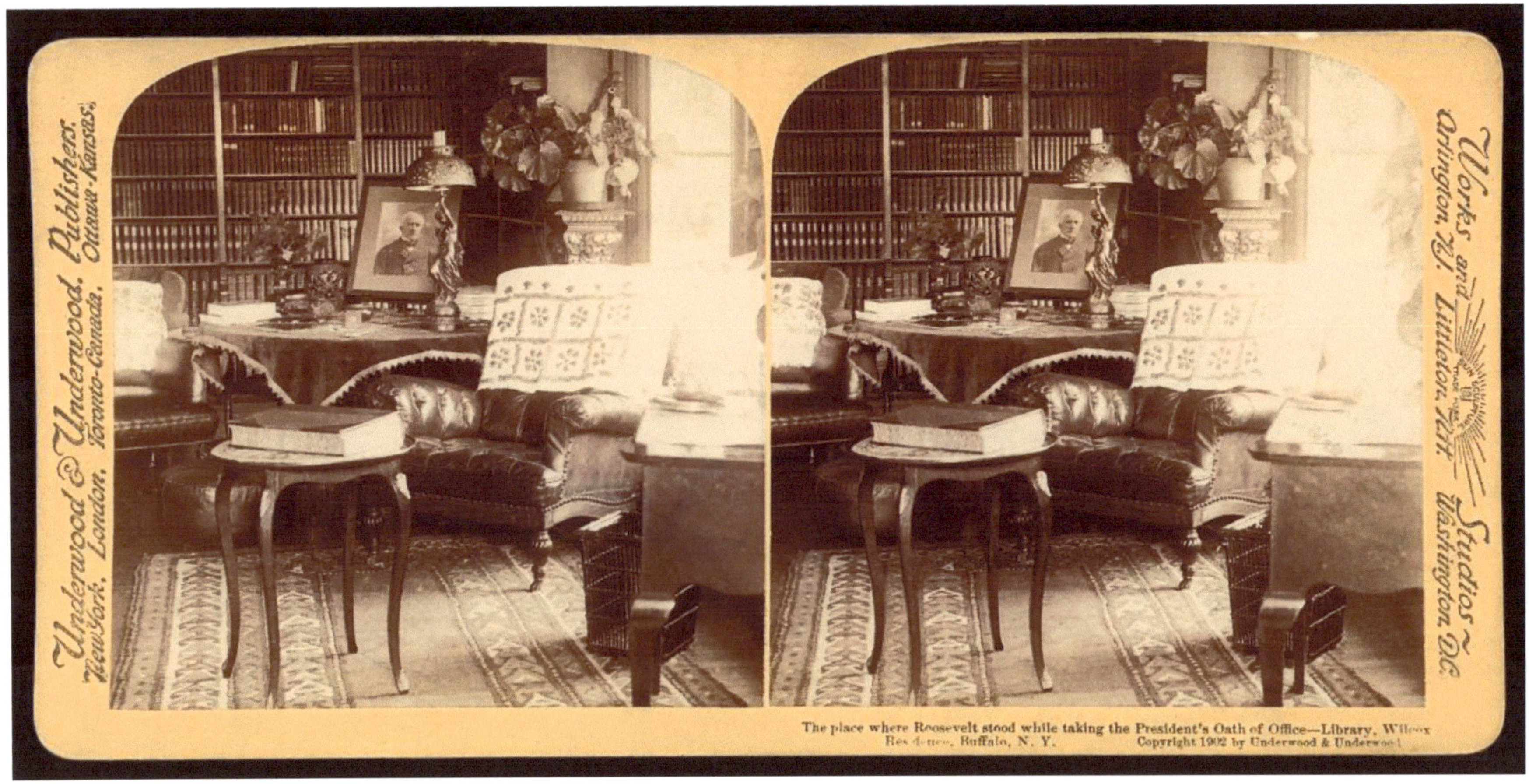

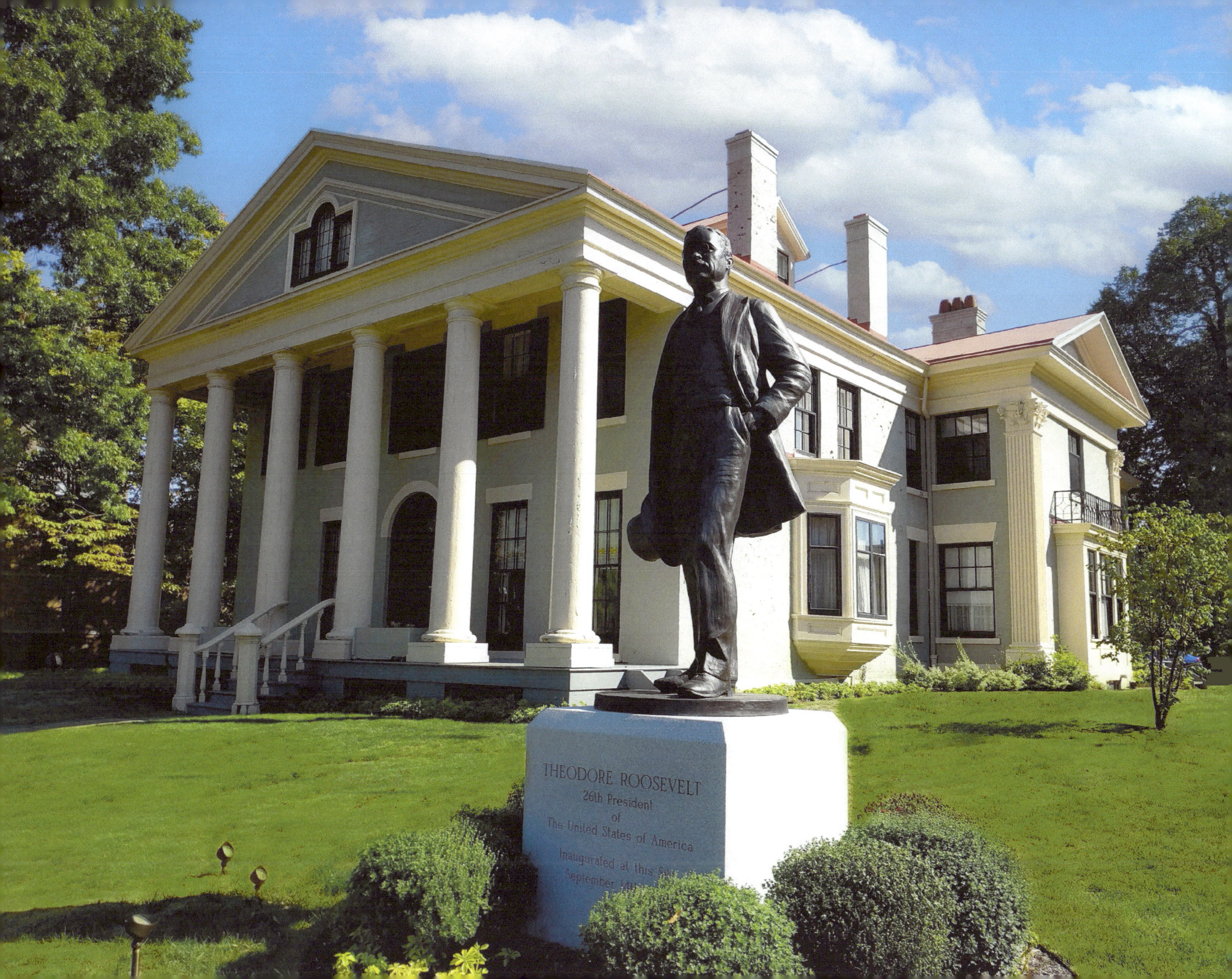
THEODORE ROOSEVELT
26th President
of
The United States of America

Buffalo Transportation Pierce-Arrow Museum

Pierce-Arrow was once one of the most recognized and respected names in the burgeoning automobile industry. For 38 years, the Buffalo-based Pierce-Arrow Motor Car Company produced some of the finest automobiles in the world, supplying cars to the White House for the use of the President for more than 20 years. In 1906, the company built a large automotive plant in Buffalo. After making what were arguably the best bicycles in the world, they turned their attention to high-end, luxury cars.

(Right:) You will find a selection of significant transportation items with an emphasis on Pierce-Arrow, the E.R. Thomas Motor Company, and other Buffalo-made automobiles and their accomplishments.

(Opposite:) Thomas Flyer, the American car that won the 1908 NY to Paris Automobile Race, beating both the German and Italian teams. It is considered one of the greatest automobile feats of all time.

(Below:) Archer radiator cap hood ornament on a 1931 Pierce Arrow 43 Club Sedan

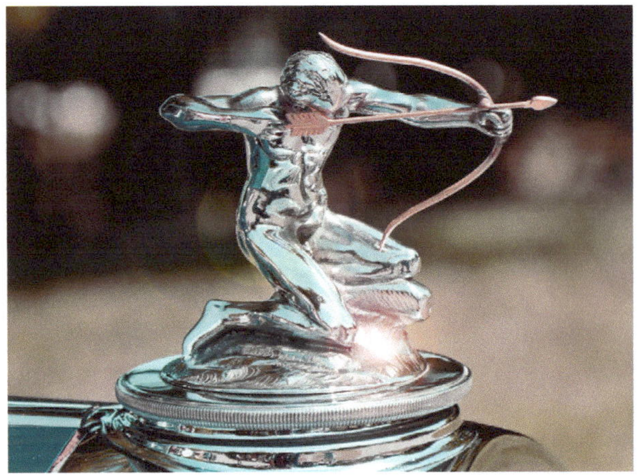

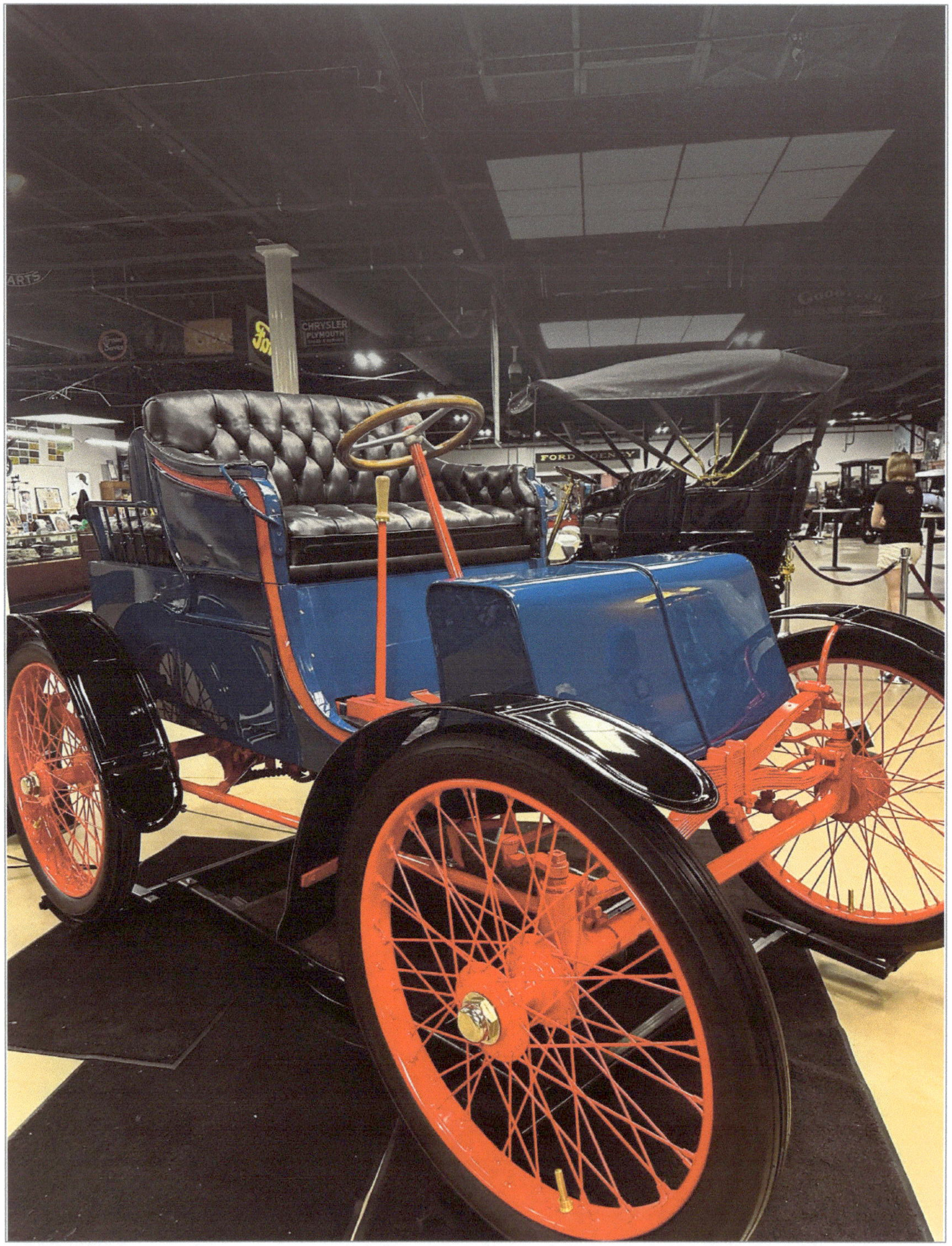

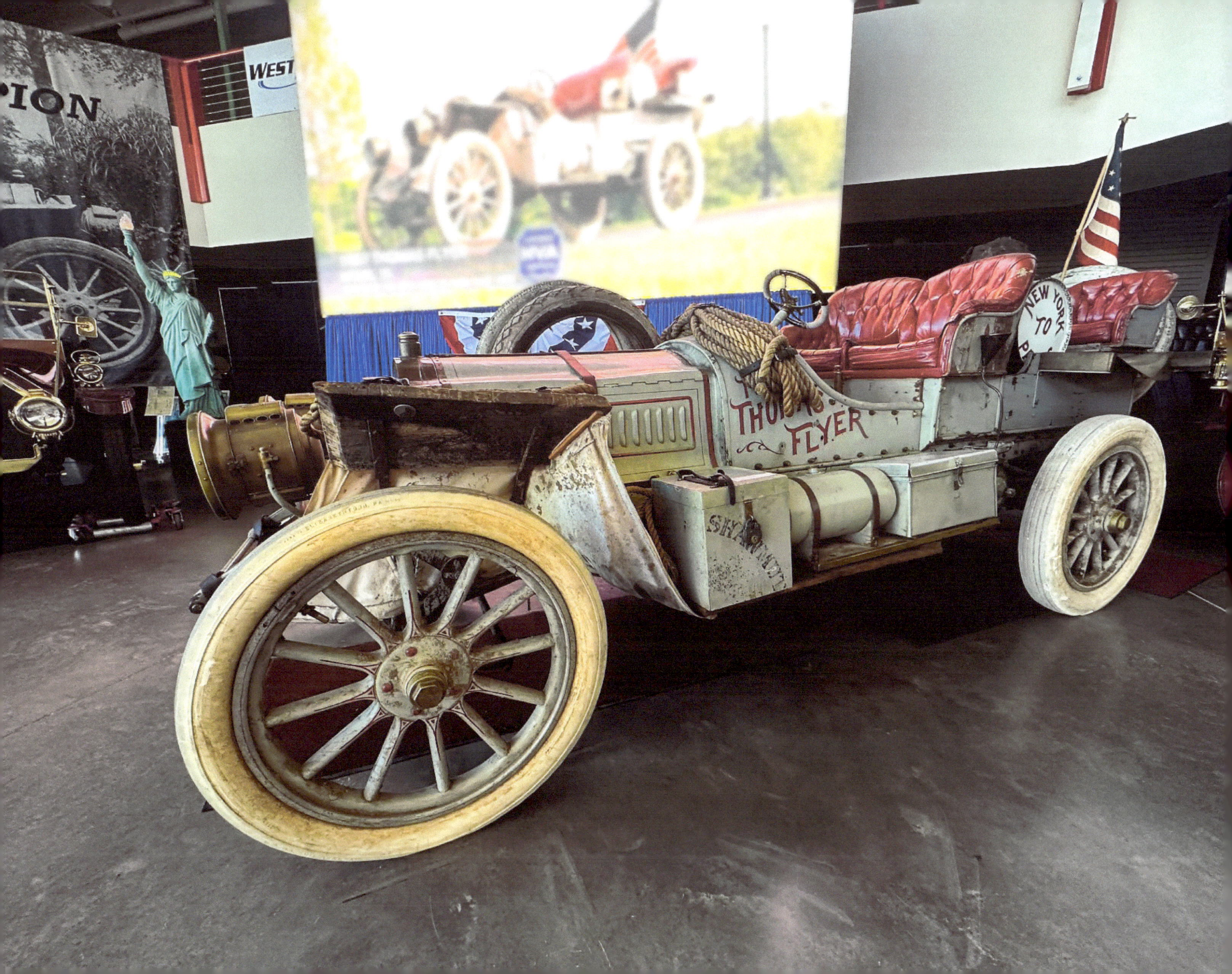

FLYER
NEW YORK
TO

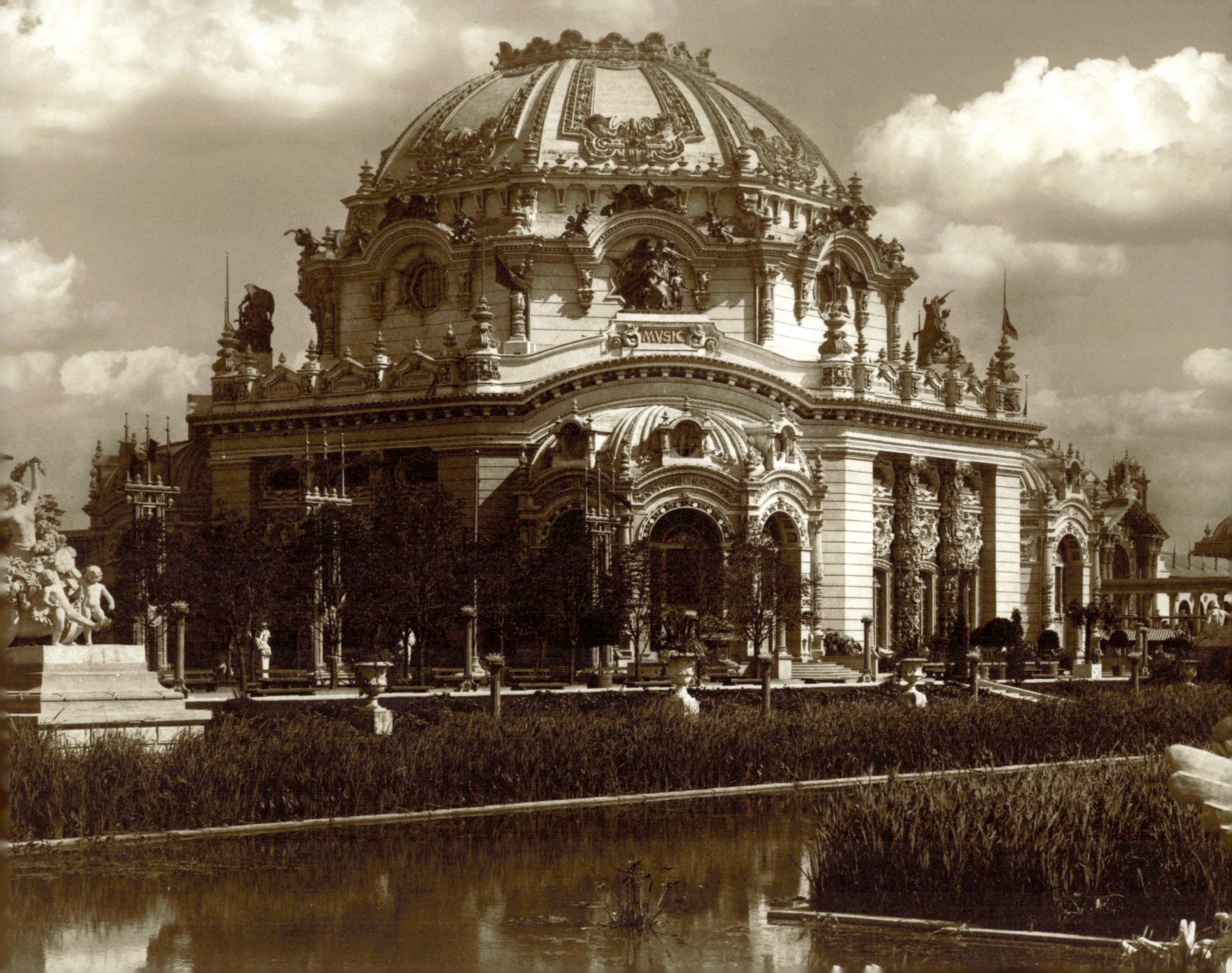
MVSIC

Pan American Exposition

The 1901 World's Fair, known as the Pan-American Exposition, was held here in Buffalo. The Exposition included many extensive exhibits and a midway with rides, shows, and other curiosities. The exhibitions showcased the latest advancements in science and technology, most notably electricity.

Electric Tower *(Right:)*
The massive 410-foot-tall Electric Tower was a central focus of the Exhibition and acted as a great light beacon. In addition to showcasing electricity, other technologies newly invented at the time, such as incubators for infants and X-ray machines, were on display along with many types of machinery. Alternating current produced at Niagara Falls was transmitted to Buffalo and powered the "Rainbow City lights," including almost a quarter-million colored 8-watt bulbs.

There is also a hint of the Pan-American Exposition in downtown Buffalo: the iconic Electric Building is patterned after the Exhibition's Electric Tower's design.

Temple of Music *(Opposite:)*
The Temple of Music was one of the most beautiful of the Exposition buildings and was situated west of the central fountain of the Esplanade. It was a concert hall and auditorium capable of seating 2,200 people built for the Exposition. John Philip Sousa and his band performed there, and daily organ recitals were given by the most celebrated organists, one of the largest pipe organs ever built in the United States.

The Pan-American Exposition turned tragic when it became the location of President McKinley's assassination. On Sept. 6, 1901, while in a receiving line at the Exposition's Temple of Music, President McKinley was shot twice by anarchist Leon Czolgosz.

Like most other buildings at the Exposition, the structure was demolished when the fair ended.

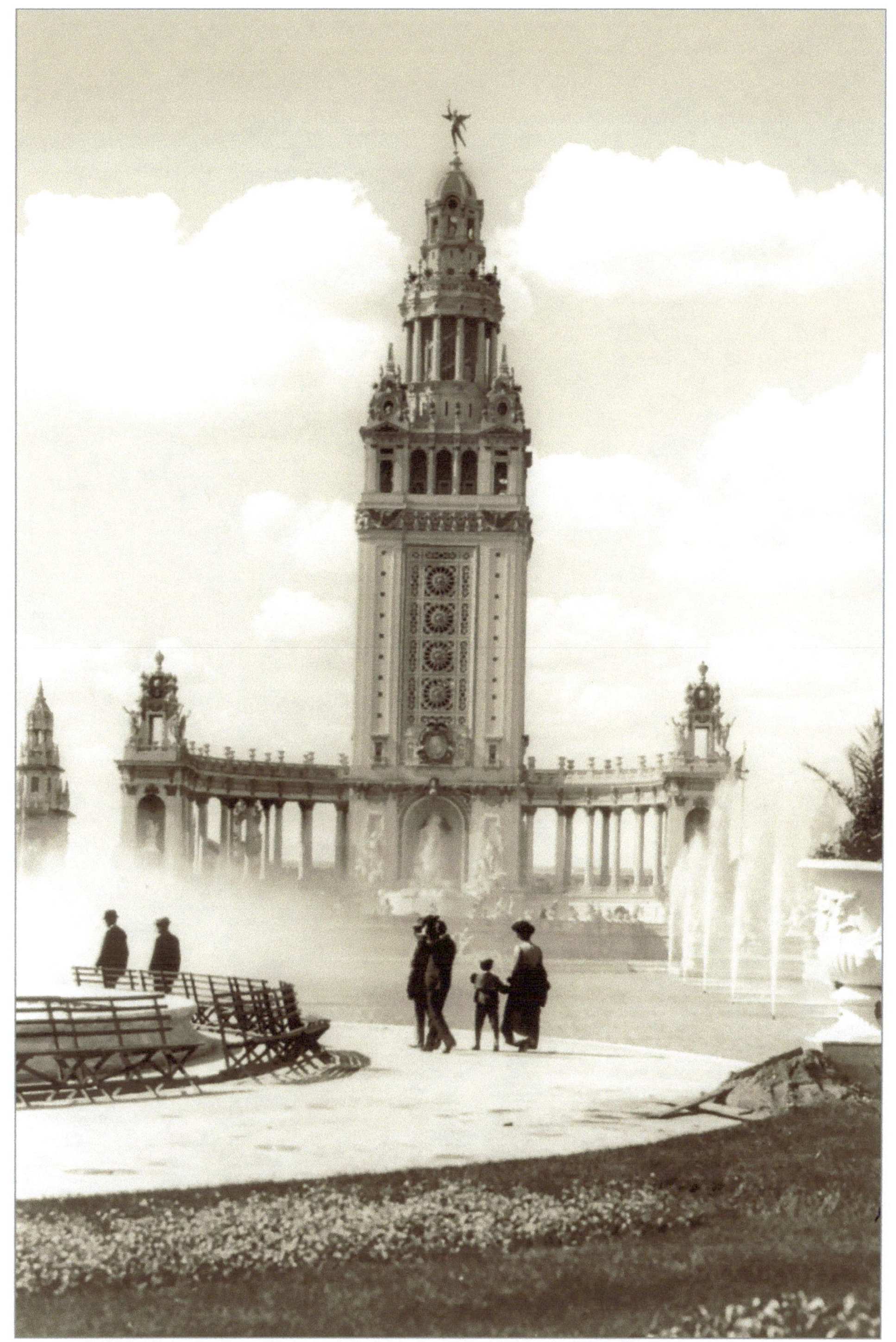

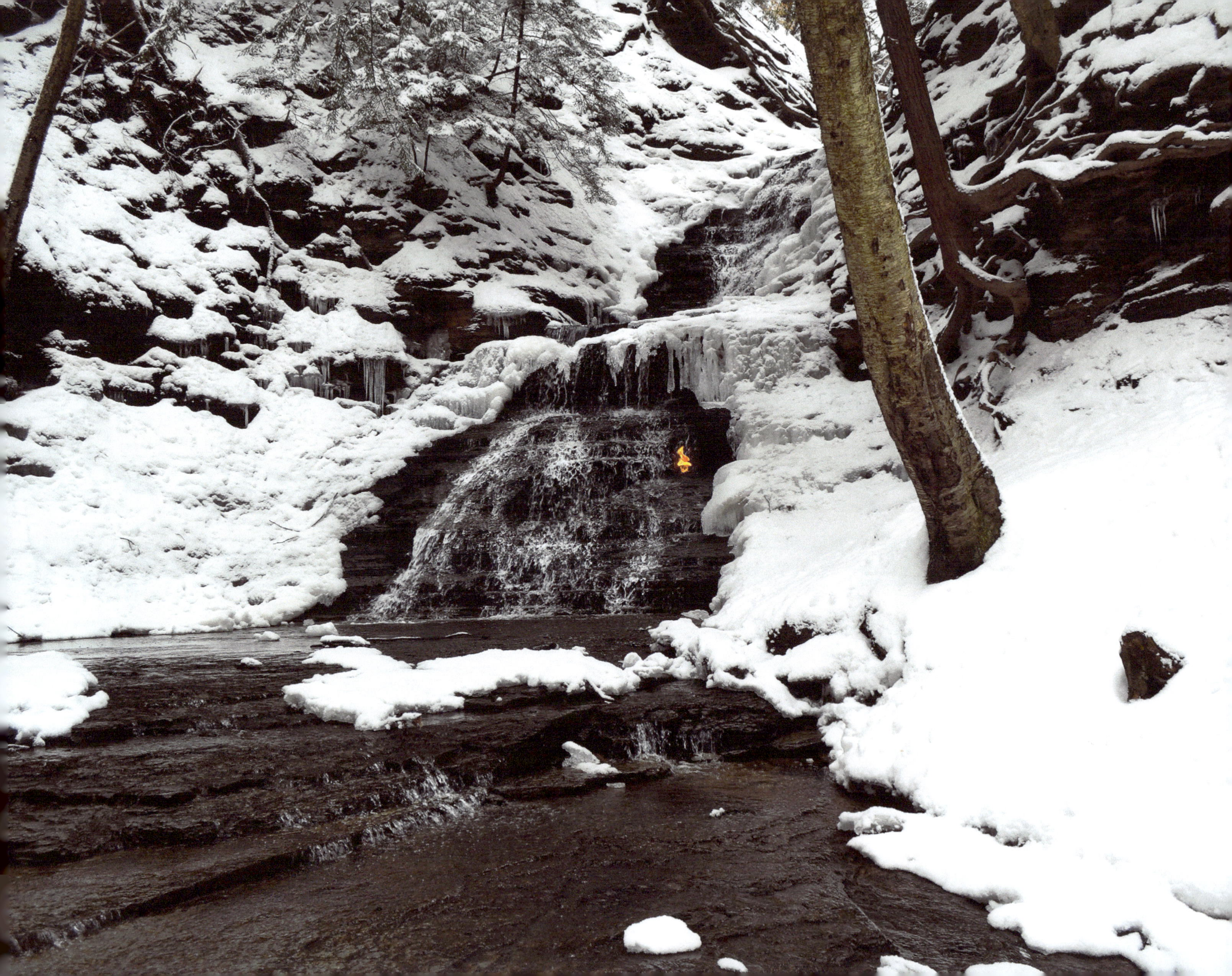

Parks & Gardens

Buffalo's parks and gardens are a wealth of cultural gems that breathe life into virtually every neighborhood. They provide the serenity of grass and trees where you most need it and bursts of color where you least expect them. During the 1901 Pan-American Exposition, Buffalo was celebrated not only as the City of Light, but the City of Trees.

Distinguished for their creativity in designing New York City's Central Park and Brooklyn's Prospect Park, Frederick Law Olmsted and Calvert Vaux were called upon by the Buffalo Parks Commission in 1868 to design parks for Buffalo.

Their unique design included not one but three parks: The Park (Delaware Park), The Parade (Martin Luther King, Jr. Park), and The Front Park, complete with connecting parkways and circles. As Buffalo expanded, Olmsted and Vaux were again called upon to enlarge the park system by adding additional parks including Riverside, Cazenovia Park, and South Park.

While the 850 acres of this historic urban park system are stellar in their own right, today it only comprises less than 75% of the city's parkland used for recreation, relaxation, and rejuvenation.

Western New York has an absolutely insatiable celebration of all things green as evidenced by our Garden Walk, the Buffalo and Erie County Botanical Gardens, WNY Peace Gardens, Niagara Falls Great Lakes Garden, and virtually everywhere else a flower will fit.

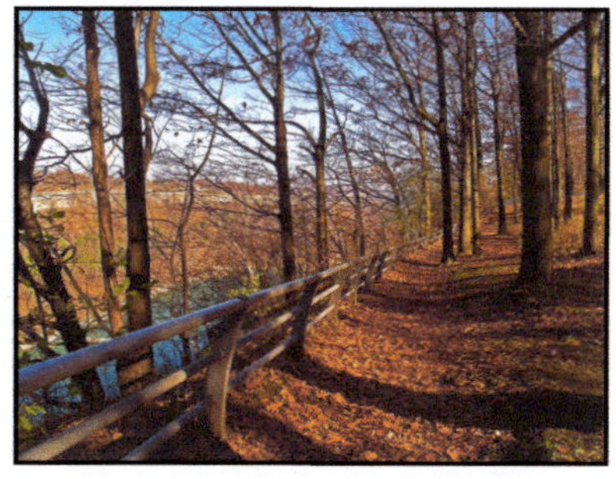

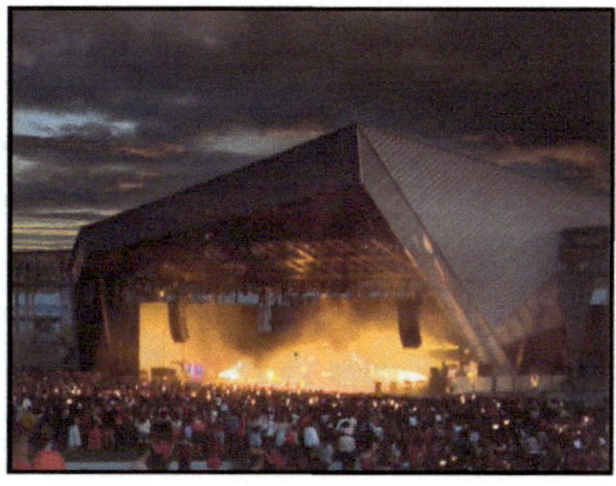

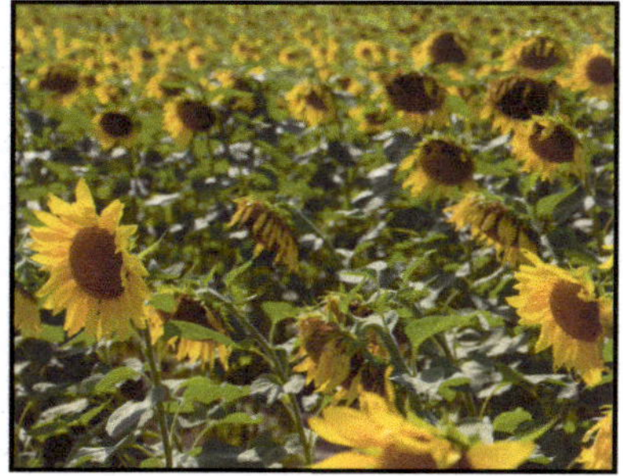

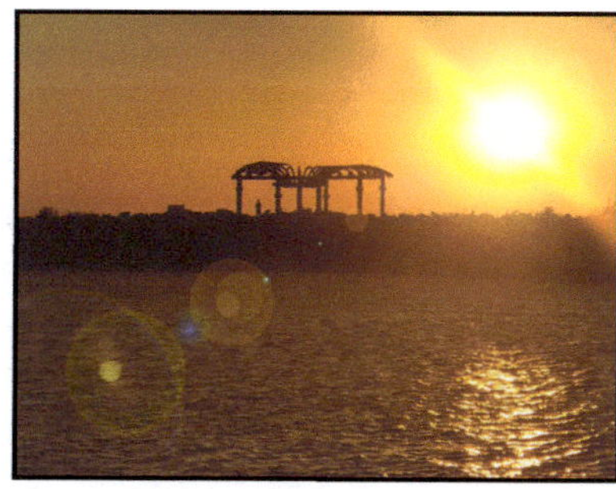

(Opposite:) The Eternal Flame Falls is a small waterfall located in the Shale Creek Preserve, a section of Chestnut Ridge Park in Western New York. A small grotto at the waterfall's base emits natural gas, which can be lit to produce a small flame.

(Left to right:) Devil's Hole State Park trail overlooking the rapids, | Concert at Terminal B on the Outer Harbor | Sunflowers of Sanborn. | Sunset at Small Boat Harbor State Park

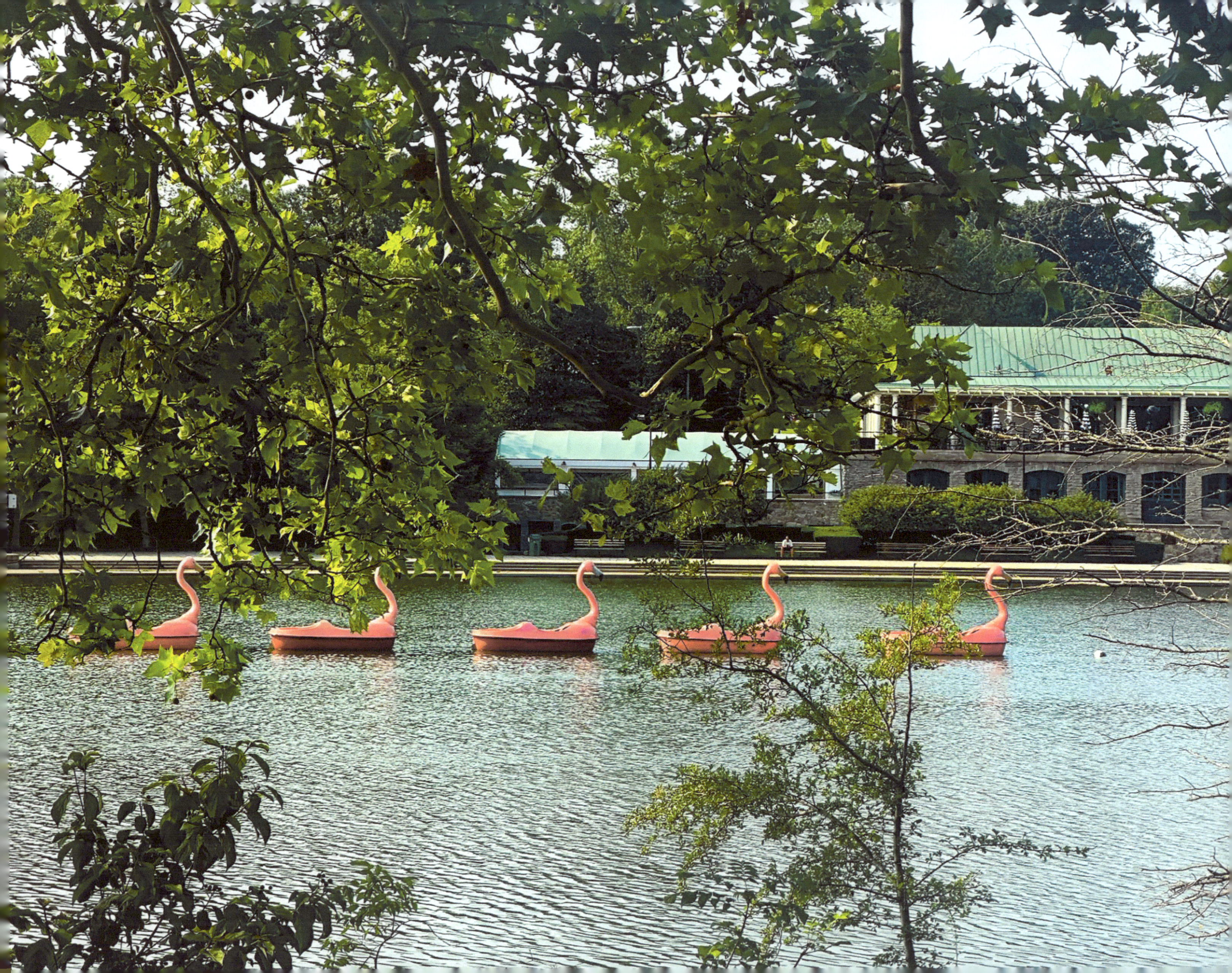

Buffalo Olmsted Parks

Many of our city's public parks and parkway systems were originally designed by Frederick Law Olmsted and Calvert Vaux between 1868 and 1896. The parkland, boulevards, and squares of Paris, France, largely inspired them. They include the parks, parkways, and circles within the Cazenovia Park, South Park, Delaware Park, and Front Park systems. They're listed on the National Register of Historic Places and maintained by the Buffalo Olmsted Parks Conservancy.

Frederick Law Olmsted described Buffalo as "the best-planned city in the United States, if not the world." With encouragement from city stakeholders, he and Calvert Vaux created an augmentation of the city's grid plan by drawing inspiration from Paris, introducing landscape architecture while embracing aspects of the countryside. Their plan would introduce a system of interconnected parks, parkways, and trails. The largest would be Delaware Park, situated across the large Forest Lawn Cemetery, to amplify the planned open land.

One of Olmsted's first three parks in Buffalo, Delaware Park serves as the focal point of the Olmsted system and today contains or borders many of Buffalo's cultural institutions such as the Buffalo History Museum, AKG Art Gallery, Shakespeare in Delaware Park, and the Buffalo Zoo. Simply named "The Park" by Olmsted, these 350 acres of meadow, forest, and lake serve as Buffalo's version of "Central Park".

(Opposite:) Hoyt Lake, the centerpiece of Delaware Park, is named in honor of William Ballard Hoyt II, a former member of the State Assembly whose vision, dedication, and concern for the environment helped beautify and preserve the lake for the people of Buffalo.

The fancy flock of FLOATmingo bright pink flamingo paddle boats on Hoyt Lake create one of the most enjoyable ways to spend time in Delaware Park. They're modeled after WNY's adopted iconic bird. It's another one of our city's mysteries - Buffalo have no wings, sponge candy isn't made of sponges, and flamingos can't swim.

(Right:) The Rose Garden and its pergola, built in 1917, is one of the main focal points of Delaware Park, featuring rose varieties from the All-America Rose Selections.

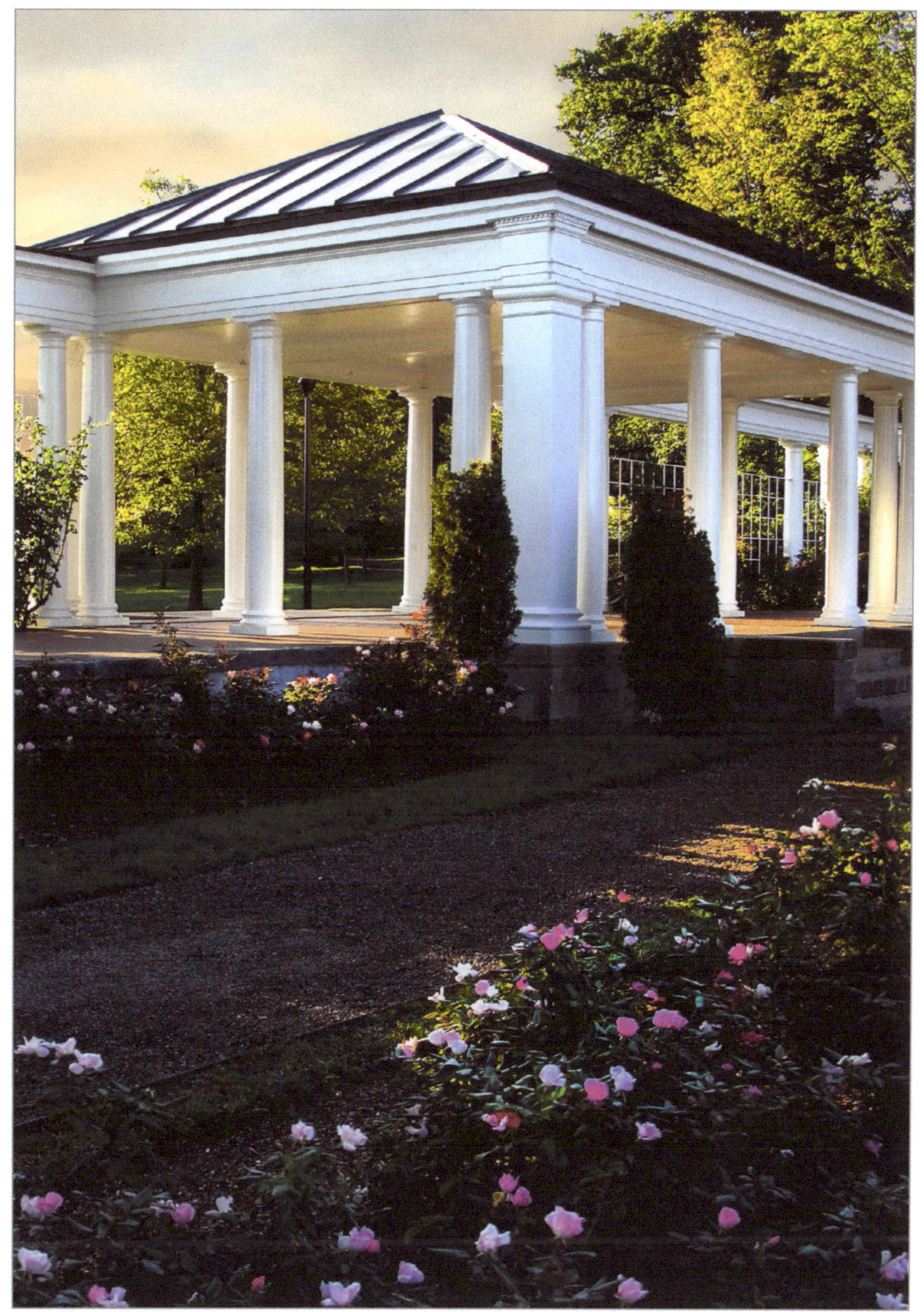

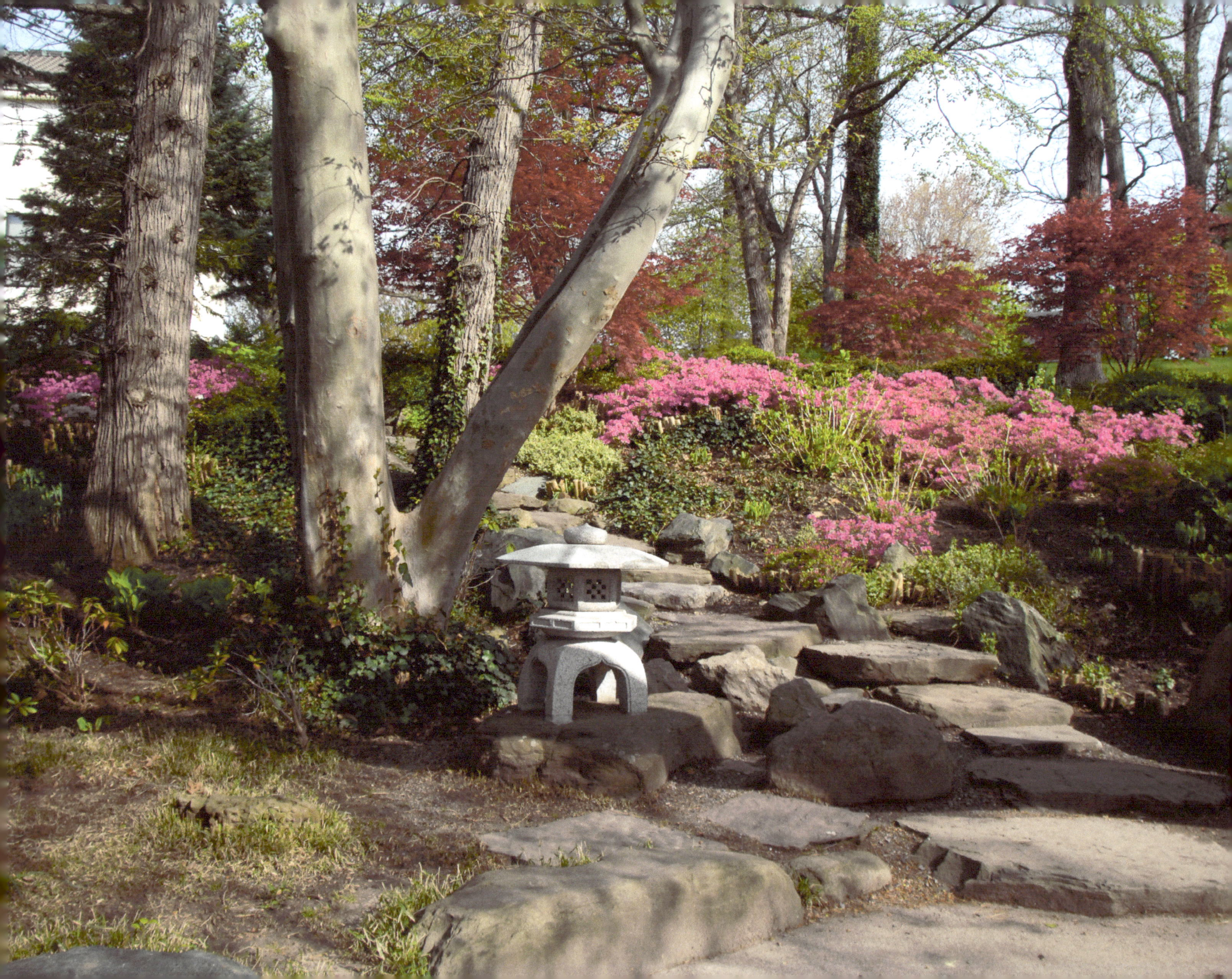

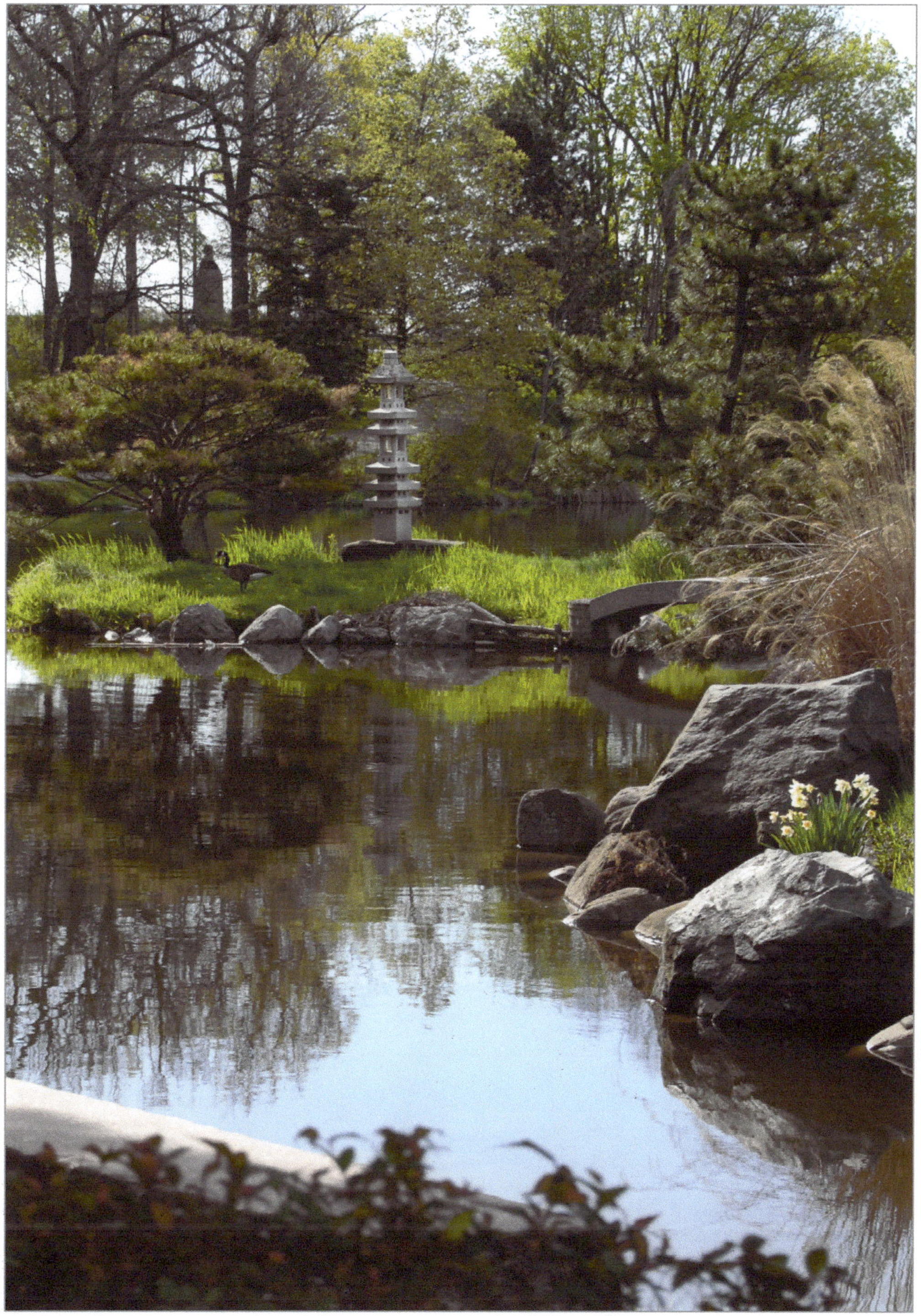

The Japanese Garden

The Japanese Garden in Delaware Park was established through a special sister-city initiative in 1962 between Kanazawa, Japan, and Buffalo. Located behind The Buffalo History Museum in Delaware Park, the lush gardens and serene lake provide a contemplative refuge for all of Buffalo to enjoy.

Started in 2014, the garden is home to the Buffalo Cherry Blossom Festival, which seeks to build awareness of Japanese culture and celebrate the blossoming of the 40 Cherry Blossom trees in the garden. In 1996, Kanazawa was primarily responsible for the significant renovations to the Japanese Garden of Buffalo, providing trees, shrubs, paths, and unique stone lanterns.

(Opposite:) A pathway across the hillside below the history museum leads directly to the heart of the hillside garden with rugged stone steps placed by master gardeners from Kanazawa.

(Left:) An arched stone bridge connects two islands, and a famous stone lantern with one foot out in the water replicates a well-known feature of Kenrokuen Garden in Kanazawa.

(Below:) Cherry blossoms and the pediment on the rear portico of the History Museum.

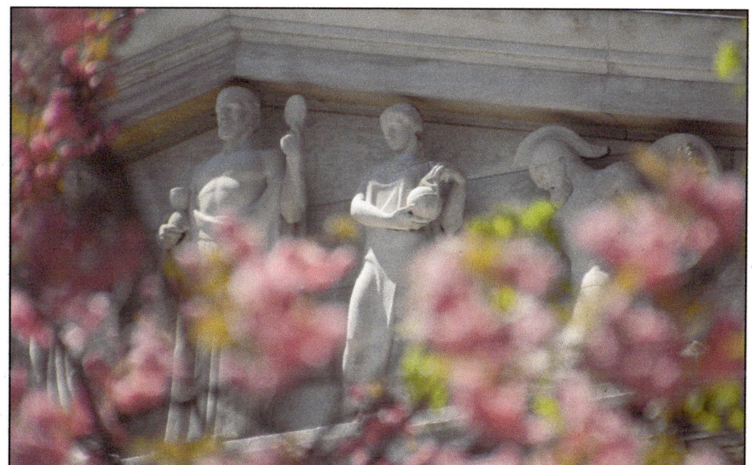

Forest Lawn Cemetery

Hiding in plain sight, right in the middle of the city, are 269 pastoral acres that define beauty and solitude. Founded in 1849, Forest Lawn is one of America's premier historic cemeteries and one of the world's finest outdoor museums.

Many of its monuments, sculptures, and mausoleums are designed by famous sculptors and architects, including Stanford White, Augustus Saint-Gaudens, Harriet Frishmuth, E. B. Green, Richard Upjohn, and Frank Lloyd Wright.

In a tradition that began more than 150 years ago, Forest Lawn remains a vital place where past and present are joined, and visitors are warmly welcomed. Picnics, tours, and creative events enrich the community's life. Such activities foster the ultimate tribute: Those departed are surrounded by vibrant life, ensuring they are perpetually remembered.

Forest Lawn's great tradition of welcoming visitors grew from a concept that originated at Père-Lachaise in 1805. This Parisian cemetery was the first to create a park-like space with bucolic vistas intended to attract the living. It encouraged families to visit and remember their loved ones. Forest Lawn became one of the first such cemeteries in America, inviting the public to enjoy its beauty and celebrate its residents.

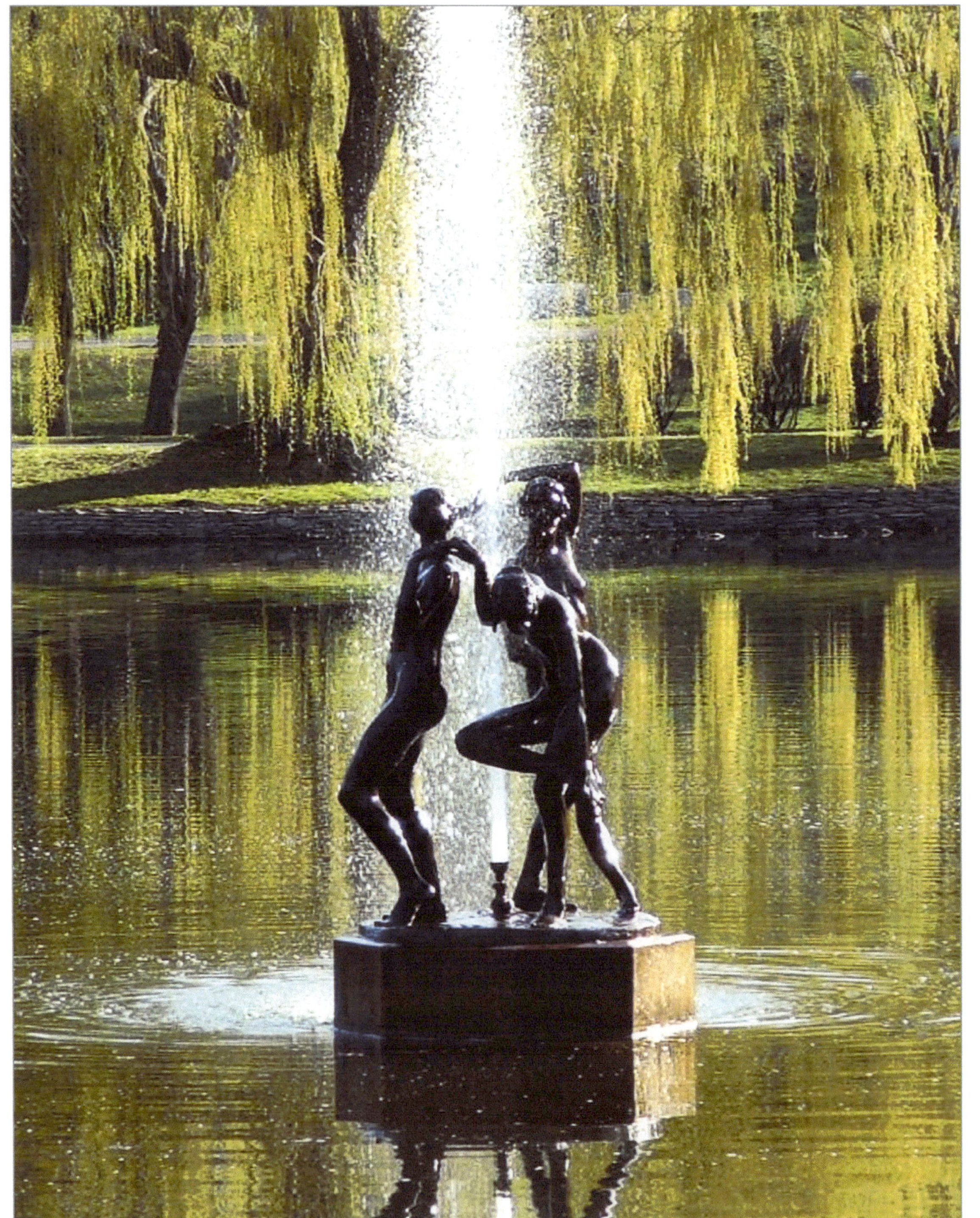

(Right:) "The Three Graces" fountain sculpture by Buffalo-born Charles Cary Rumsey (1879-1922) is located on Mirror Lake in Forest Lawn Cemetery.

(Opposite:) Blue Sky Mausoleum in Forest Lawn Cemetery in Buffalo, New York, is the 2004 completion of a 1928 design by Frank Lloyd Wright as a commercial cemetery project. The design was completed by a one-time apprentice to Wright, Anthony Puttnam.

The Mausoleum was the last of four projects Darwin D. Martin commissioned from Wright; the others were his residential complex, Graycliff, their summer house, and the Larkin Administration Building,

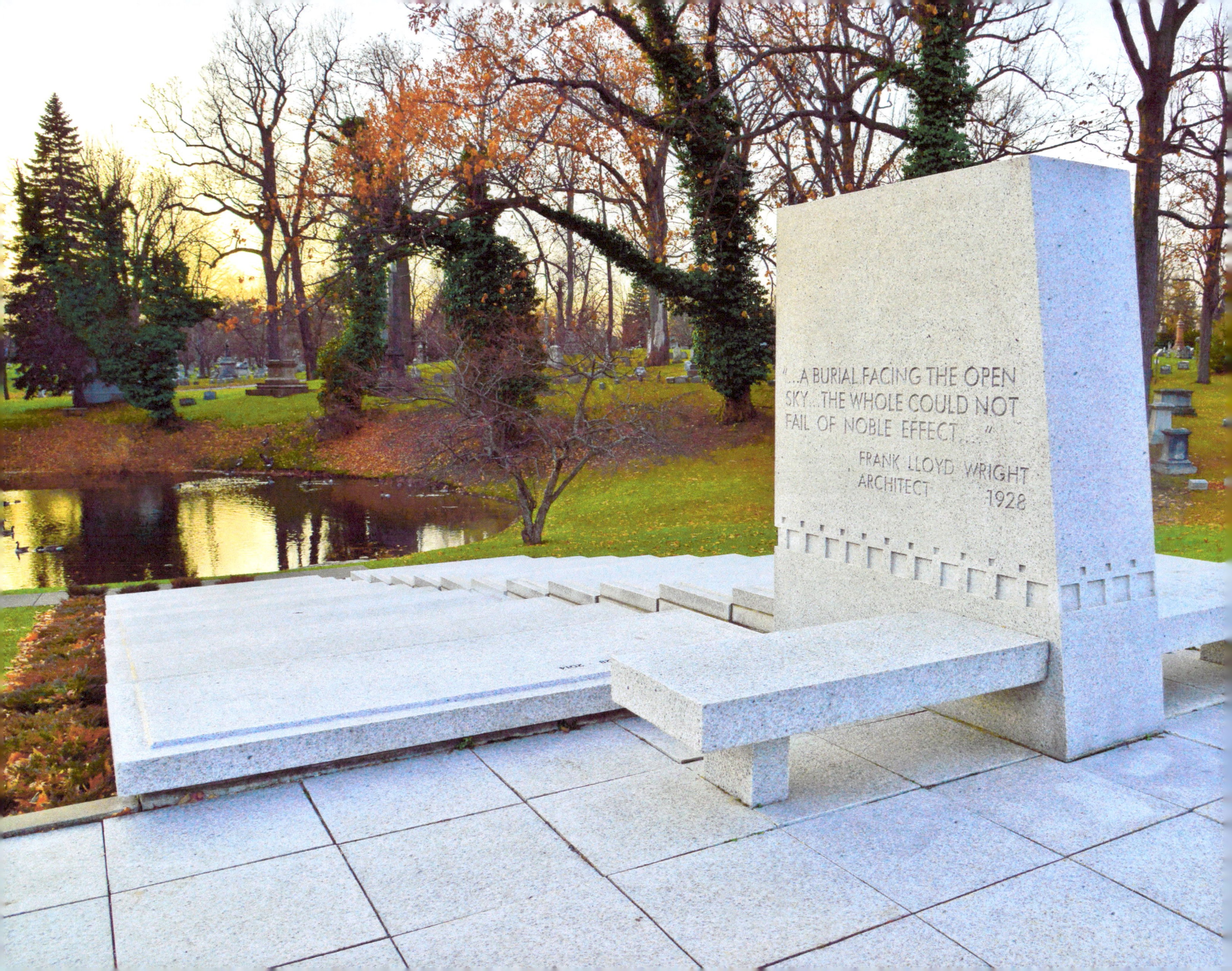
"...A BURIAL FACING THE OPEN
SKY...THE WHOLE COULD NOT
FAIL OF NOBLE EFFECT...."
FRANK LLOYD WRIGHT
ARCHITECT 1928

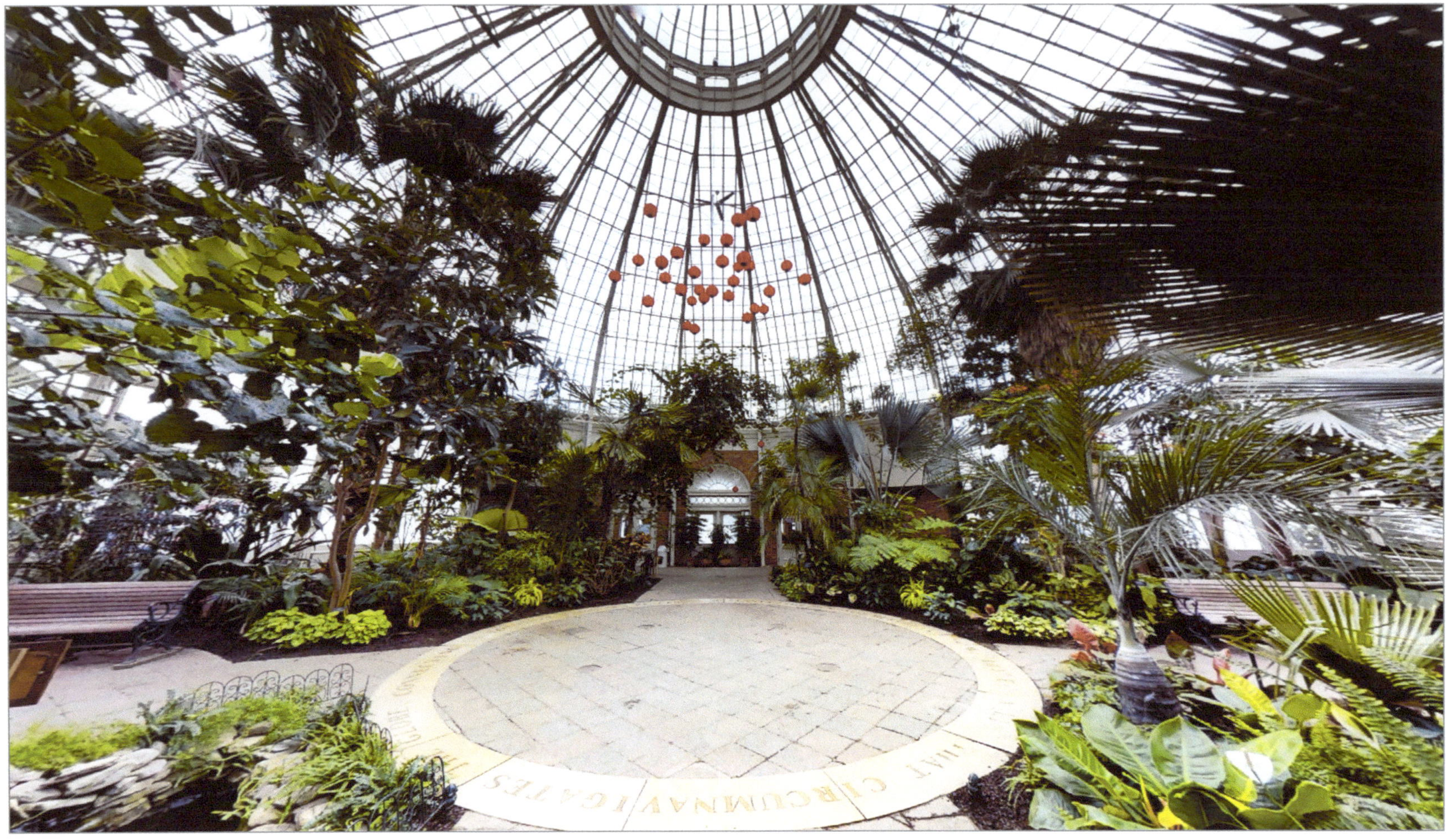

Buffalo and Erie County Botanical Gardens

A perfect respite from the daily grind, the Buffalo and Erie County Botanical Gardens is the best place in Buffalo to enjoy the beauty of plants and flowers year-round.

The conservatory was built between 1897 and 1899 by Lord & Burnham Co., the country's premier greenhouse designers and builders. In the spring of 1900, the South Park Conservatory opened its doors to the public. A prime example of Victorian architecture, it was the third-largest public greenhouse under glass in the U.S. at the time and the ninth-largest in the world.

The 1901 Pan-American Exposition in Buffalo helped to spur the success of the South Park Conservatory by providing trolley rides from downtown Buffalo to the conservatory. Tens of thousands of people visited the breathtaking conservatory and delighted in the exotic collection of plants and flowers.

In 1981, the South Park Conservatory was sold to Erie County, and its name was changed to the Buffalo and Erie County Botanical Gardens. In 1982, the Botanical Gardens was placed on the National Register of Historic Places and the New York State Register of Historic Places.

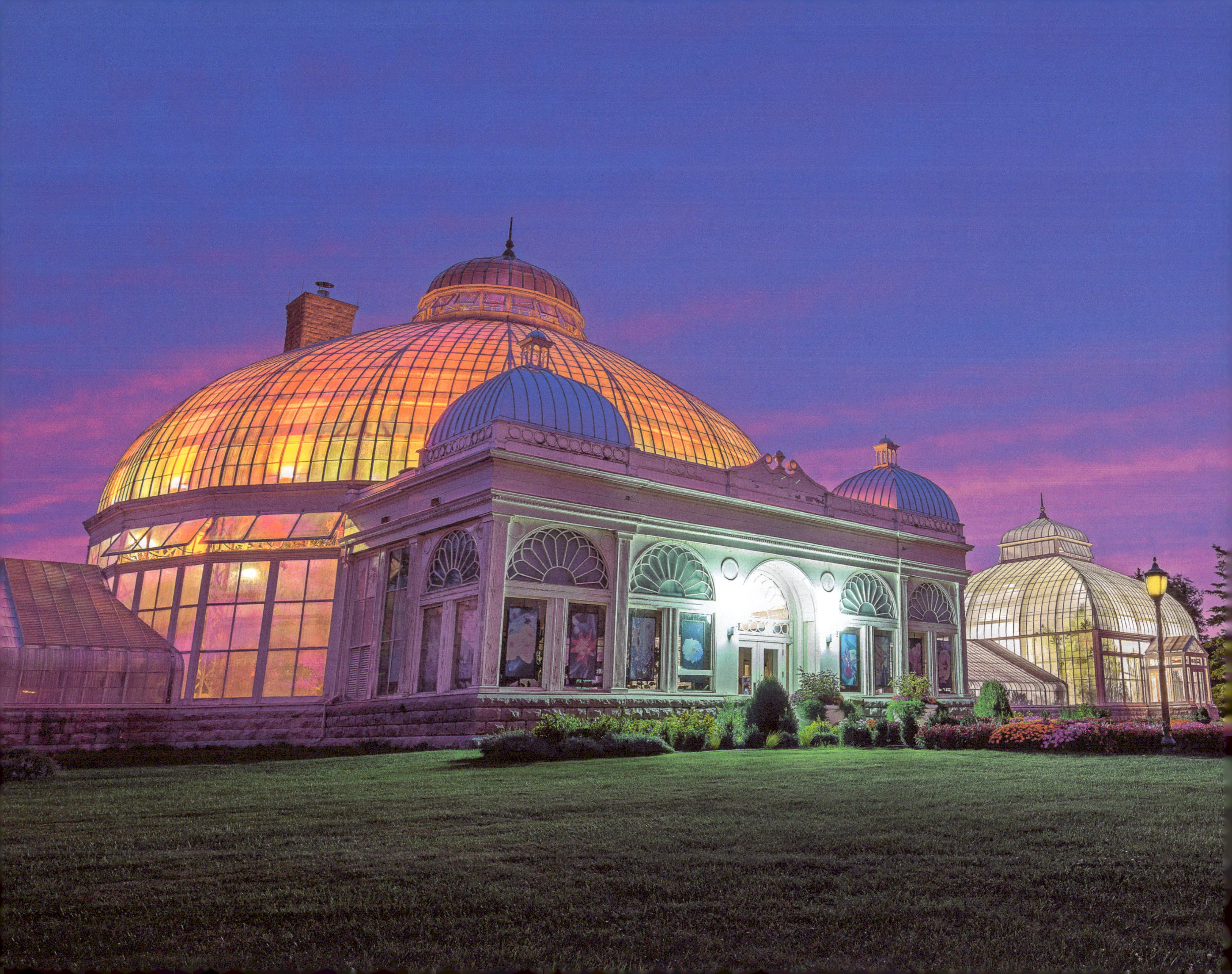

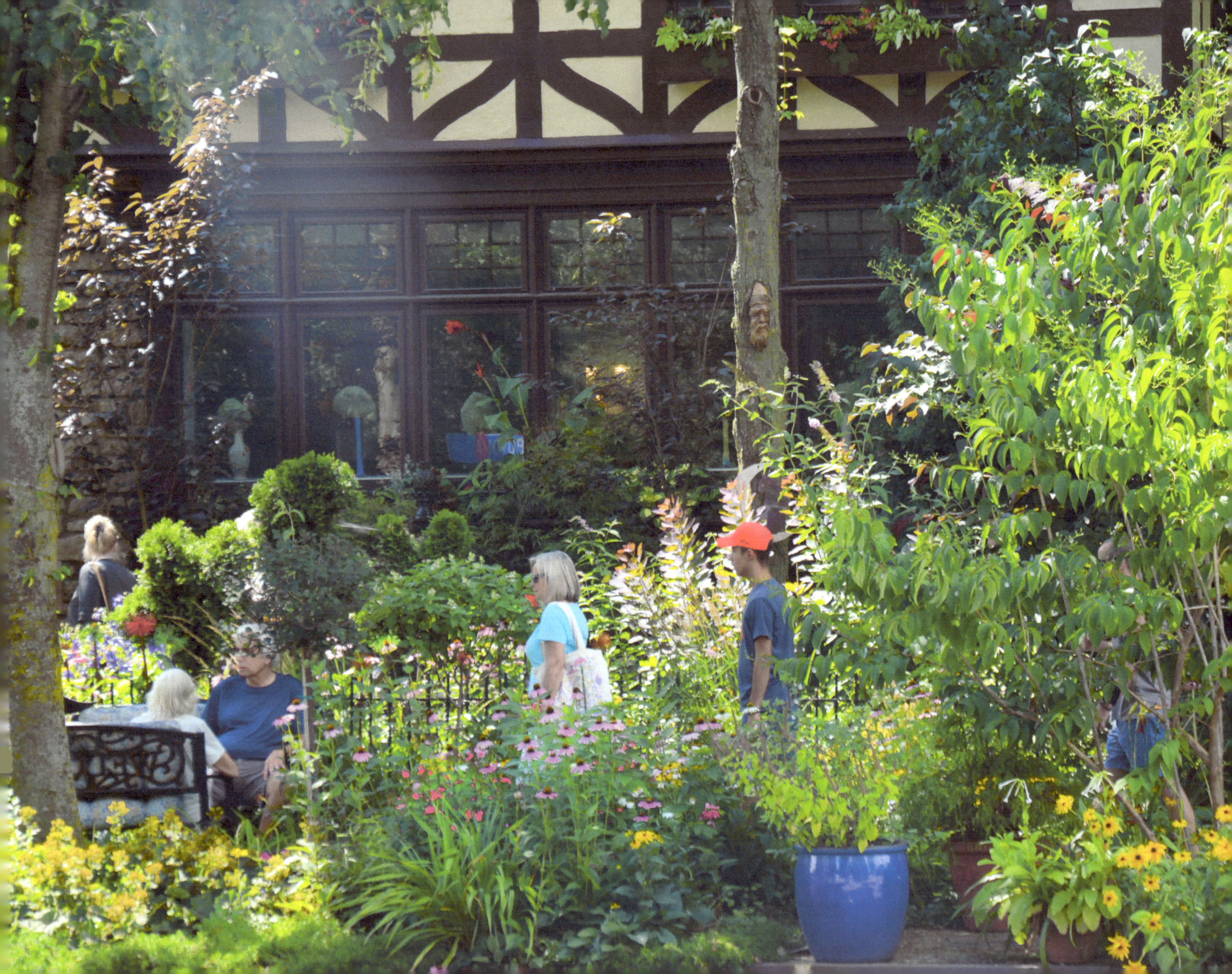

Flower Power

Garden tours in communities throughout WNY now pack our summer calendars, delighting green thumbs from near and far.

Garden Walk Buffalo Niagara *(Opposite:) is one of Western New York's most anticipated summer happenings. From its humble beginnings in 1995, which included only 29 gardens, it features more than 400 gardens and is now the nation's largest private garden tour. During the last weekend in July, an estimated 60,000 garden lovers pick up their maps and walk amidst our city's beautiful flora at homes that sport the familiar yellow signs.*

The Gardens at the Erie Basin Marina *(Right:)are more than just a fantastic explosion of floral color; it's a test garden for companies that hybridize flowers for the home gardener. Brimming with over 300 varieties of annuals gracing our waterfront, this is an essential proving ground supported by many seed companies testing flowers in this climate and location.*

The Village Pocket Park *(Below:) is located between Williamsville Village Hall and the Williamsville Library. The mural, "A Butterfly's View of the Garden" was created by Buffalo artist Chris Piontkowski.*

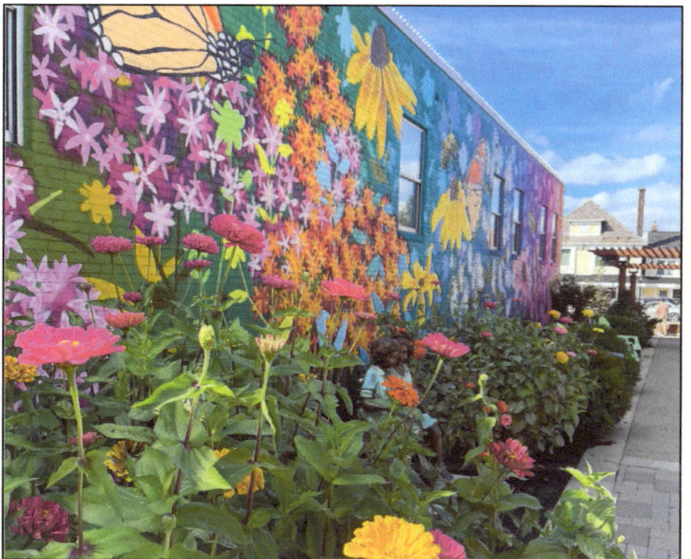

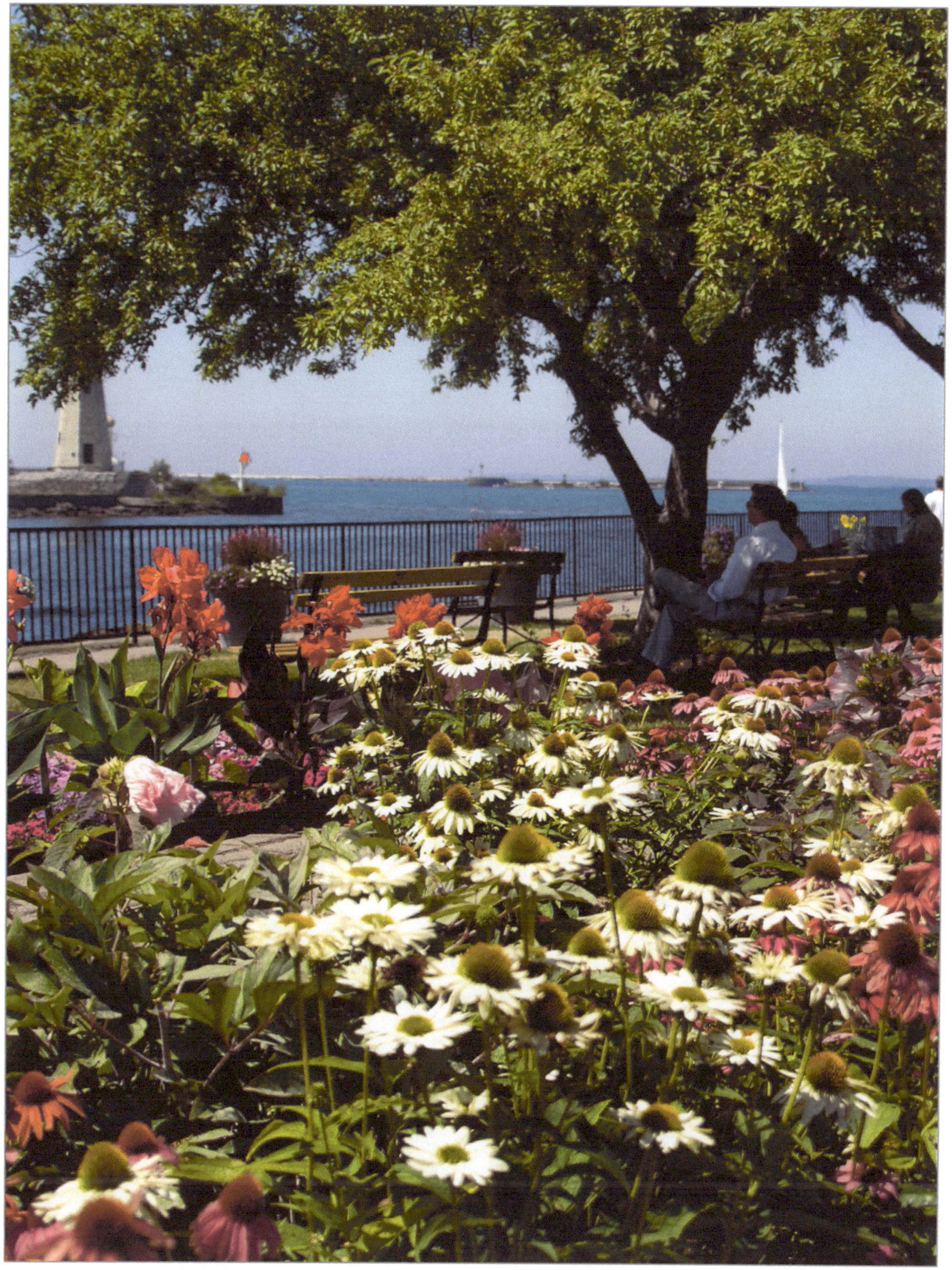

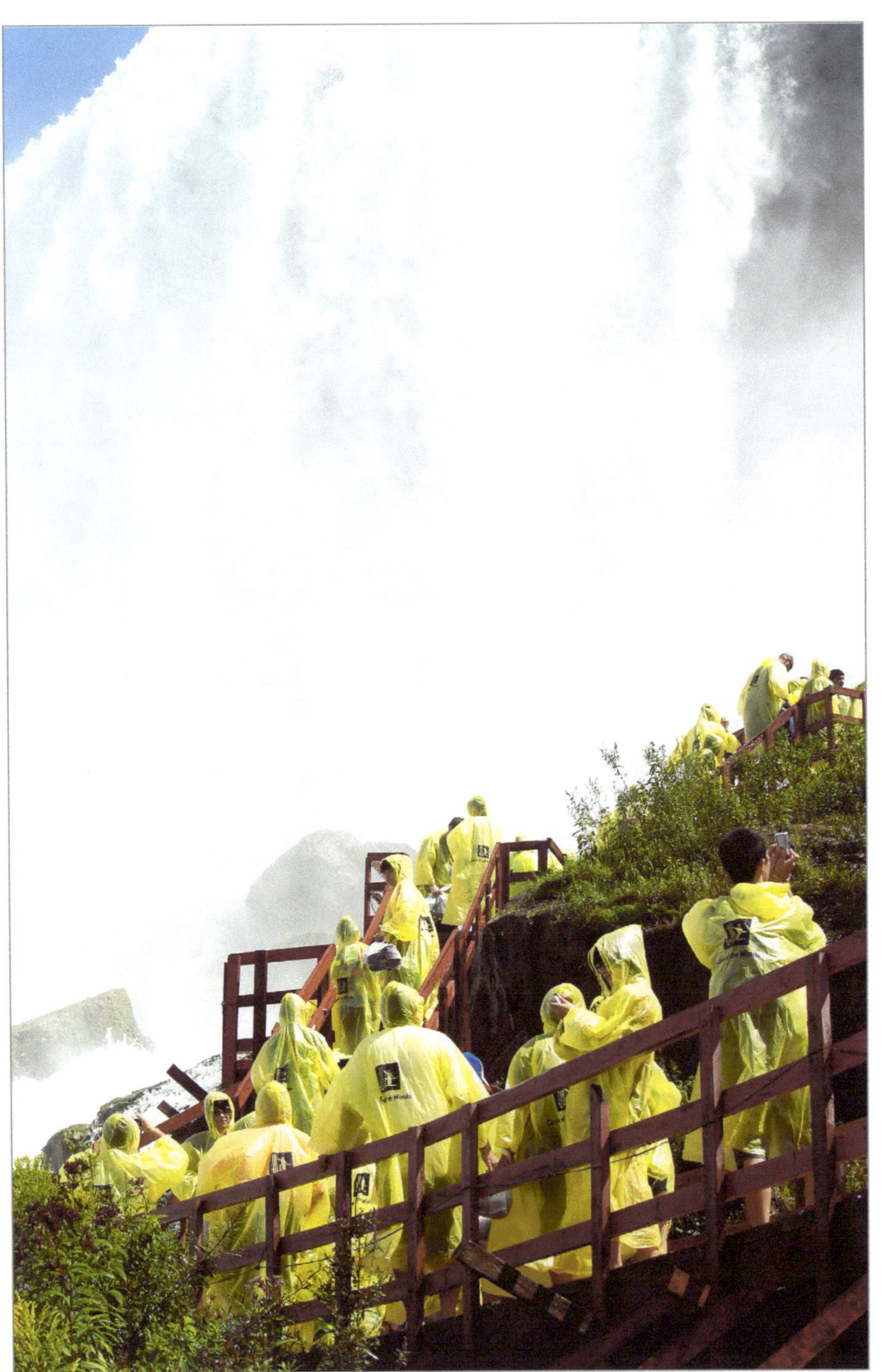

Niagara Falls State Park

Niagara Falls State Park, established on July 15, 1885, is the model from which all other state parks were created. Niagara Falls State Park's magical combination of water, cliff, and gravity, America's oldest state park, has mesmerized multiple generations. Each year, millions of visitors come to view the millions of gallons of water roaring over Niagara Falls every minute – about 750,000 gallons each second!

Niagara Falls State Park provides unparalleled access to experience this wonder from every angle. You can stand within feet of the brink of the Falls at Prospect or Teripin Points. View from a point jutting out over the Niagara Gorge from the Observation Deck at the Cave of the Winds. Feel the mist on your face as you climb the stairs midway up the Falls to the Eagle's Nest. Discover why they provided rain ponchos and water sandals at the Cave of the Winds Hurricane Deck as waterfalls thundered from incredible heights. Or sail into the belly of the beast as the Maid of the Mist fights its way through the churning rapids directly below the Horseshoe Falls.

The Falls are stunning by night, bathed in colorful lights, and spectacular when illuminated by nightly fireworks displays. Niagara Falls State Park is a visual delight in all seasons, from the warmth of summer to the blaze of fall leaves and the breathtaking frozen mounds in winter.

Remaining faithful to the vision of park designers Fredrick Law Olmsted and Calvert Vaux, who believed that parks should be places of natural beauty where "the masses could be renewed," the historic Niagara Falls State Park still carries on as a unique natural respite. Well-integrated alongside the inspiring wonder of the world is the solitude of a park filled with nature to be discovered and scenic terrain to be explored. Niagara Falls State Park is a stunning counterpoint to its more commercial neighbor across the border, from the floral Great Lakes garden to the Three Sisters islands and all the miles of beautiful trails that connect them.

(Opposite:) A field of frozen mounds surrounds the Horseshoe Falls in winter.

(Left:) A parade of colorful rain ponchos making their way to the Hurricane Deck at the Cave of the Winds.

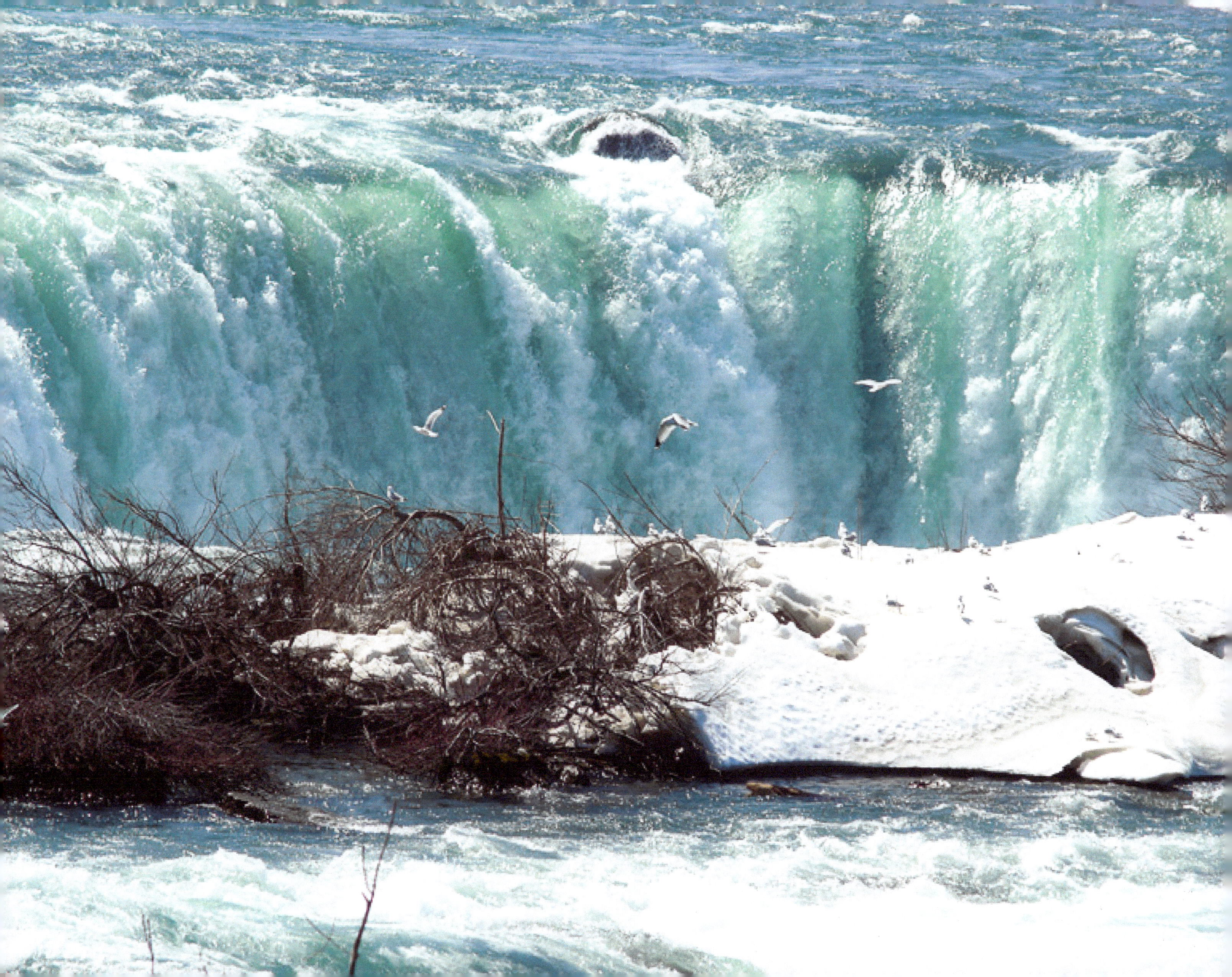

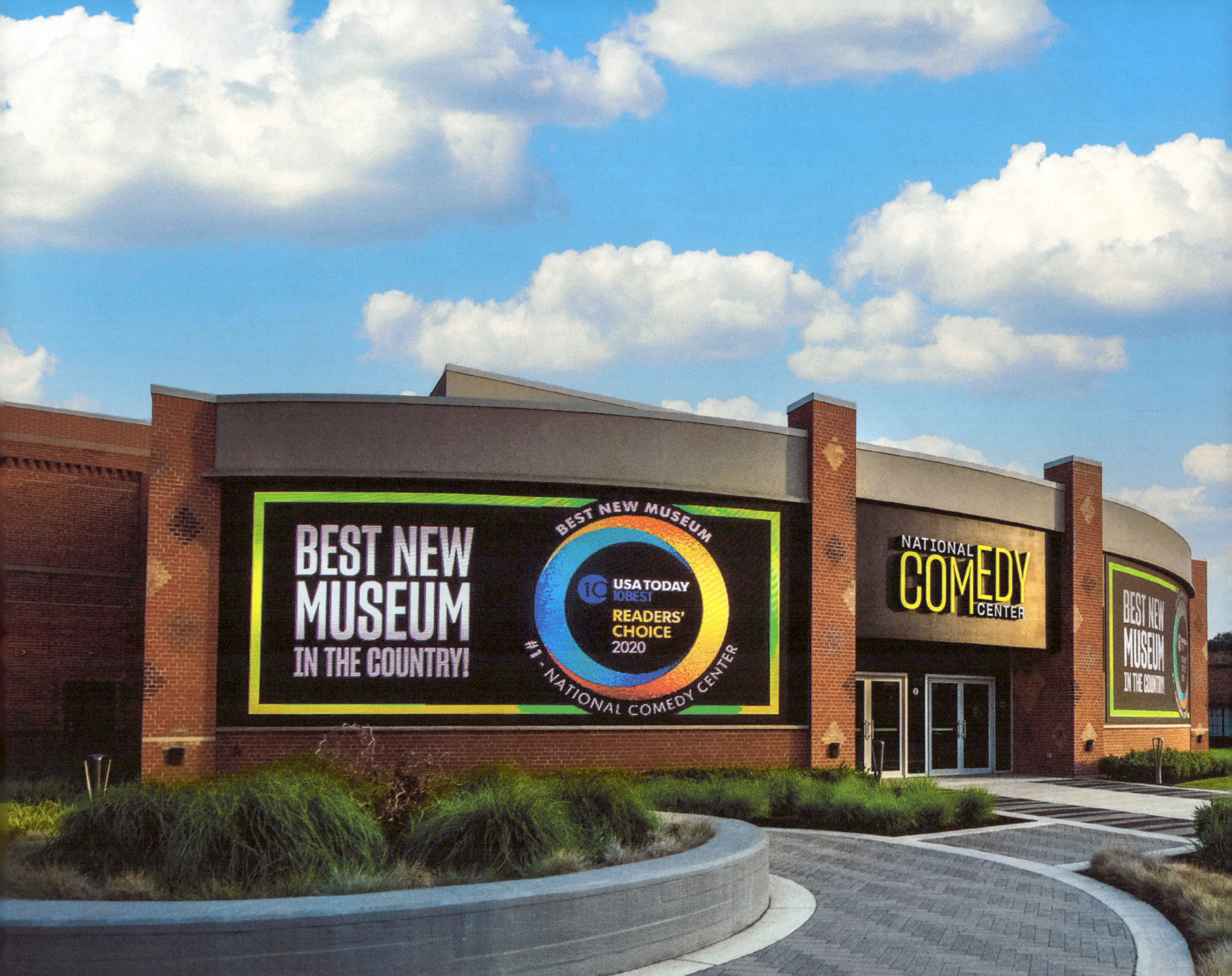
BEST NEW MUSEUM IN THE COUNTRY!
BEST NEW MUSEUM
USA TODAY 10BEST
READERS' CHOICE 2020
#1 - NATIONAL COMEDY CENTER
NATIONAL COMEDY CENTER

Arts & Culture

Arts, culture, and architecture aren't just an important part of our quality of life, they're a key driver of our region's renewal. And quite frankly, we're spoiled rotten. Buffalo Niagara's embarrassment of cultural wealth is difficult to hide. Humility takes a back seat in a region that can boast a world-class philharmonic orchestra, internationally acclaimed art galleries, and award-winning theater. We are home to a mind-boggling array of music, theater, and dance, housed in some of the most unique venues ever built to experience them.

We can explore the vibrant colors of our regional palette with more than its fair share of great art and great art galleries. From the AKG Art Gallery, one of the finest collections of modern and contemporary art anywhere in the world, and permanent collections like the Burchfield Penney, Castillani, Anderson, and CEPA, to hundreds of small, local galleries and studios, ours is a bustling region of the arts.

We're spoiled by sharing a backyard with the awe-inspiring Buffalo Philharmonic Orchestra, sizzling jazz at the Colored Musicians Club, Shakespeare in Delaware Park, an outstanding array of museums, the Chautauqua Institution, Artpark, Shea's Performing Arts Center, and dozens of professional theater companies.

The possibilities are virtually endless: Dig fossils. See how electricity is made. Get up close and personal with everything from dinosaurs and polar bears, to wooden horses. You can take a walk through history, escape as a run away slave to freedom, and reenact historic battles.

It's hundreds of cultural experiences to get your hands on and mind around to recharge your creative batteries.

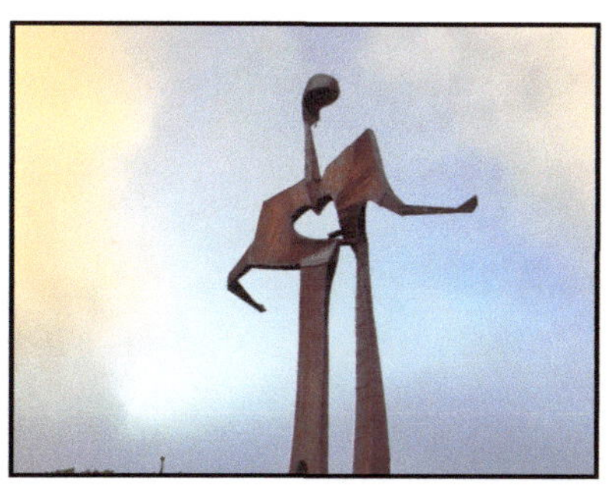

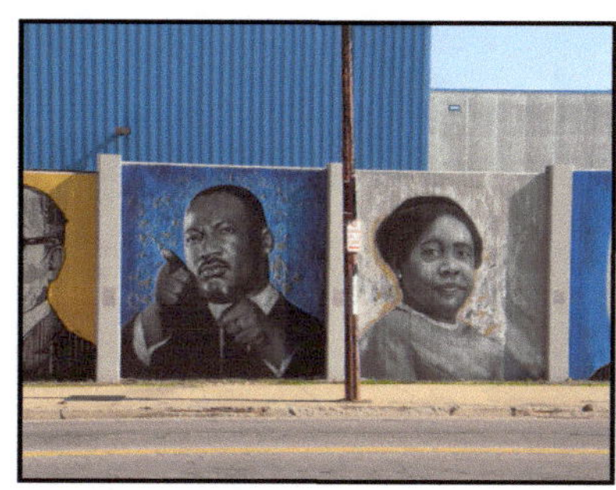

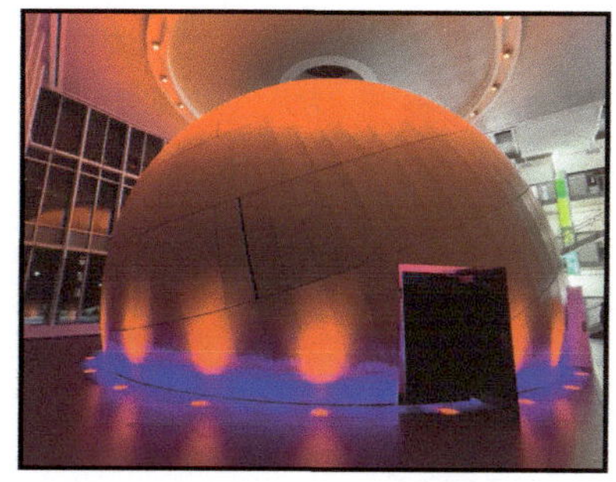

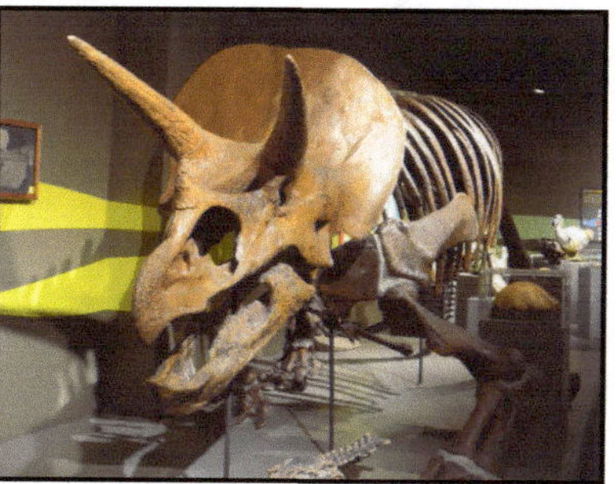

(Opposite:) The National Comedy Center in Jamestown, NY, is a world-class attraction based on the celebration of comedy.

(Left to right:) Griffis Sculpture Park, one of the largest sculpture parks in the United States, features over 250 large-scale sculptures dispersed through miles of hiking trails.

- The 300-foot Freedom Wall features 15-foot tall portraits of 28 different influential Black Americans throughout history.

- The Whitworth Ferguson Planetarium at SUNY Buffalo State brings the wonders of the Universe to Western New York—their state-of-the-art software and projection systems present opportunities for visualizations of the night sky and far beyond.

- The Rethink Extinct exhibit at the Buffalo Museum of Science takes you on a journey through time, starting in the Paleozoic Era 542 million years ago.

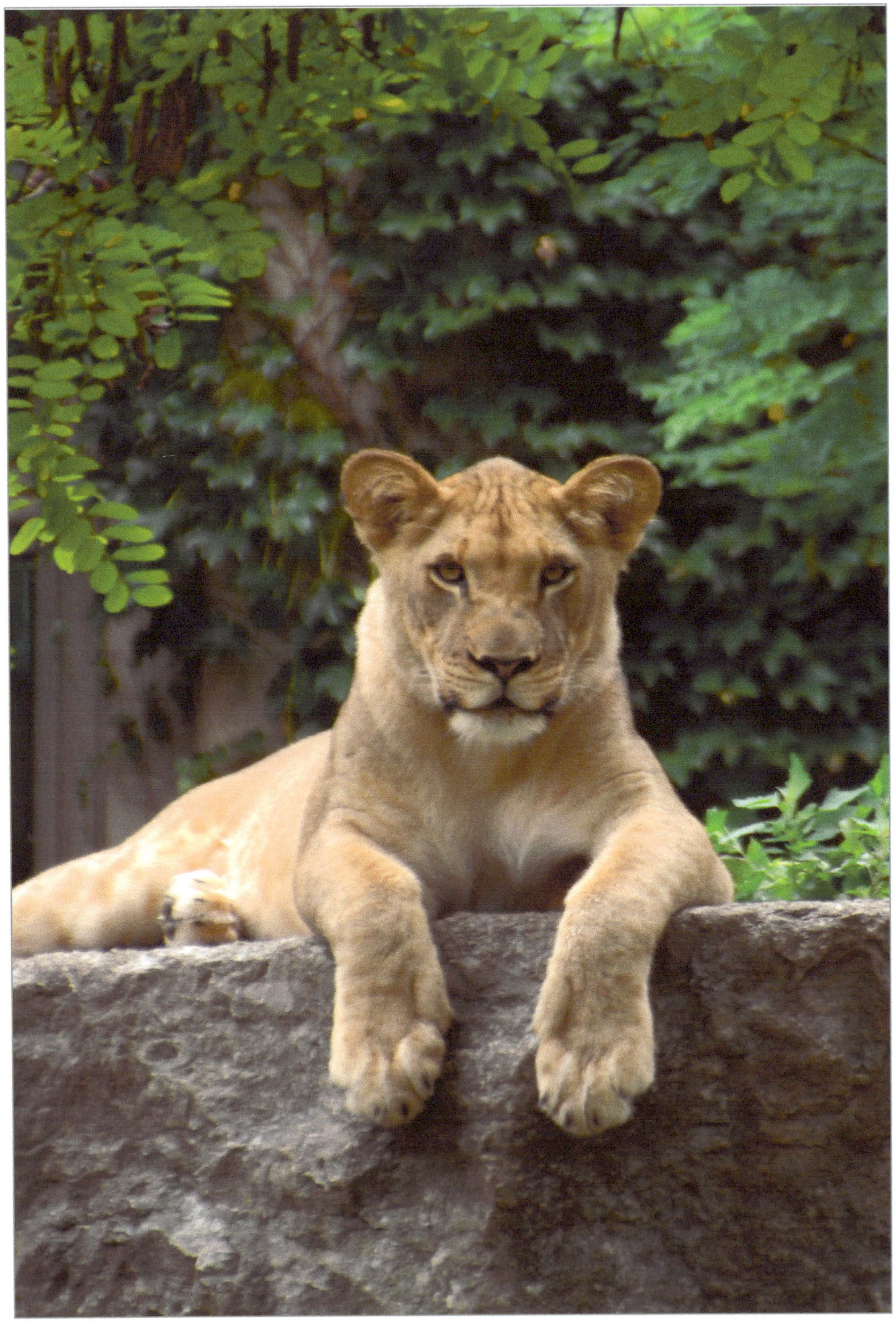

The Buffalo Zoo

The Buffalo Zoo is a vibrant collection of wild and exotic animals and houses more than 320 species of plants. Founded in 1875, it's the third oldest zoo in the U.S. and is listed on the National Historic Register. Located on 23.5 acres of Buffalo's Delaware Park and open year-round, the zoo is a recreation, education, and conservation source for more than 400,000 visitors annually.

At Sea Lion Cove, families get a commanding view of a group of charismatic, vocal sea lions. Visitors can view these large, graceful mammals from below the water and the 220-seat amphitheater.

The Arctic Edge focuses on the snowy, frozen climate of the Arctic Circle. Visitors get an up-close look at the bears' playful antics and enclosures that feature Arctic wolves, lynxes, and the majestic bald eagle.

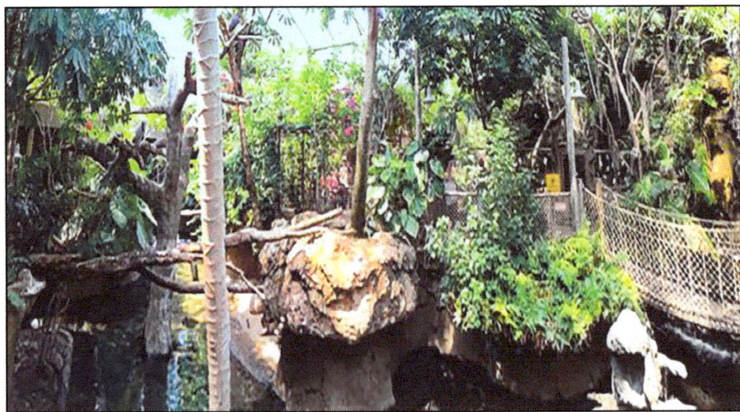

(Above:) Rainforest Falls, a year-round zoo attraction, replicates the unique geology and ecology of Venezuela's Canaima National Park, home to Angel Falls, the highest waterfall in the world. In addition to showcasing a wide variety of wildlife, the exhibit's back wall resembles a flat-topped mountain with a live, working waterfall.

(Left:) In June 2023, the Buffalo Zoo welcomed four newborn lion cubs.

(Opposite:) Parents and children line up to be amazed, amused, and much more aware of the world and the animals that fill it.

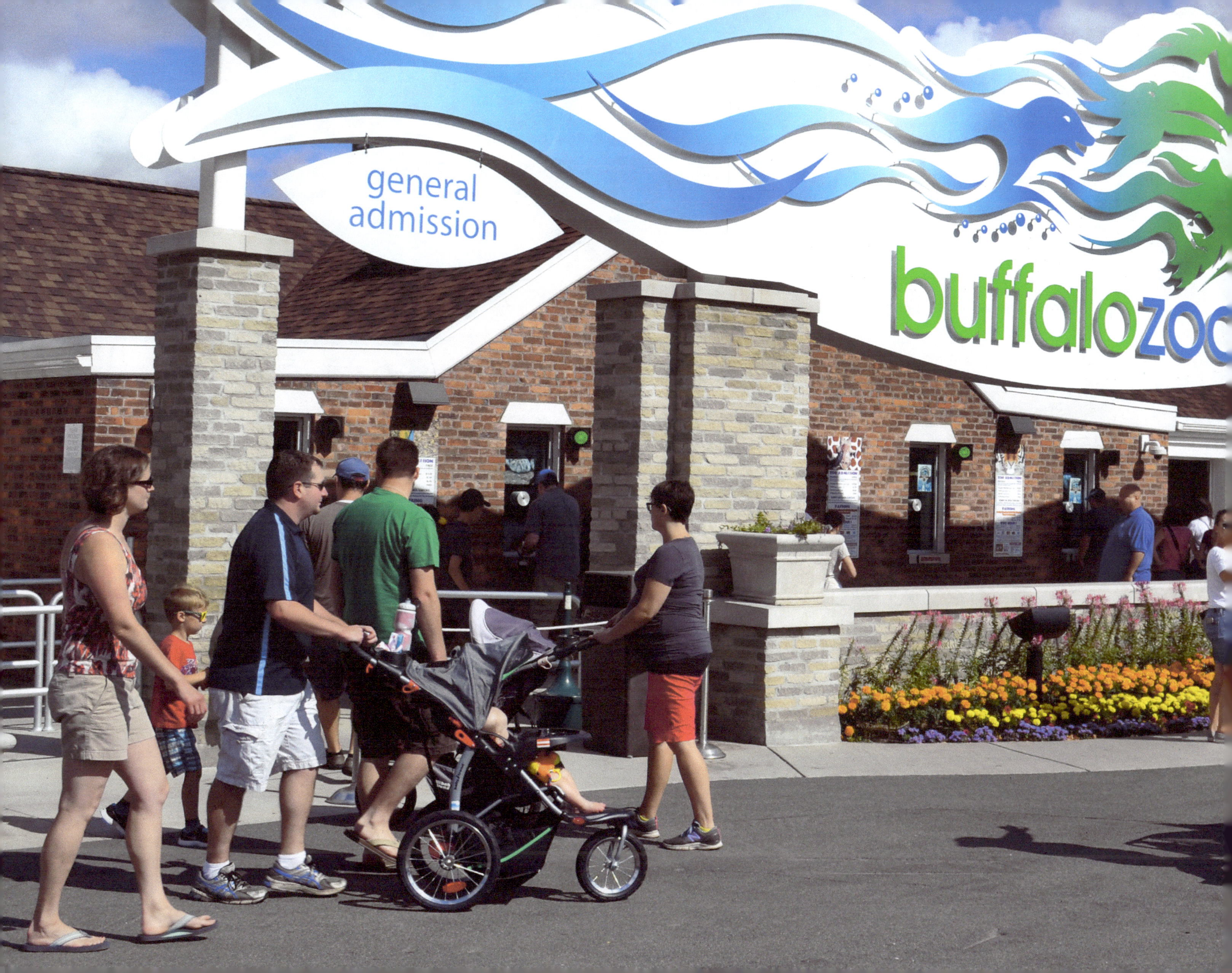
general
admission
buffalo

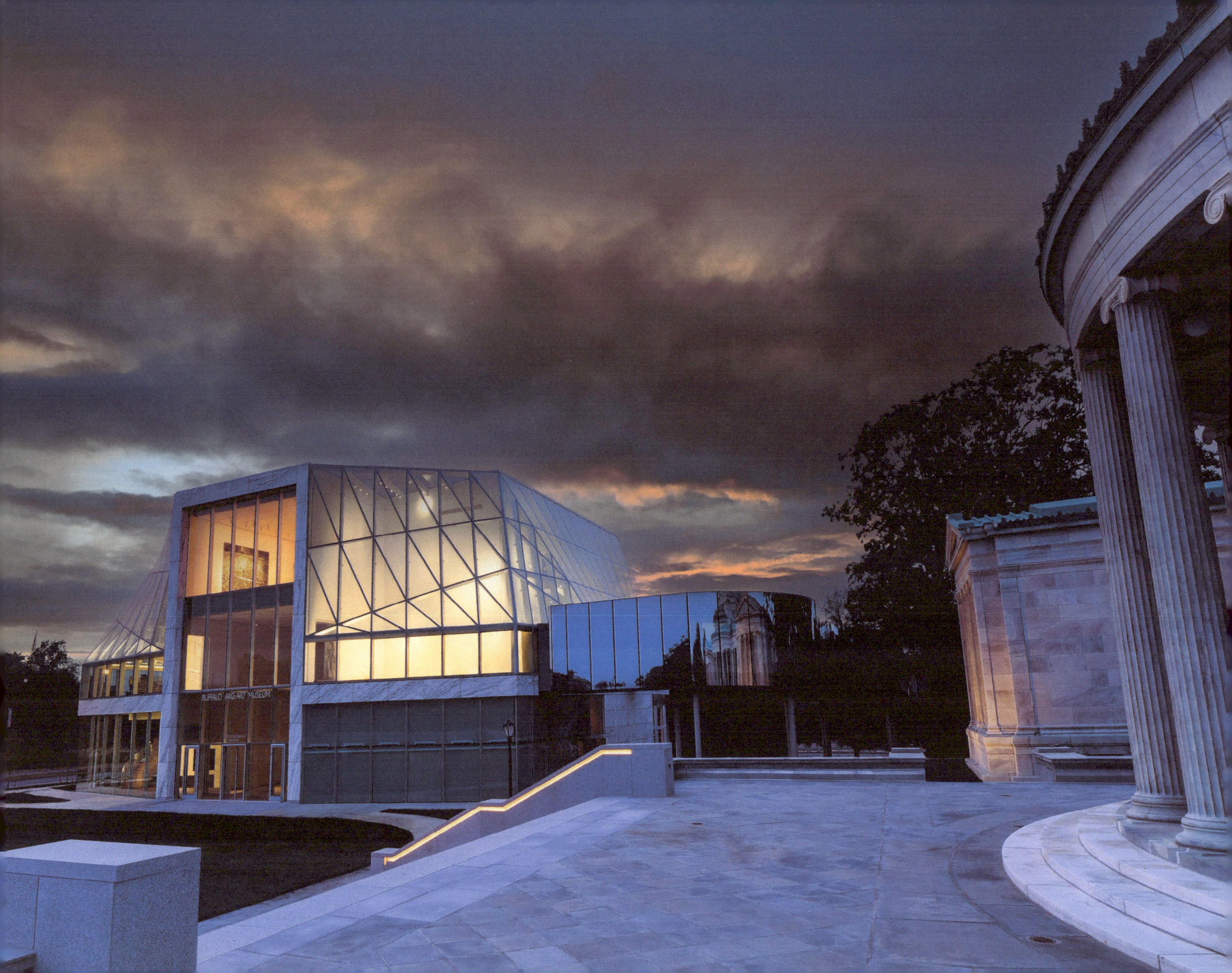
BUFFALO AKG ART MUSEUM

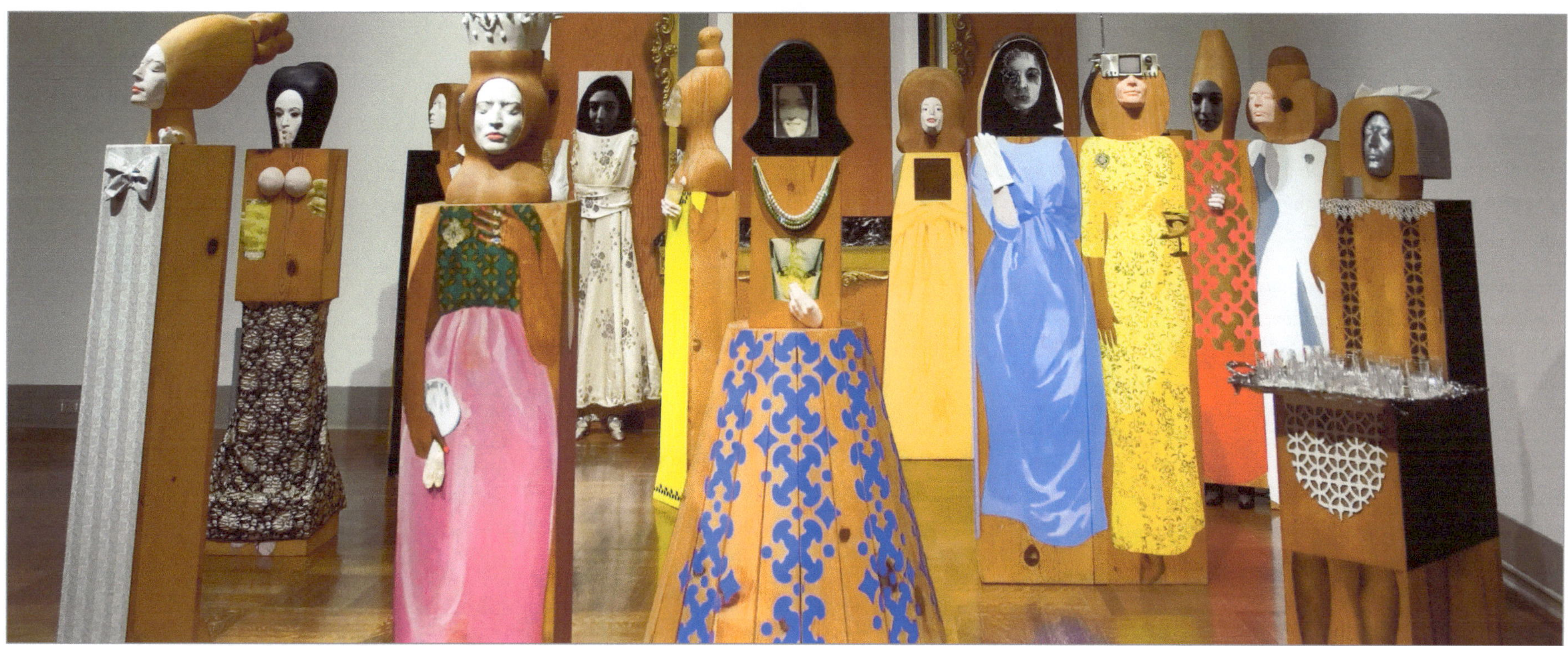

The AKG Art Gallery

The Buffalo AKG Art Museum, formerly known as the Albright–Knox Art Gallery, is a major showplace for modern and contemporary art. It was expanded beginning in 2021 and reopened in June 2023. It is now named after three major donors: John J. Albright, Seymour H. Knox II, and Jeffrey Gundlach. Before its expansion, the Buffalo AKG Art Museum exhibition space could accommodate only 200 works – 3% of its 6,740-piece collection.

The parent organization of the Buffalo AKG Art Museum is the Buffalo Fine Arts Academy, founded in 1862, one of the oldest public arts institutions in the United States. It was initially to be used as the Fine Arts Pavilion for the Pan-American Exposition in 1901. Still, delays in its construction caused it to remain uncompleted until 1905.

The gallery's expansive collection includes works spanning Impressionistic and Post-Impressionistic styles by artists of the nineteenth century, such as Paul Gauguin, Edgar Degas, Claude Monet, and Vincent van Gogh.

Twentieth-century styles such as abstraction, cubism, surrealism, and constructivism are represented in works by artists like Pablo Picasso, Henri Matisse, Piet Mondrian, and Georgia O'Keeffe.

The Abstract Expressionism movement is widely represented in the collection with works by artists including Jackson Pollock, Robert Motherwell, Helen Frankenthaler, and Clyfford Still.

(Opposite:) In addition to creating another entry point to the museum, the Gundlach Building features 13 new galleries totaling 27,000 sq. ft, plus an enclosed 6,100 sq. ft sculpture terrace.

(Above:) Marisol: A Retrospective - The Party, 1965–66

Buffalo History Museum

The Buffalo History Museum, formerly The Buffalo and Erie County Historical Society, collects and preserves over a million artifacts and records of Western New York. Founded in 1862, the Historical Society's first president was Millard Fillmore.

Buffalo architect George Cary designed the museum building and is the only permanent structure erected for the Pan-American Exposition, which took place in 1901. It was designated a National Historic Landmark in 1987.

All three floors of the building offer exhibits, including Continuum: A History of Erie County. Created in coordination with Erie County's bicentennial celebration, Continuum offers a glimpse into our region's history, dating back thousands of years. Visitors will discover the people, events, and innovations that helped build our county and view unique artifacts illuminating its past. Among the many objects on display are a rare Lewis lighthouse lens from early Buffalo and the Iver-Johnson revolver used to shoot President McKinley in 1901.

Continuum also features nine cutting-edge augmented reality experiences available through your phones or tablets.

(Opposite:) TThe front enterance of the Buffalo and Erie County Historical Society at night.

(Right:) Overlooking Hoyt Lake from the museum's portico is Lincoln, The Emancipator, a bronze statue mounted on black marble by sculptor Charles H. Niehaus. It was commissioned by the Lincoln Birthday Association, founded by Buffalo druggist Julius E. Francis. Francis unsuccessfully petitioned Congress 1873 to make Lincoln's birthday a n ational holiday. On Feb. 12, 1874, the following year, he began in Buffalo what has become the longest continuous celebration of Lincoln's birthday, with people gathering each year in the museum to mark the date.

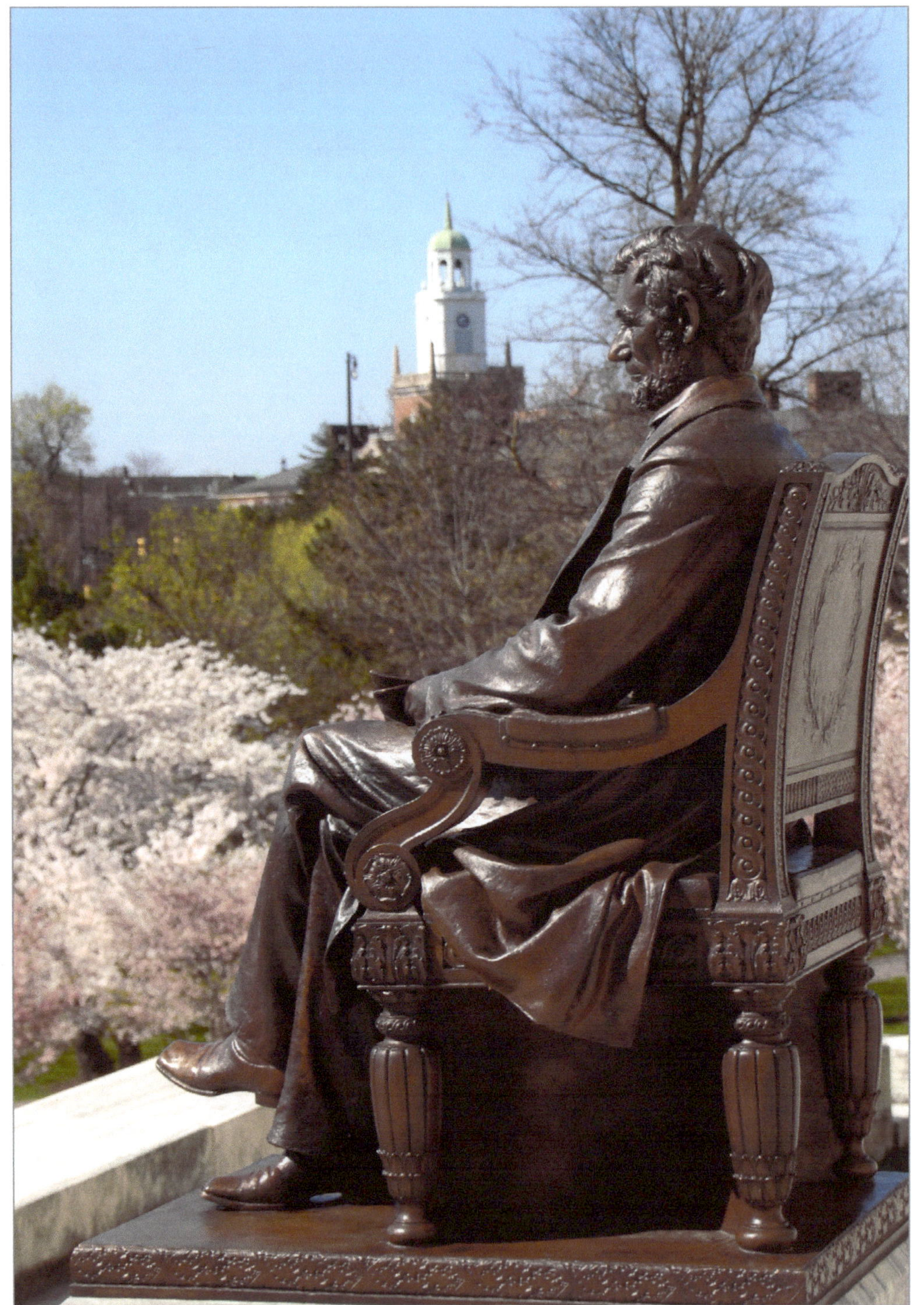

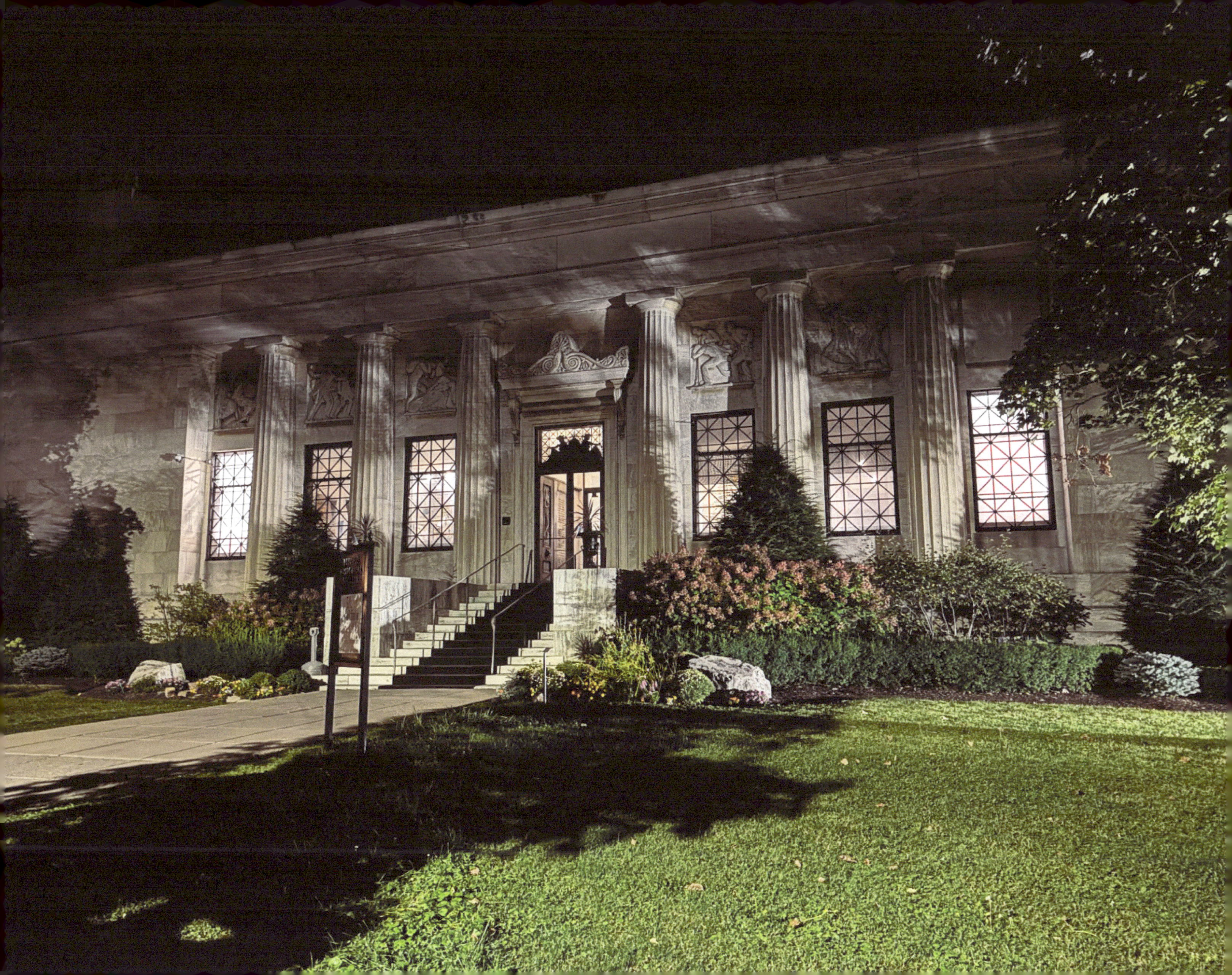

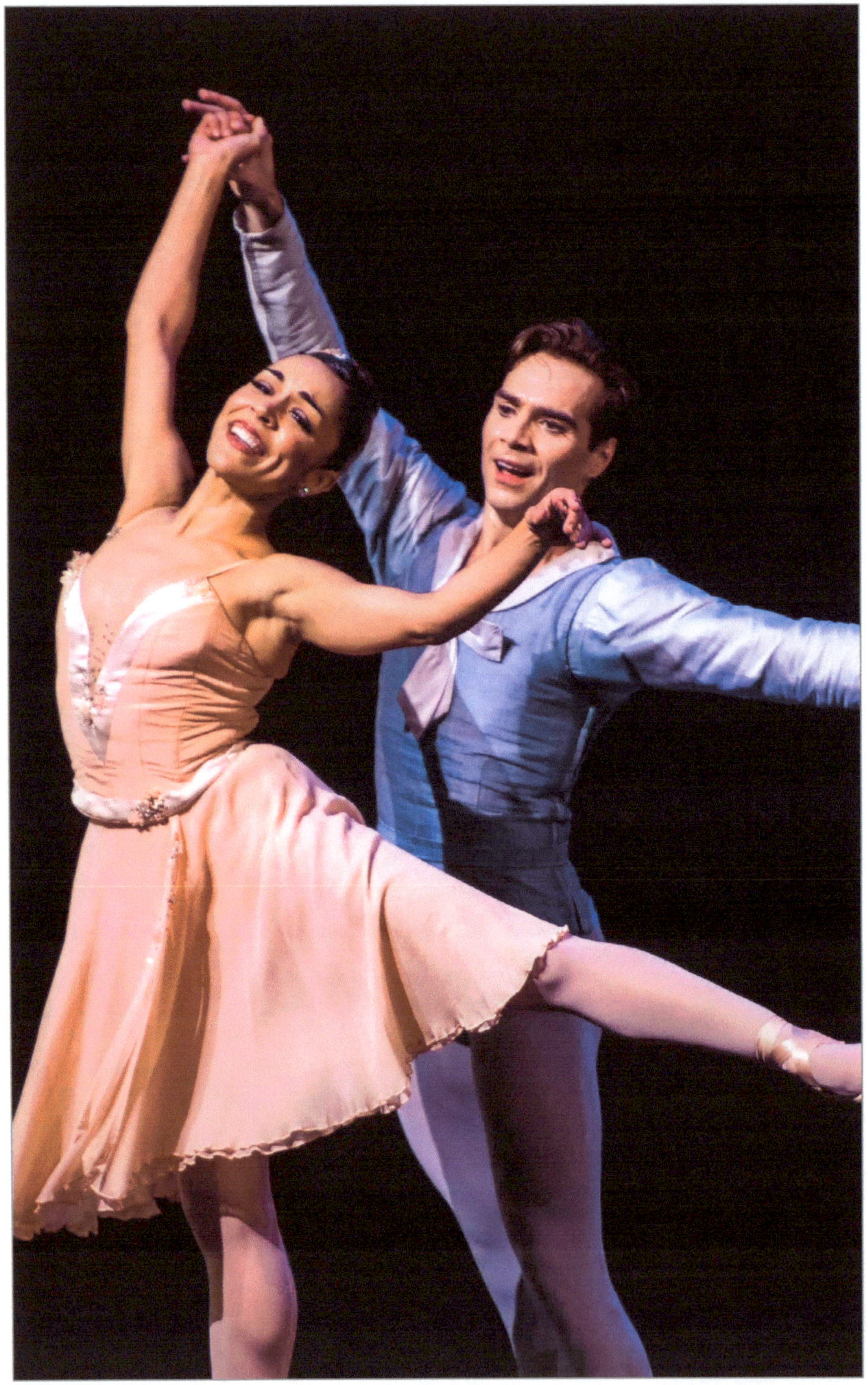

The Chautauqua Institution

The Chautauqua Institution is a not-for-profit, 750-acre educational center beside Chautauqua Lake in southwestern New York State, where approximately 7,500 persons are in residence on any day during a nine-week season, and over 100,000 attend scheduled public events. Over 8,000 students enroll annually in the Chautauqua Summer Schools, which offer courses in art, music, dance, theater, writing skills, and a wide variety of special interests.

Chautauqua as a community celebrates, encourages, and studies the arts and treats them as integral to all of learning. With symphony, opera, theater, dance, visual arts, and a renowned music school, Chautauqua produces an "eclectic mix" of programming that can be found nowhere else.

Chautauqua is dedicated to the exploration of the best in human values and the enrichment of life through a program that explores the important religious, social, and political issues of our times; stimulates provocative, thoughtful involvement of individuals and families in creative response to such issues; and promotes excellence and creativity in the appreciation, performance, and teaching of the arts.

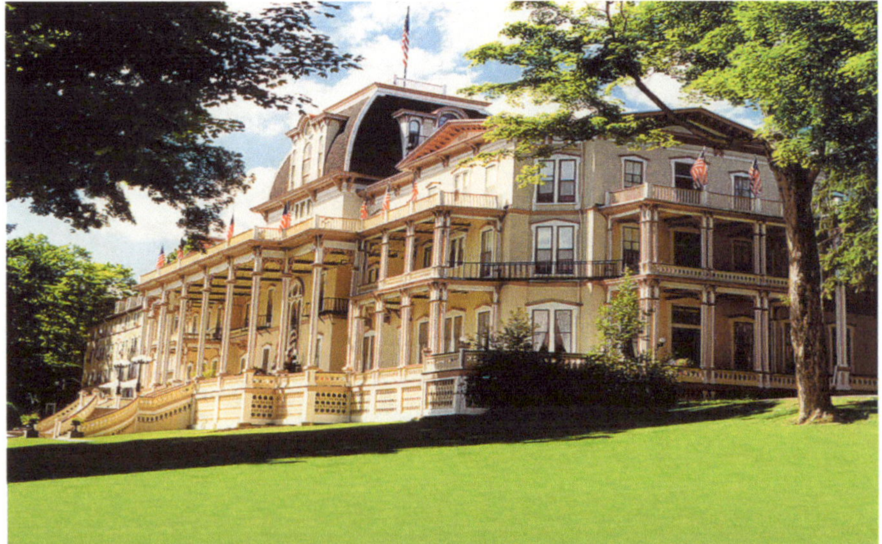

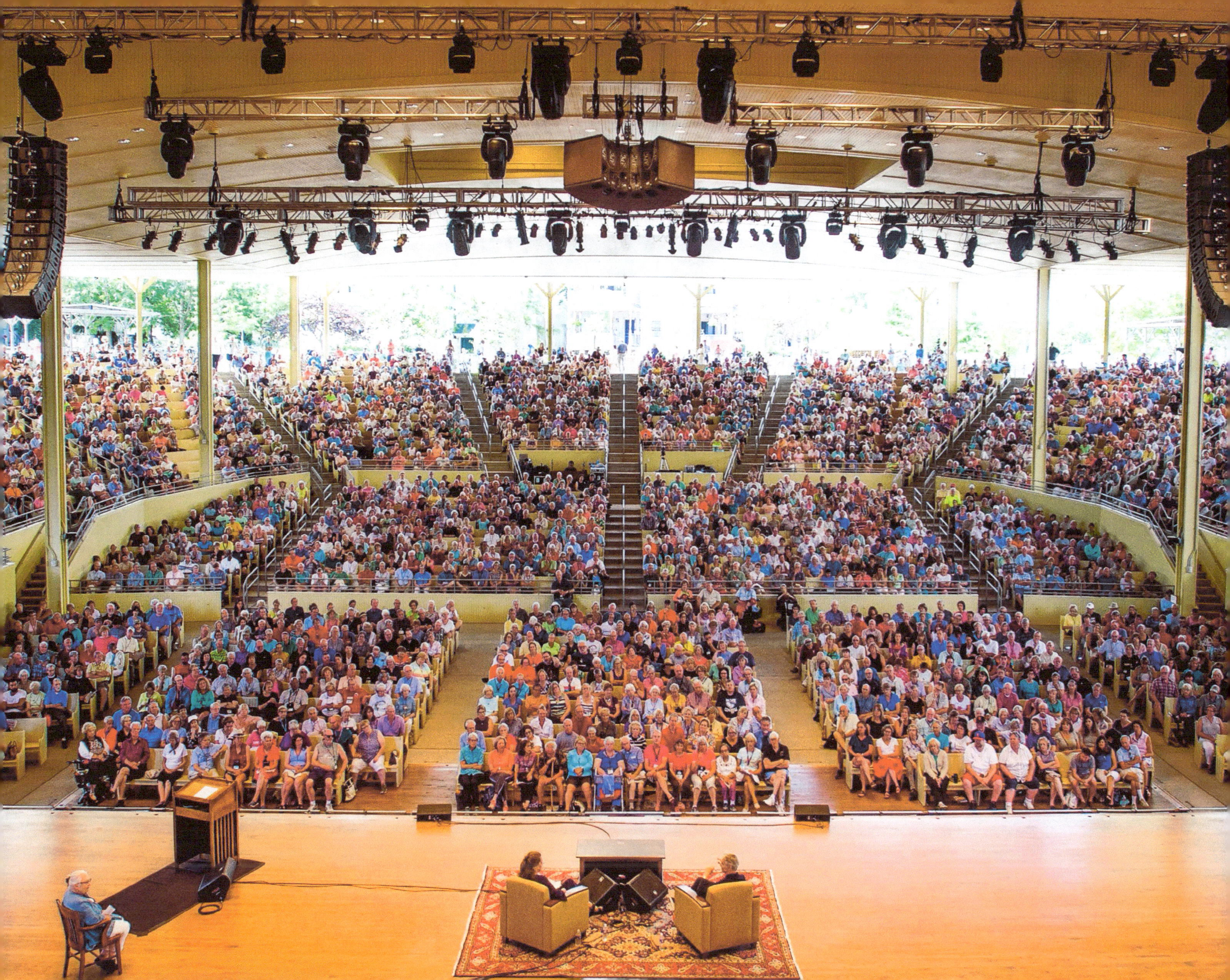

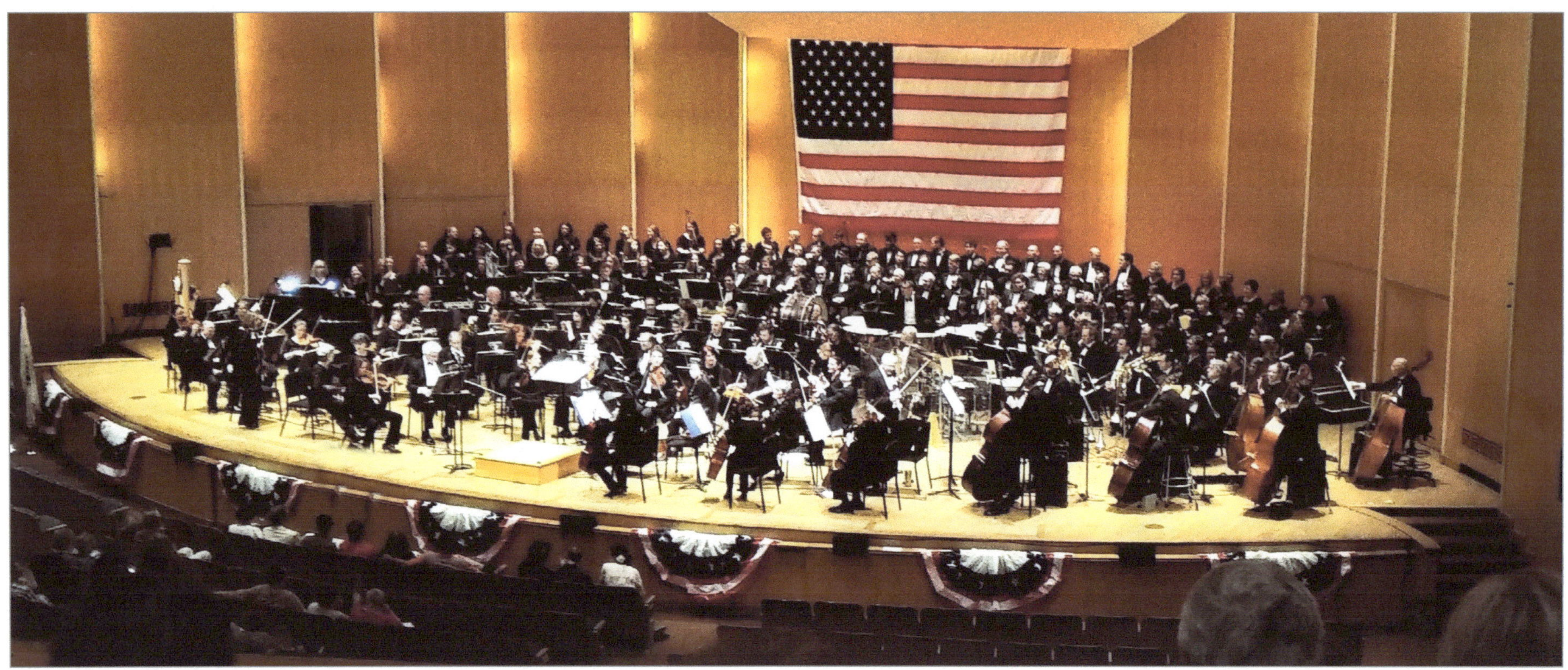

© Photo by Nickel City Studio

Buffalo Philharmonic Orchestra

The Buffalo Philharmonic Orchestra is one of the brightest jewels in our long list of cultural treasures. Since its inception in 1938, the artistic excellence of the BPO has consistently enriched the quality of life in Western New York.

In fall and winter, the BPO performs at the orchestra's permanent home at Kleinhans Music Hall, a National Historic Site with an international reputation as one of the finest concert halls in the United States. And when the weather breaks, theybecome road warriors, mesmerizing crowds at dozens of diverse locations from Bison's games, Artpark, and Canalside to the Shaw Festival and even Carnegie Hall.

As Buffalo's cultural ambassador, the Grammy Award-winning BPO, under the leadership of music director JoAnn Falletta, presents more than 120 Classics, Pops, and Youth Concerts each year and reaches over 40,000 students across all eight counties of Western New York.

"I've enjoyed every place I've conducted, but there's a rightness about this place. Yes, we can make good things happen here. We can play for a community we know and love. That is truly a collaborative relationship, and it's rare."

JoAnn Falletta
Music Director
Buffalo Philharmonic Orchestra

(Opposite:) © Photo by David Adam Beloff

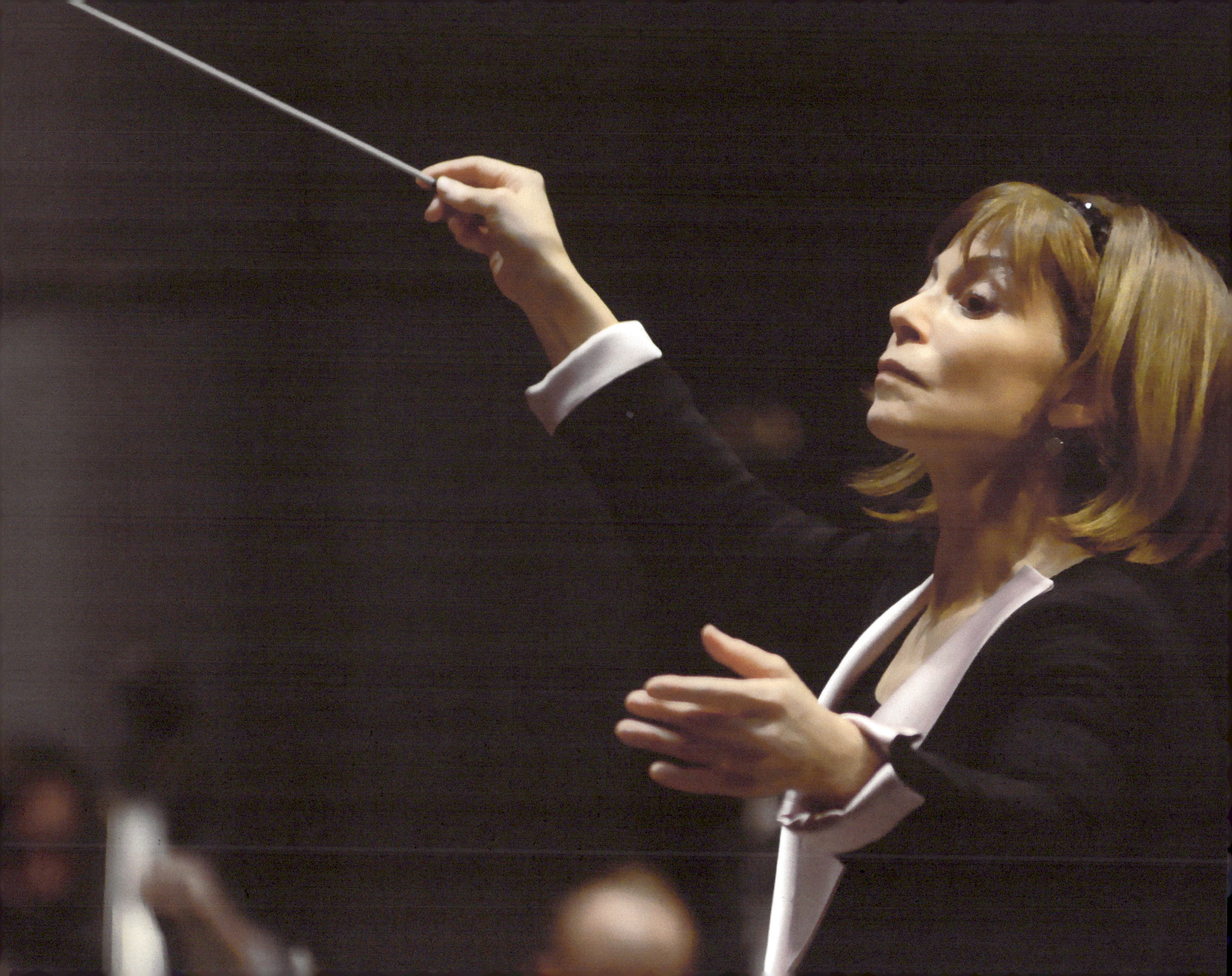

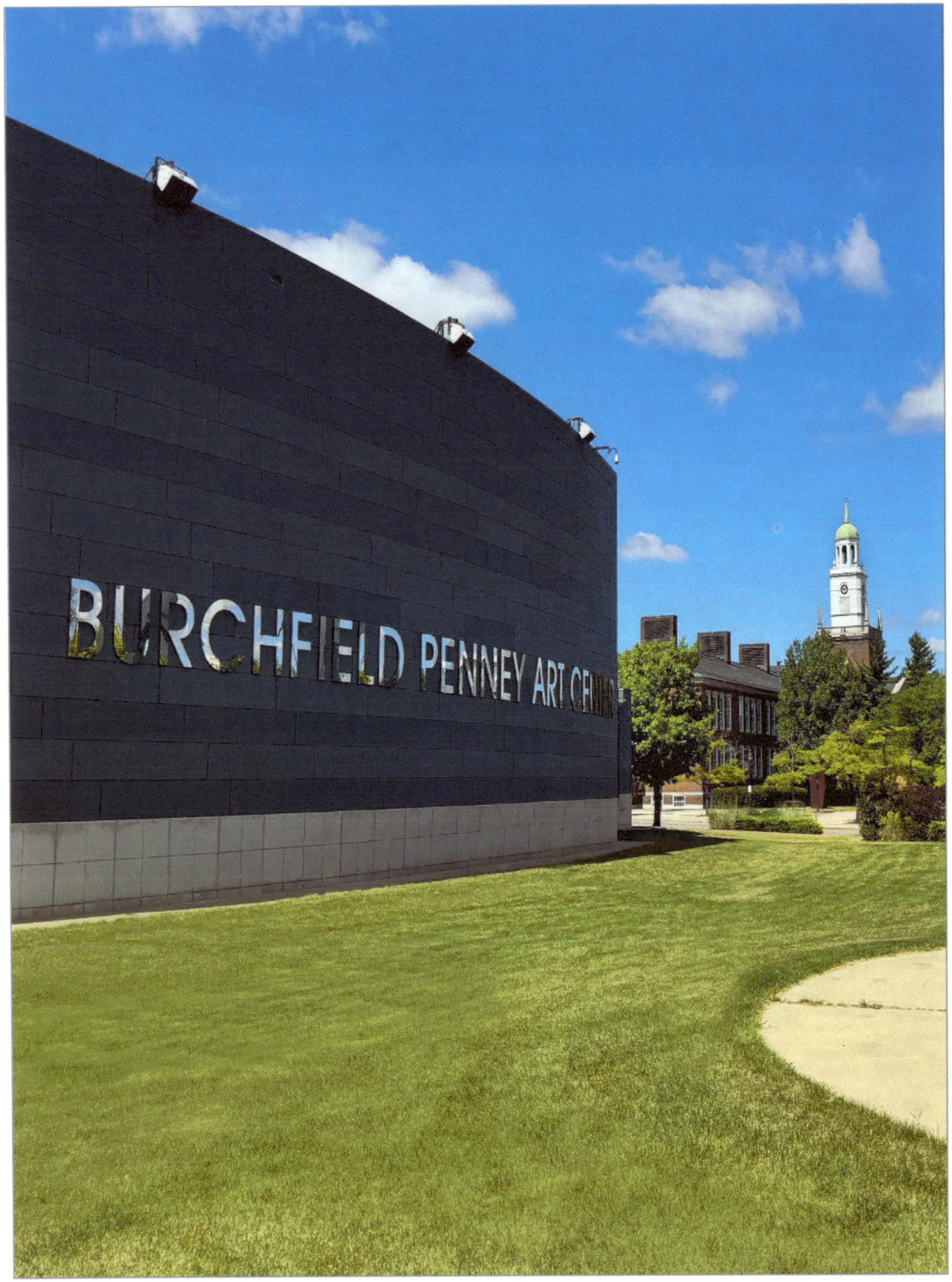

Burchfield Penney Art Center

The Burchfield Penney Art Center is a museum dedicated to the art and vision of Charles E. Burchfield and distinguished artists of Buffalo Niagara and Western New York. Through its affiliation with Buffalo State College, the museum encourages learning and celebrates our richly creative community.

In addition to its visual arts offerings, the Burchfield Penney has diverse programming, regularly presenting concerts, literary readings, lectures, symposia, workshops, and special events.

The Burchfield Penney Art Center holds the most extensive public collection of works by Charles E. Burchfield (1893–1967), as well as an archive of more than 10,000 pages of handwritten journals, 25,000 drawings, and other ephemera, including a scale re-creation of the artist's studio. Best known for his romantic, often fantastic depictions of nature, watercolorist Charles Ephraim Burchfield (1893–1967) developed a unique style of watercolor painting that reflected distinctly American subjects and his profound respect for nature.

(Left:) The front of the Burchfield Penney with the familiar clock tower of Rockwell Hall at Buffalo State College is in the background.

(Below:) Charles Burchfield's studio.

(Opposite:) The Center's main gallery

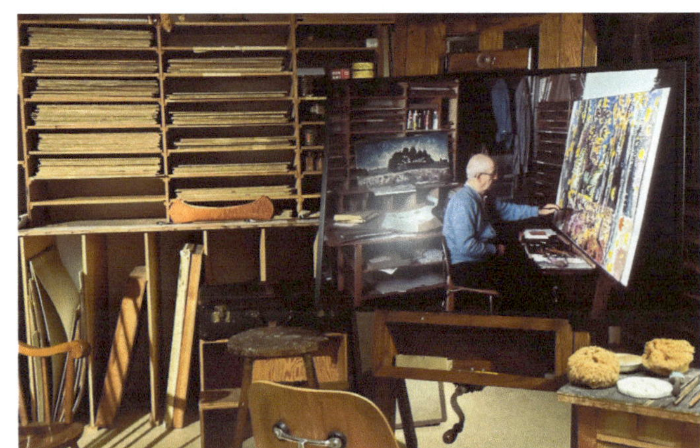

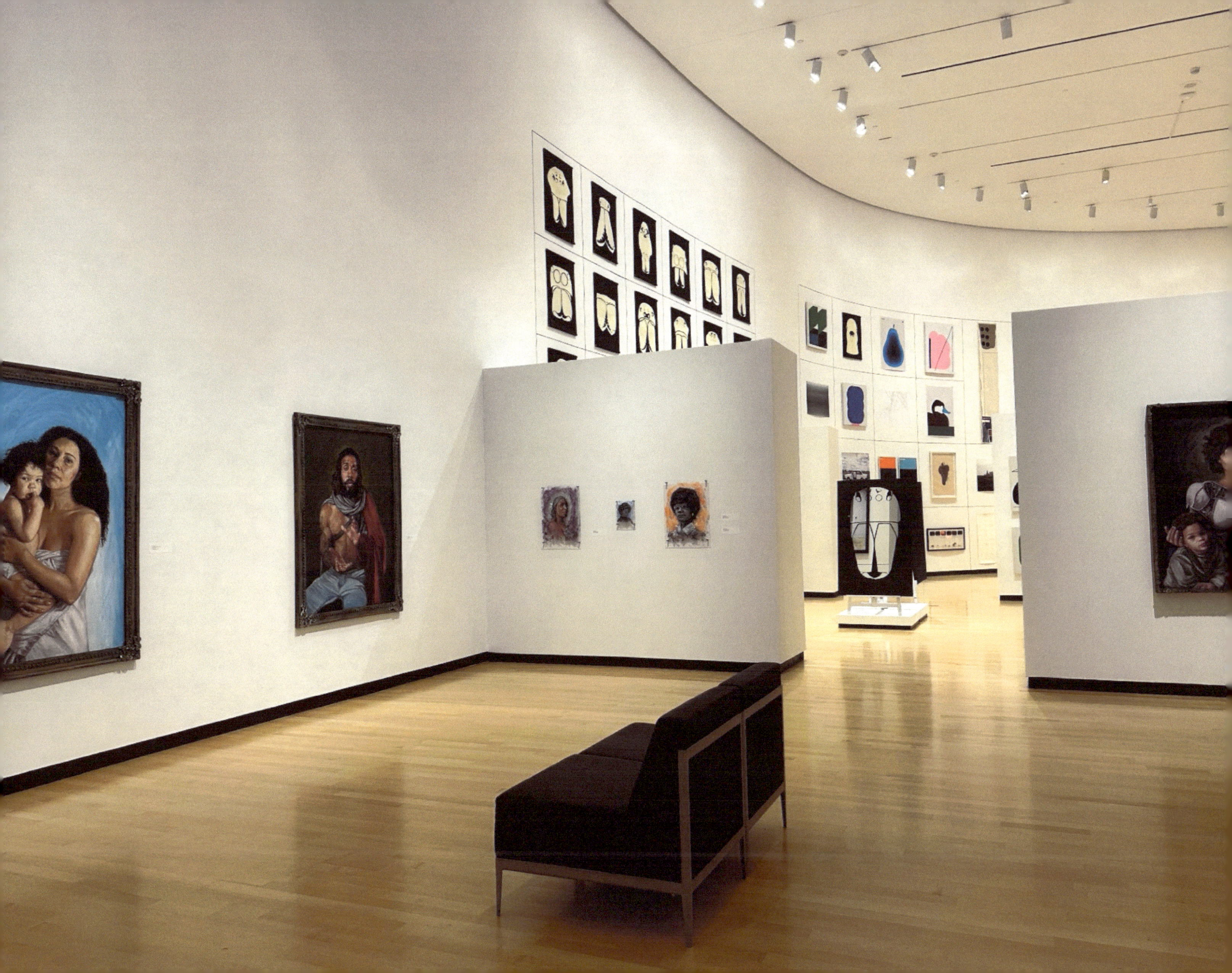

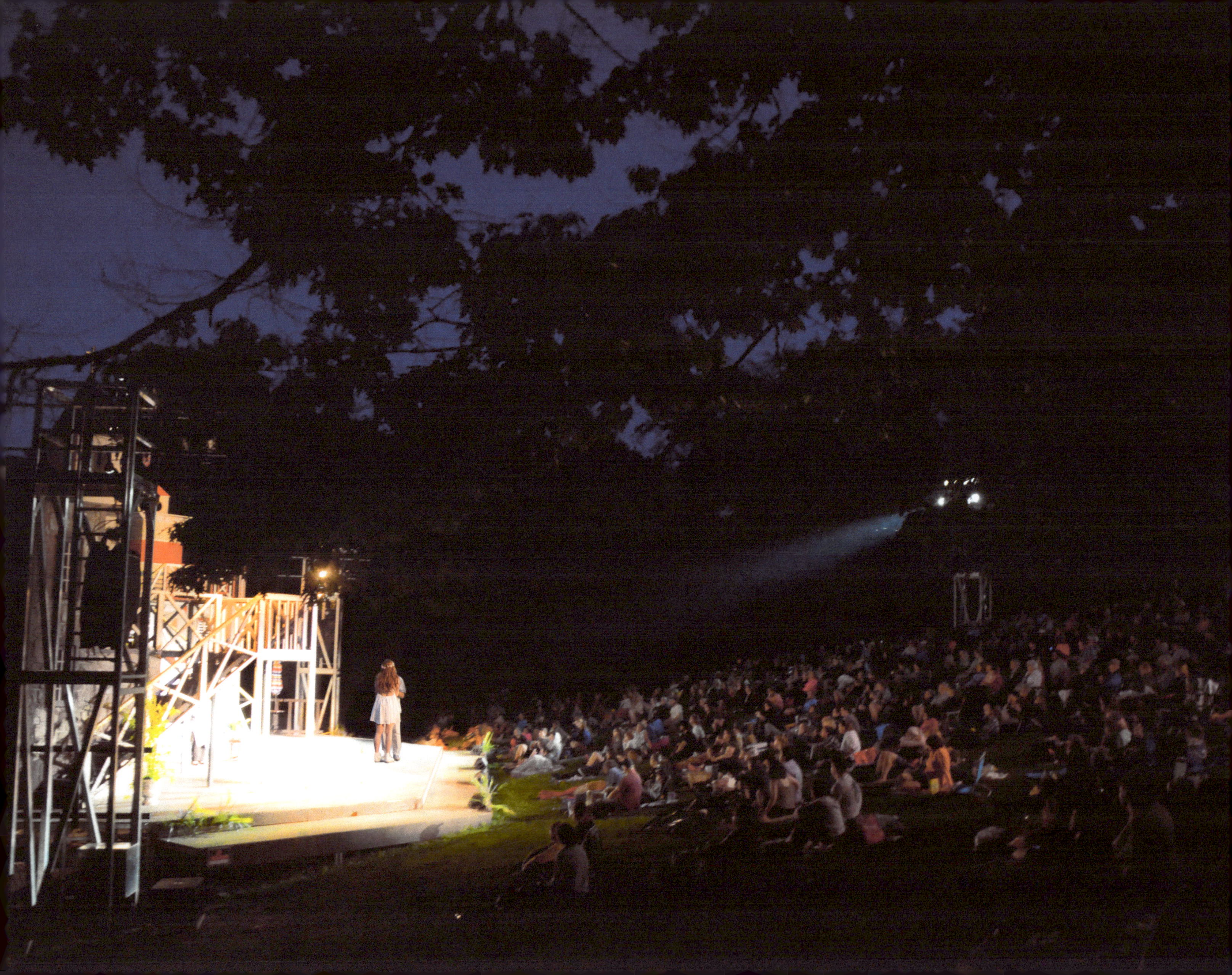

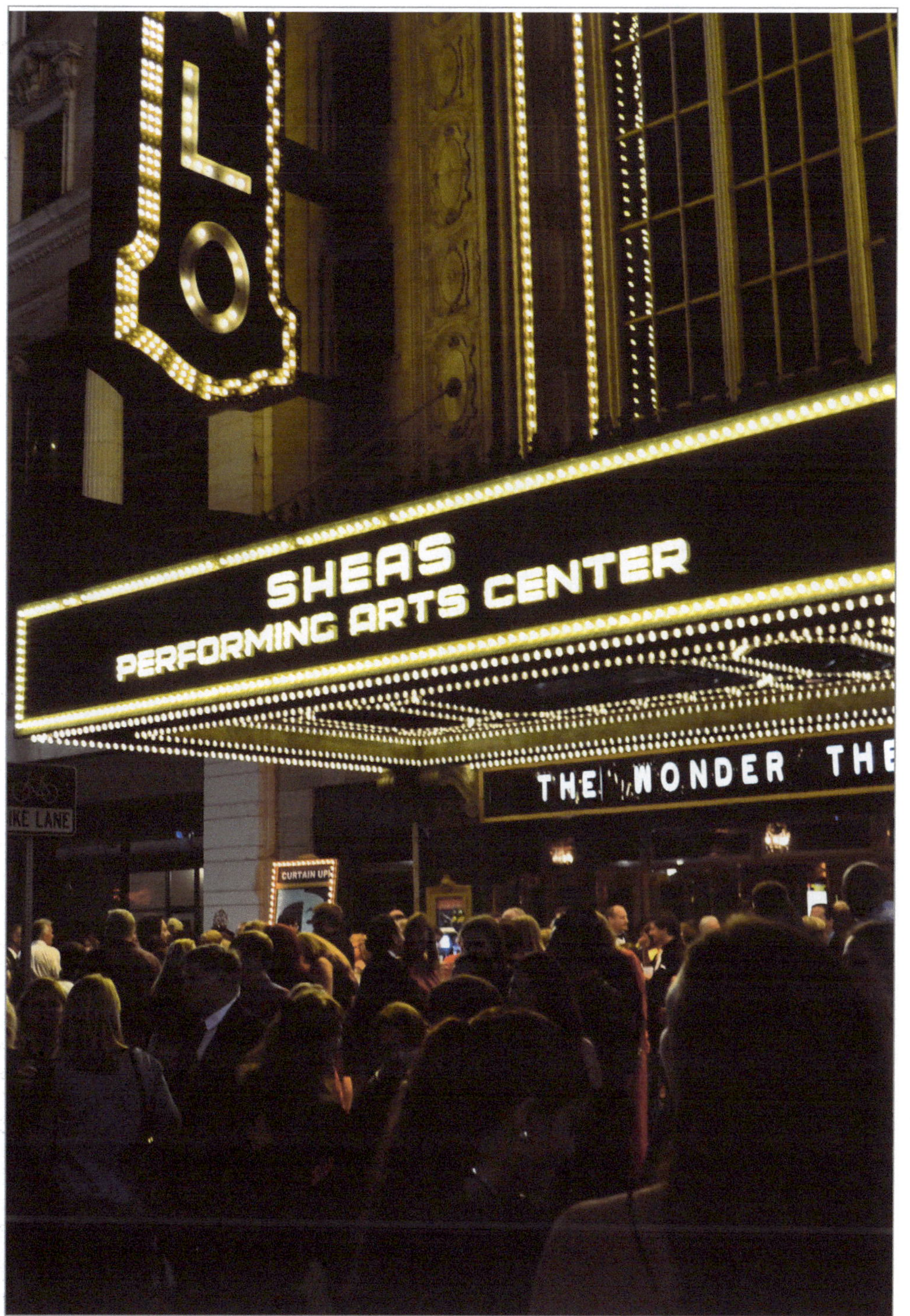

Great Theater, On the Boards and on the Grass

WNY's vibrant performing arts scene is home to 22 professional theater companies. They span from the touring Broadway musicals at Shea's Performing Arts Center, classic and contemporary musicals at MusicalFare Theatre, dramatic literature at the Irish Classical Theatre Company, to work by up-and-coming and undiscovered playwrights at the Alleyway Theatre, and child-centered productions from Theatre of Youth.

Sheas Performing Arts Center *(Left:)*
Over 250,000 patrons attend Sheas Performing Arts Center annually, a spectacularly restored European-style opera house designed by Cornelius and George Rapp in 1926. Listed on the National Registry of Historic Places, it is one of the only remaining Tiffany-designed theaters in the country. Originally an elaborate silent movie house, Sheas became a place for live vaudeville shows with stars like the Marx Brothers, Bing Crosby, Frank Sinatra, Cab Calloway, George Burns, and Gracie Allen.

Shakespeare in Delaware Park *(Opposite:)*
An audience, complete with wine, cheese, and a sea of blankets, enjoying a captivating performance of Shakespeare in Delaware Park. Directly behind the rose garden stands a grand Tudor-style stage on a sweeping hill of green. In this beautiful setting under the stars, Shakespeare's stories live on to explore the truths of the human heart: tragedy, jealousy, foolishness, passion, laughter, and love.

Shakespeare in Delaware Park has been a Buffalo summer tradition since 1976. It is the country's second most successful outdoor Shakespeare festival in terms of audience, attracting an average of 50,000 patrons each summer. They are a not-for-profit, professional theater company dedicated to providing free, high-quality public theater to the widest possible audience.

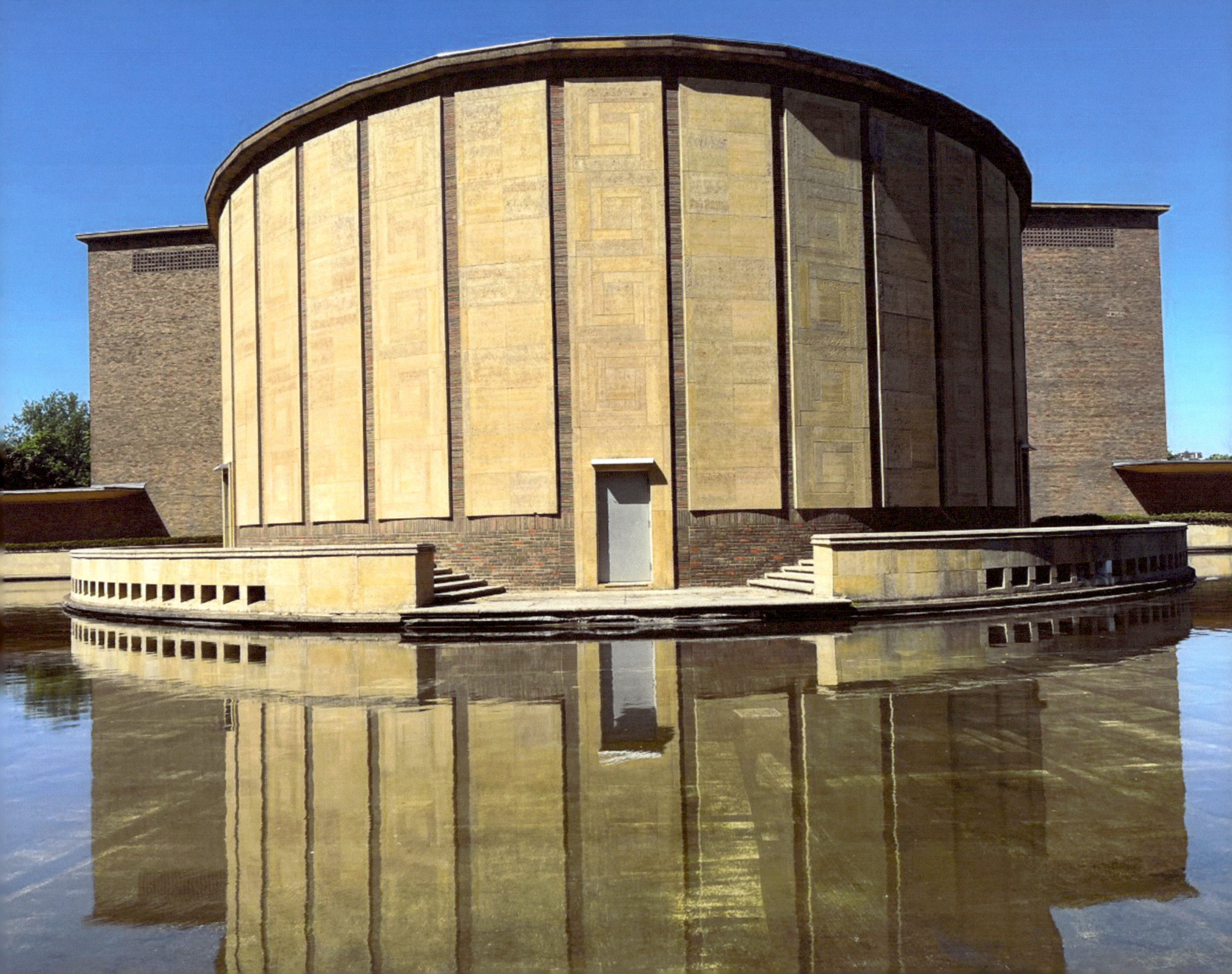

Architecture

Here in Western New York, we not only have the privilege of standing on the shoulders of giants – we also get to live in their houses. Our city is a walkable encyclopedia of amazing architecture, told through the works of internationally renowned masters such as Frank Lloyd Wright, Louis Sullivan, H. H. Richardson, Daniel Burnham; McKim, Mead & White; Eliel and Eero Saarinen, and dozens of great local architects including E.B. Green and Louise Blanchard Bethune.

Buffalo also contains many buildings designed by modern architects, including Minoru Yamasaki, Toshiko Mori, Harrison & Abramovitz, and Mehrdad Yazdani of CannonDesign.

These masterworks are framed by the radial street plan designed by Joseph Ellicott and a series of parks and parkways by Frederick Law Olmsted and his partner Calvert Vaux.

"Buffalo was founded on a rich tradition of architectural experimentation. The architects who worked here were among the first to break with European traditions to create an aesthetic of their own, rooted in American ideals about individualism, commerce, and social mobility."

–Nicolai Ourousoff
The New York Times

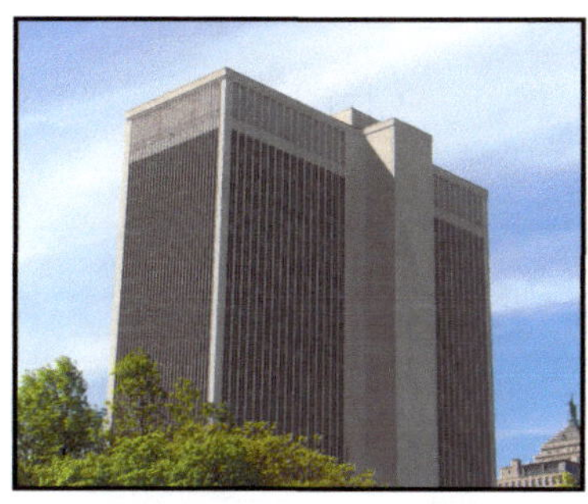

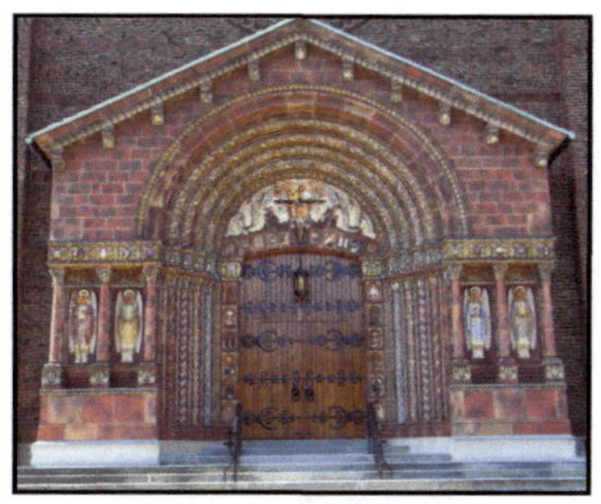

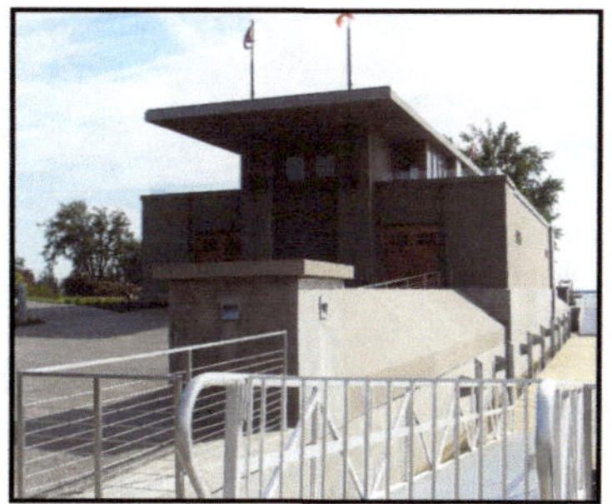

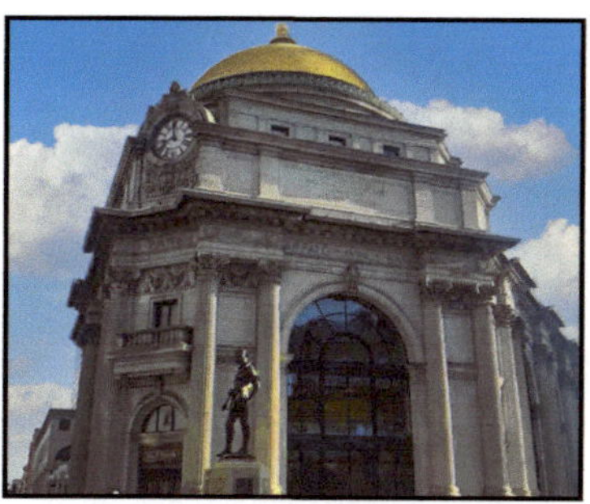

(Opposite:) The reflection pool at Kleinhans Music Hall was designed in 1938 by Eliel & Eero Saarinen,the internationally famous Finnish architects. The concert hall, internationally renowned for its acoustic excellence, was initially built for and is currently home to the Buffalo Philharmonic Orchestra.
(Left to right:) One M&T Plaza was designed by Minoru Yamasaki and completed in 1966. If the design looks familiar, Yamasaki also designed the former World Trade Center in New York City. • Blessed Trinity Roman Catholic Church • Frank Lloyd Wright's Fontana Boathouse, the home of the West Side Rowing Club • Originally the Buffalo Savings Bank, now part of M&T Bank, this building was designed by the prolific Buffalo architects Green & Wicks in 1901.

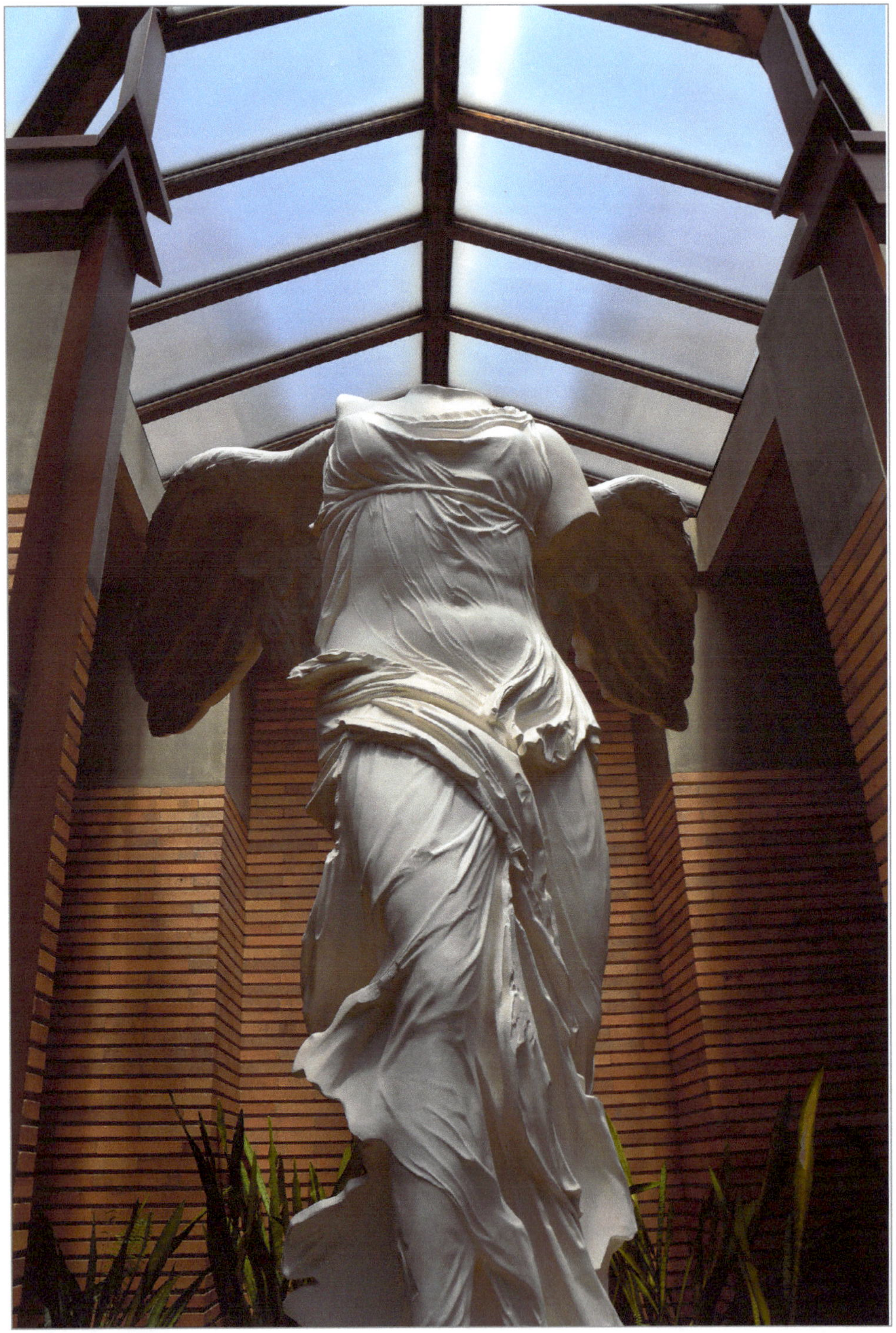

Frank Lloyd Wright's Darwin Martin Complex

Frank Lloyd Wright's 1904 masterwork, the Darwin D. Martin House Complex, is a residential estate that has become one of the most important works of his career. It is a seminal design built at the height of his Prairie House era and a rare Wright commission incorporating multiple structures for an extended family.

The complex includes a spectacular main house for Darwin and his wife, Isabelle, a conservatory, and a stable, all connected by a magnificent pergola. A smaller residence built for Darwin Martin's sister and brother-in-law shares the site.

The multi-phase restoration of the Martin House Complex has been ongoing since 1996 and includes a spectacular interpretive center designed by Toshiko Mori.

(Left:) Visitors are greeted with a dramatic 180-foot view from the Martin House front door down a walkway connected to a sunlit interior garden in the conservatory and a replica statue of the Nike of Samothrace.

(Opposite and below:) Darwin Martin House south façade

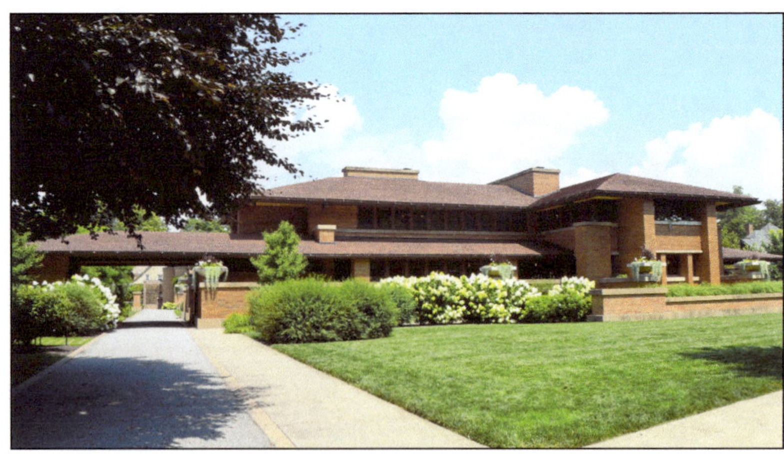

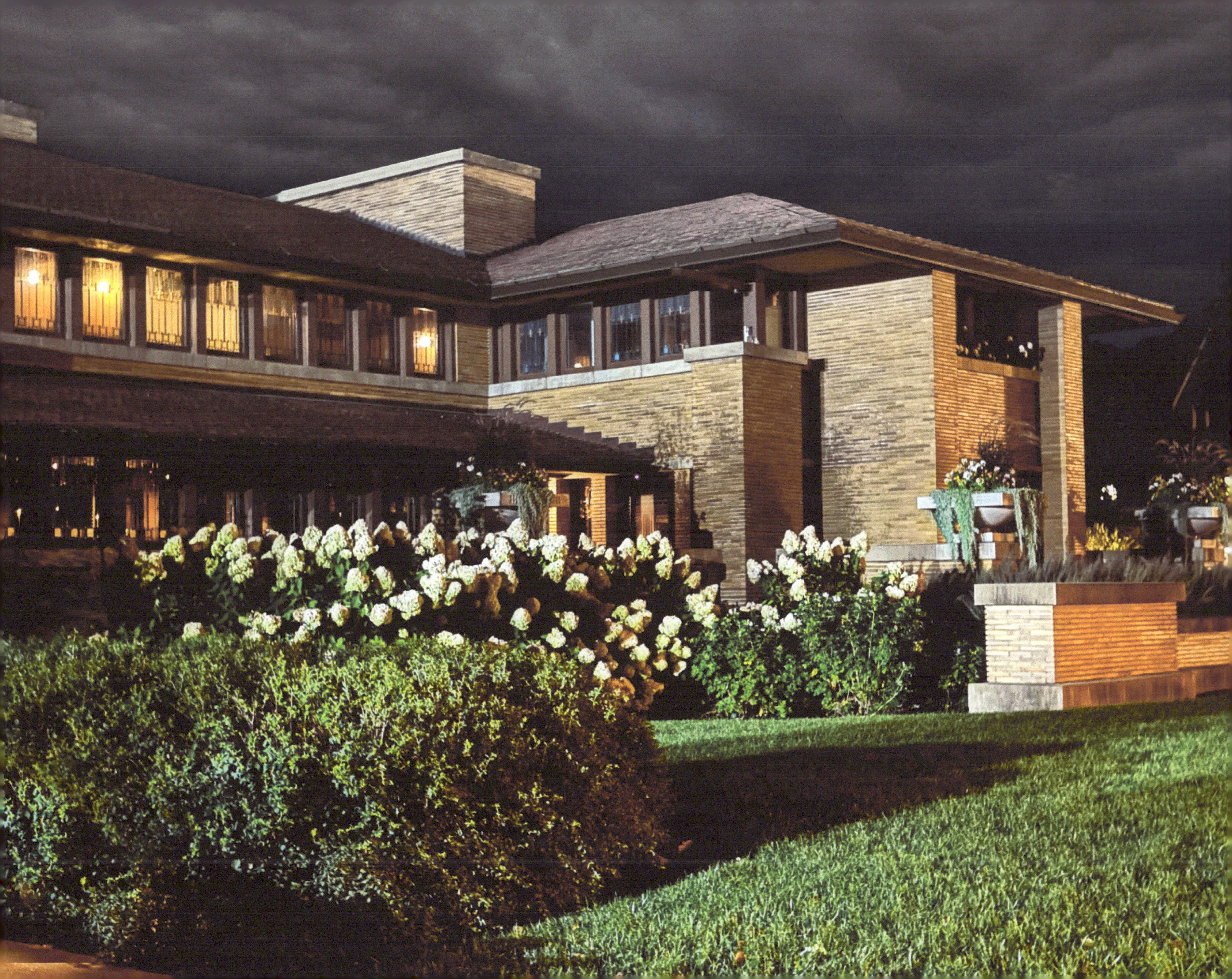

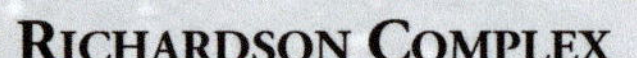

RICHARDSON COMPLEX

The Richardson Olmsted Complex, originally known as the Buffalo State Asylum for the Insane, is internationally regarded as one of the nation's great architectural treasures.

Construction began in 1870 and was completed almost twenty years later. It was designed by one of America's premier architects, Henry Hobson Richardson, along with the legendary landscape team of Frederick Law Olmsted and Calvert Vaux. Its distinctive soaring towers characterized it and a pastoral landscape that created a therapeutic environment in its day, considered the most progressive treatment available for mental illness.

Still relatively unknown when the complex was commissioned, H. H. Richardson was the first American architect to achieve international renown. He introduced a style that became so popular it was named after its originator – Richardson Romanesque.

A National Historic Landmark and one of Buffalo's most iconic buildings, the Richardson Olmsted Complex is now being renewed after many years of neglect. It is being adaptively reused as a hospitality venue and cultural asset for the city as The Richardson Hotel Buffalo.

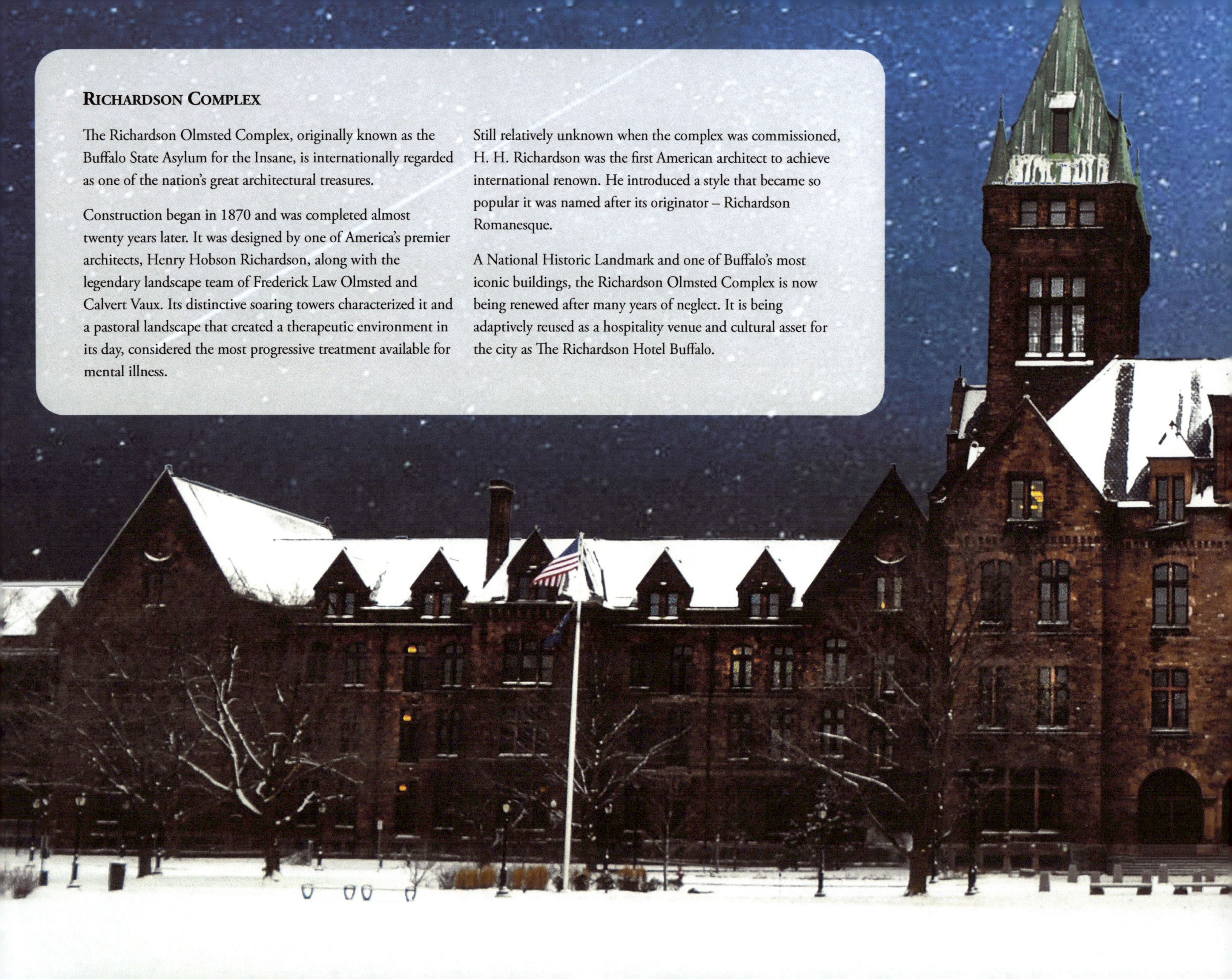

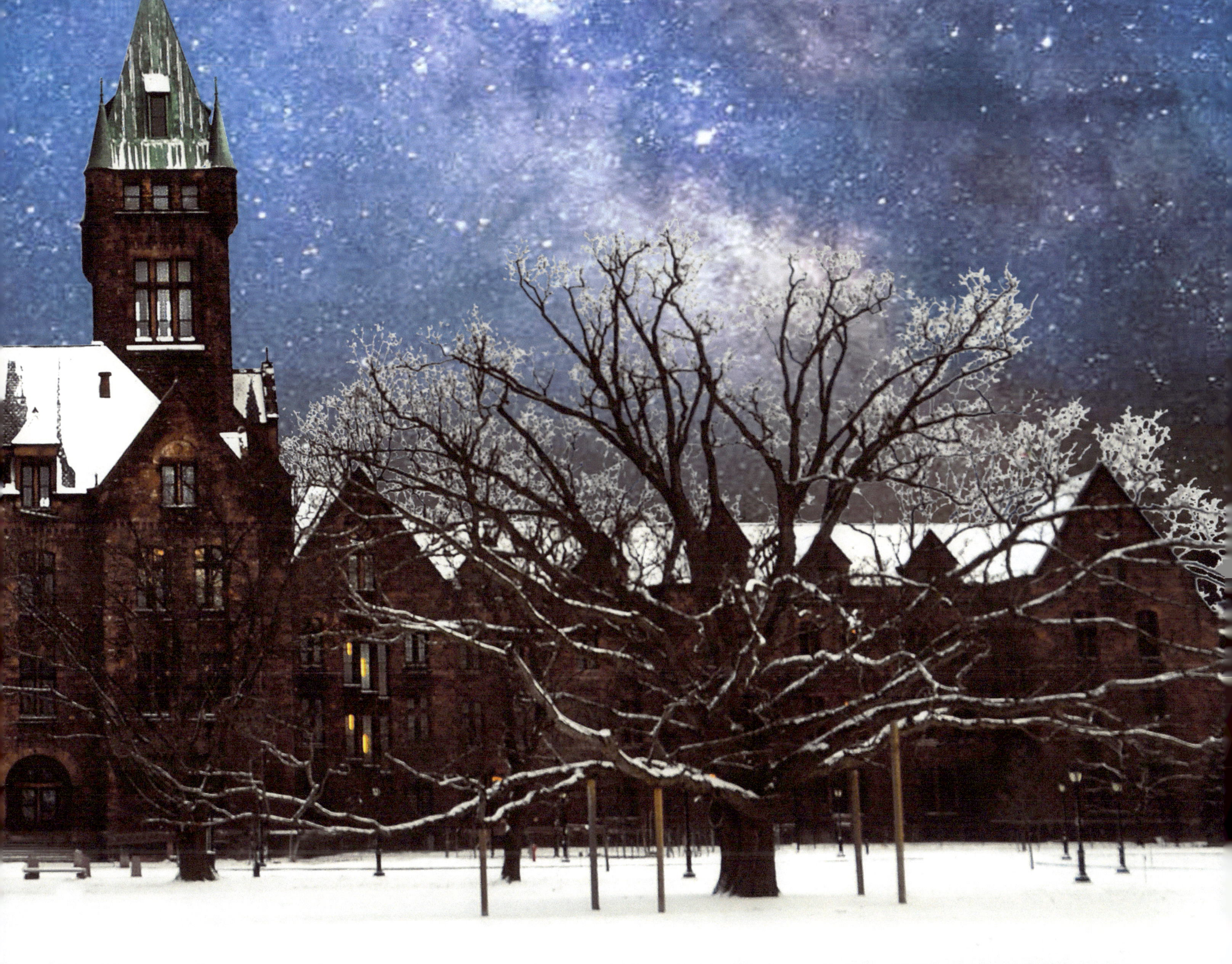

Louis Sullivan's Guaranty Building

Standing at thirteen stories, the Prudential, also known as the Guaranty Building, was one of the first steel-supported buildings in the world and the archetype of the modern skyscraper. It was the tallest building in Buffalo when architect Louis Henry Sullivan and partner Dankmar Adler designed it in 1896.

Louis Sullivan richly covered all exterior surfaces with ornate terra-cotta featuring stylized foliage and geometric shapes.

The Guaranty stands as the pinnacle of Sullivan's forward-thinking designs. His belief that form follows function earned him the title "The Father of Modern Skyscrapers." His uniquely American style of architecture greatly influenced the young Frank Lloyd Wright, who once worked for Adler and Sullivan.

The building was renamed the Prudential Building in 1898 to acknowledge the refinancing provided by the Prudential Insurance Company. Both names adorn the entrances.

The building was added to the National Register of Historic Places in 1973. After many years of decline and a fire in 1974, the Guaranty Building avoided calls for demolition and has undergone a series of restorations to take its place as one of Buffalo's premier office buildings.

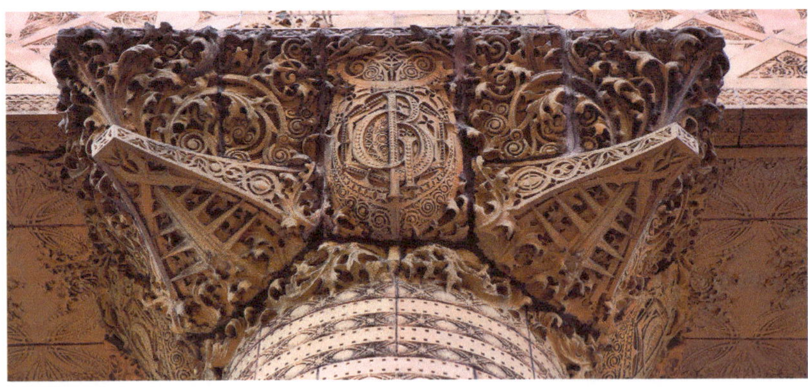

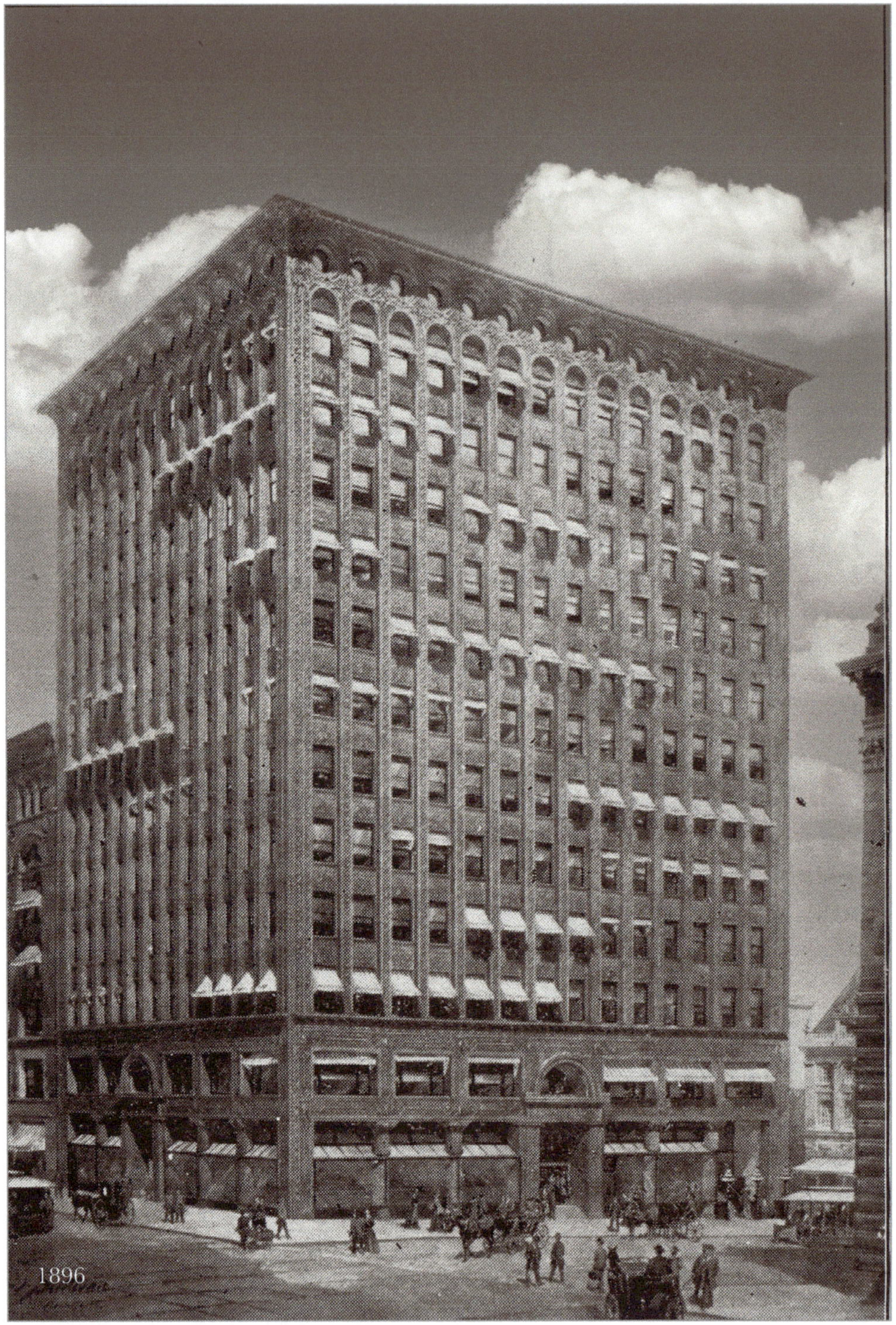

1896

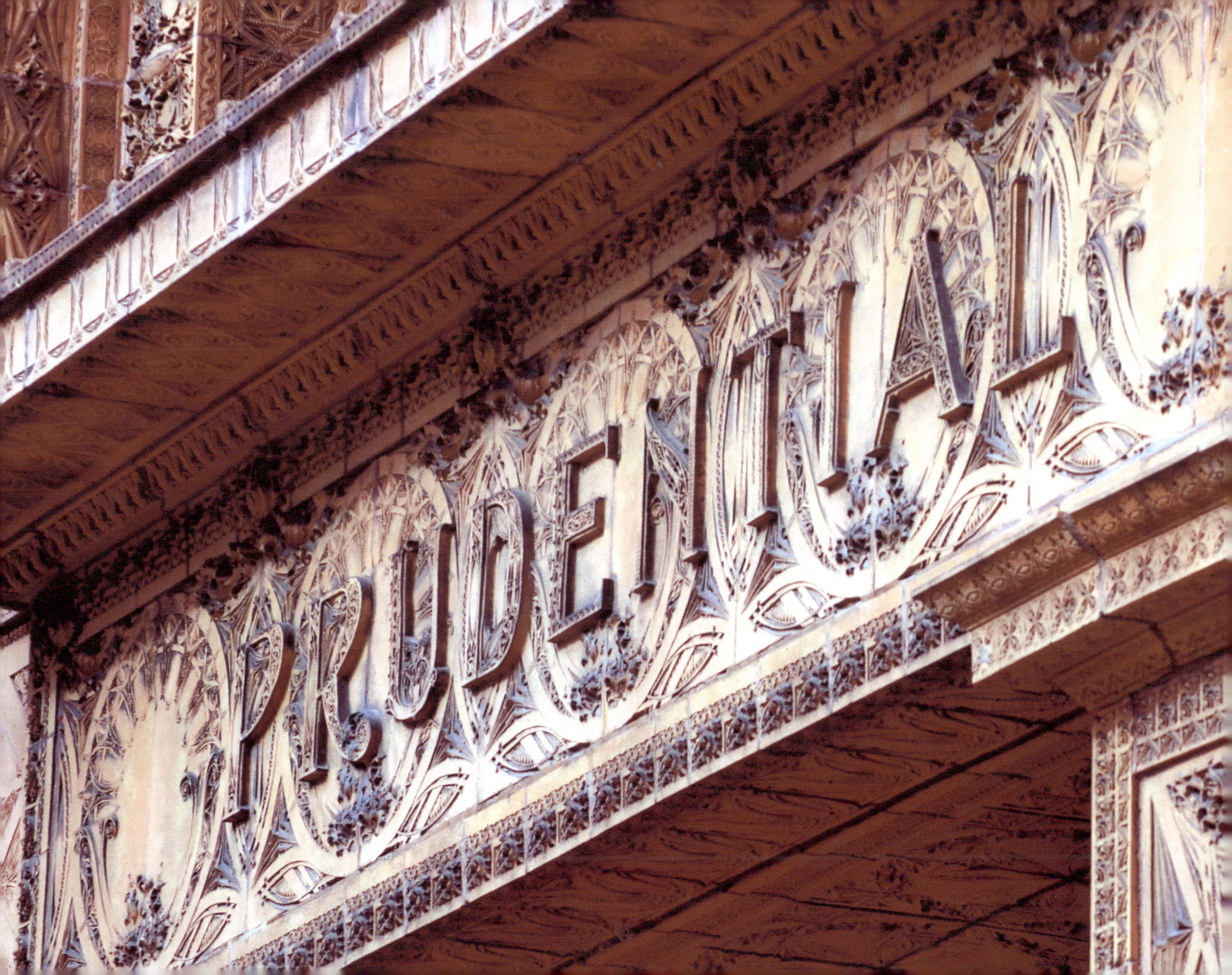
PRUDENTIAL

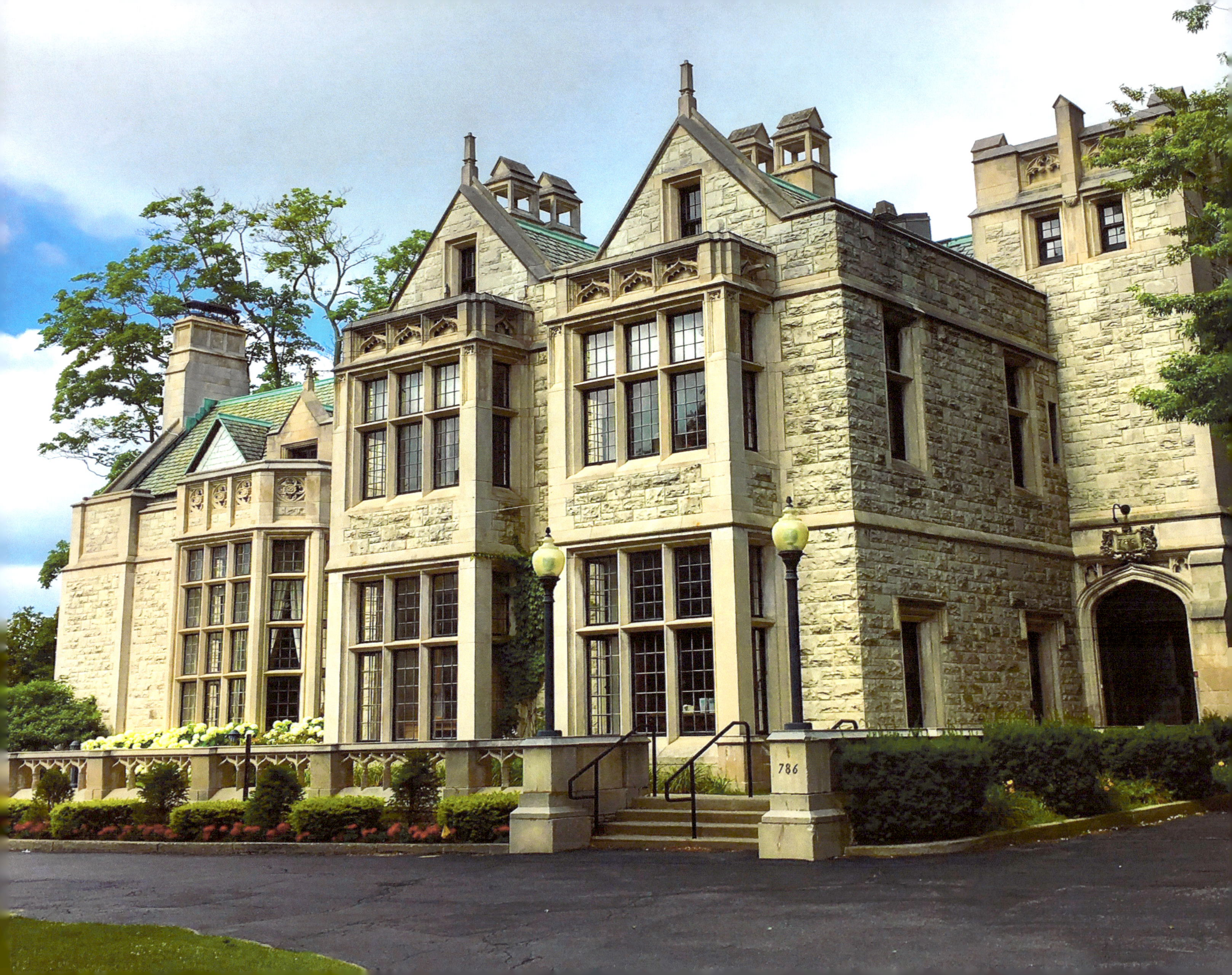
786

MILLIONAIRES' ROW

Nine elegant 19th-century mansions on Delaware Avenue, once home to the city's most conspicuously wealthy, are evidence of the Gilded Age grandeur found along Buffalo's "Millionaires' Row". These stunning examples of turn-of-the-century extravagance are of such astonishing size and opulence that they are used today as schools and offices for major corporations and not-for-profit organizations such as the American Red Cross. During Buffalo's heyday, more millionaires lived here in the Queen City than in any other city in the United States.

(Opposite:) Built-in 1914 on the lots of three previous homes, the Clement House was built for Stephen M. Clement, president of Marine Bank, and his wife Carolyn, by Buffalo architects Green & Wicks. Stephen died before the Delaware Mansion was completed. This home was the scene of many important social functions for thirty years. Two years before her death in 1943, Carolyn donated her palatial mansion to the American Red Cross, which still occupies the house today.

(Right:) The Forman-Cabana House is a Beaux Art Classical style mansion completed in 1893. Initially built for early oil magnate George V. Forman, it is now the home of Child and Family Services Conners Children's Center.

(Below left:) The Richmond-Lockwood House - 844 Delaware Avenue

(Below right:) George Brewster Mathews House - 830 Delaware Avenue

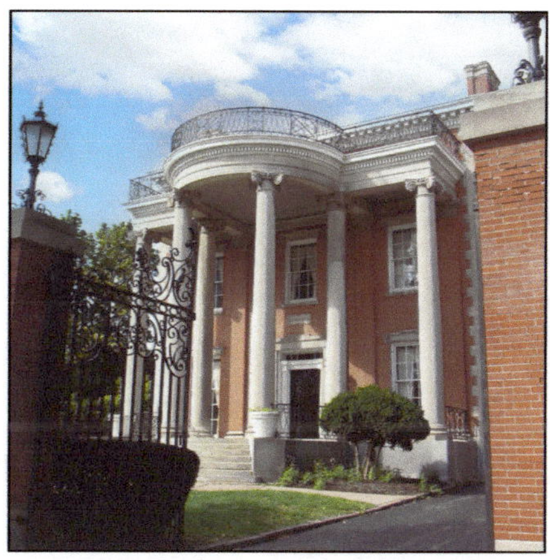

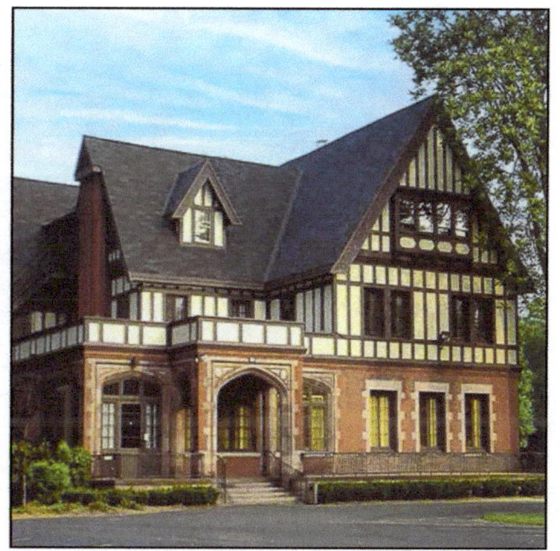

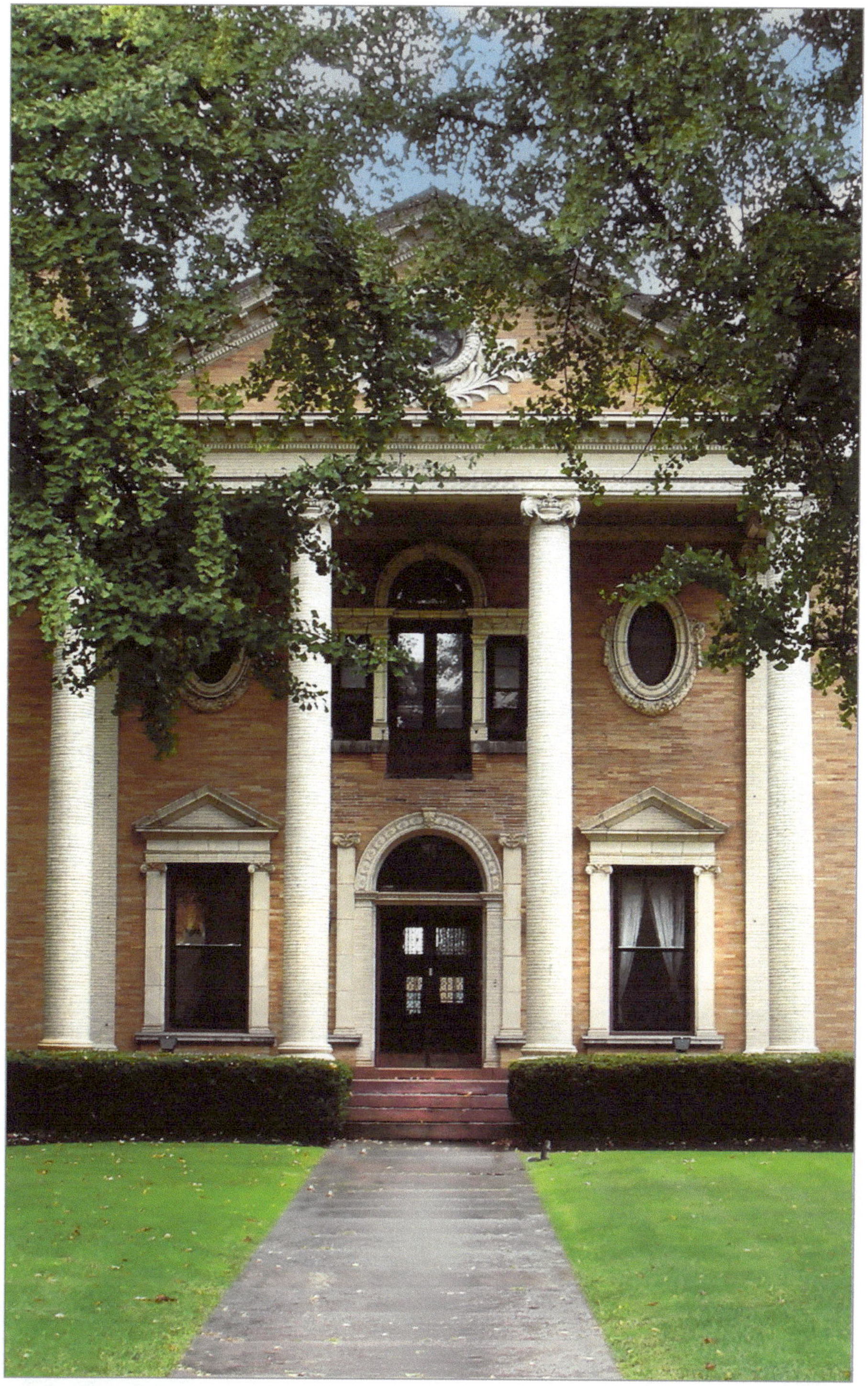

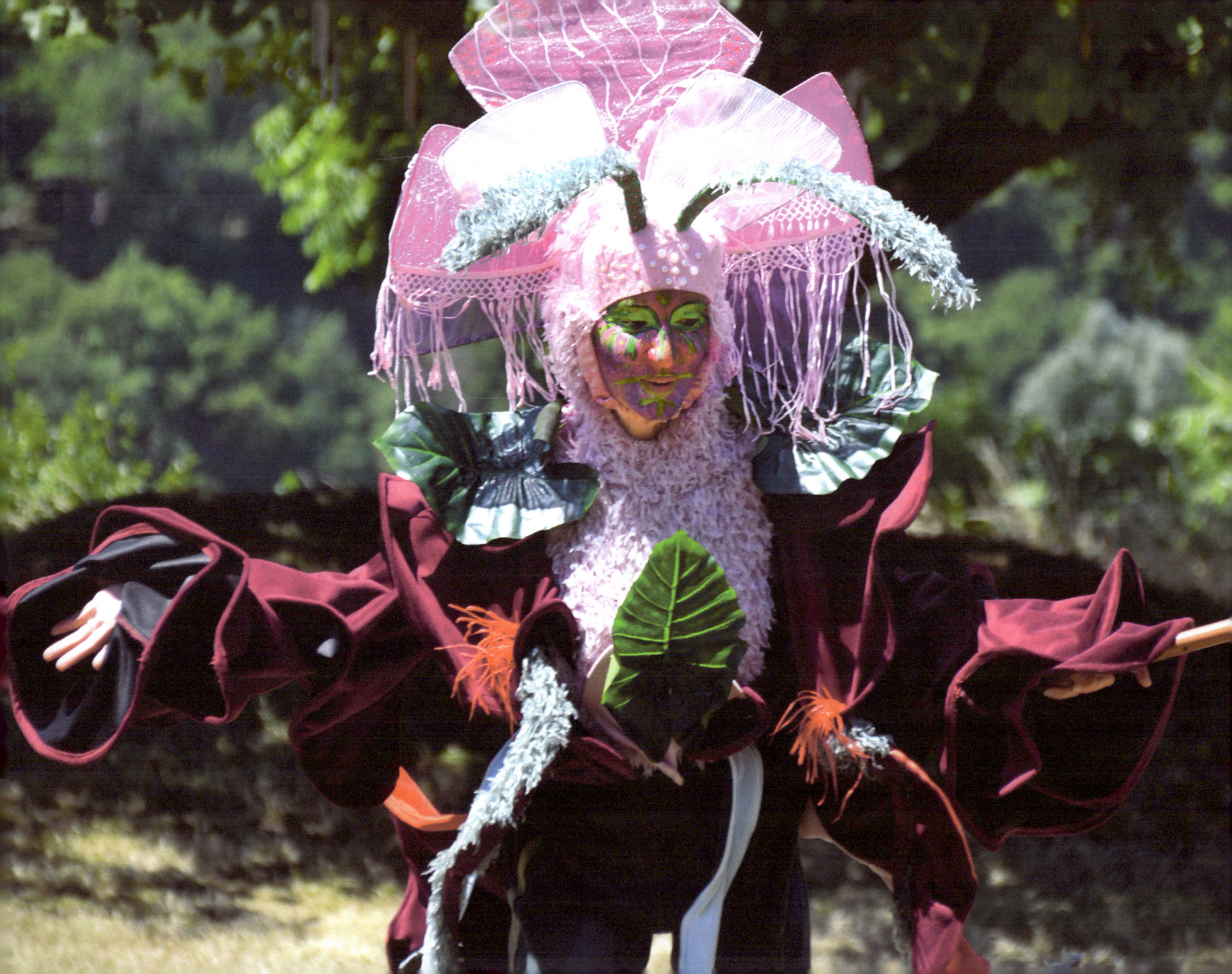

Fairs & Festivals

"If it's a weekend during the summer,
there's a festival to enjoy."
– Just ask anyone

Whether celebrating a once-discarded chicken part, removing the ice boom, or attending a parade on the coldest day in March, here in Western New York, we aren't real fussy about what excuse we use to throw a party for 100,000 of our closest friends.

We have festivals for corn, beer, canals, gardens, chalk, sexual orientation, pumpkins, fairies, and more beer. If you're Greek, Irish, German, Scottish, Puerto Rican, African-American, Italian, or any one of a dozen other nationalities, you've got your own festival. We have an art festival that lines the street to kick off the summer and an art festival that lines the road to bring it to a close. We've even stated the obvious and defined music as art and throw a festival for that.

On the Monday following Easter, the people of Buffalo celebrate Dyngus Day, an odd Polish courting ritual. This massive party on the city's East Side is so much a part of our cultural DNA that it's included as an official holiday in city labor contracts.

In short, we love everything that makes a living and working in Western New York unique and find inventive ways to enjoy them all to their fullest.

Opposite: Artpark Fairy House Festival has evolved from an art walk of the miniature fairy houses installed in the park by both local community and professional artists to an international, interdisciplinary, and immersive performing arts festival with European street theater groups, modern dance, interactive performances by local actors, and music presented in the setting of the park overlooking the stunning Niagara Gorge. Visitors can marvel at the fairy house creations and enjoy the whimsical and enchanting Artpark Fairies and roaming musicians.

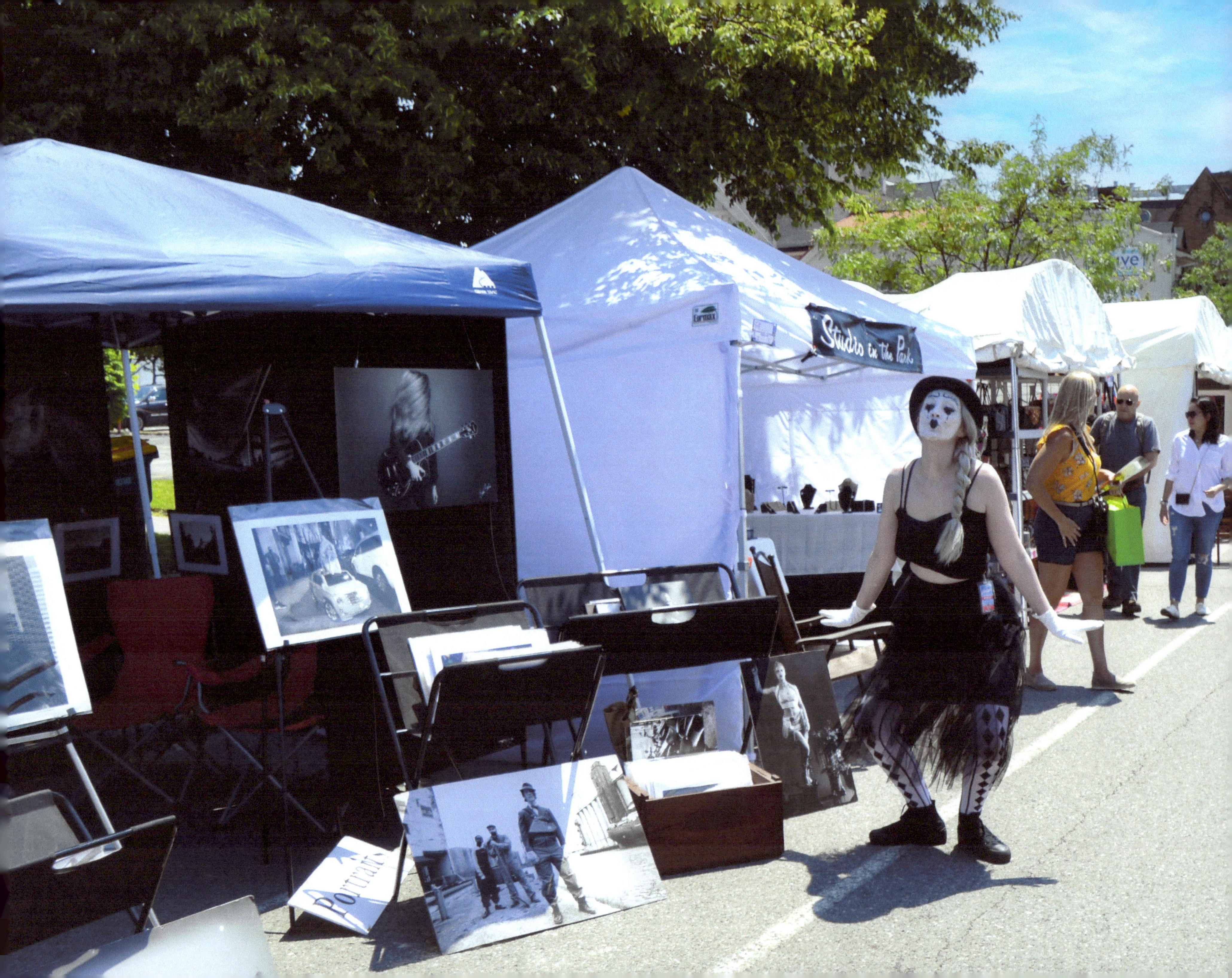
Studio in The Park
Portrait

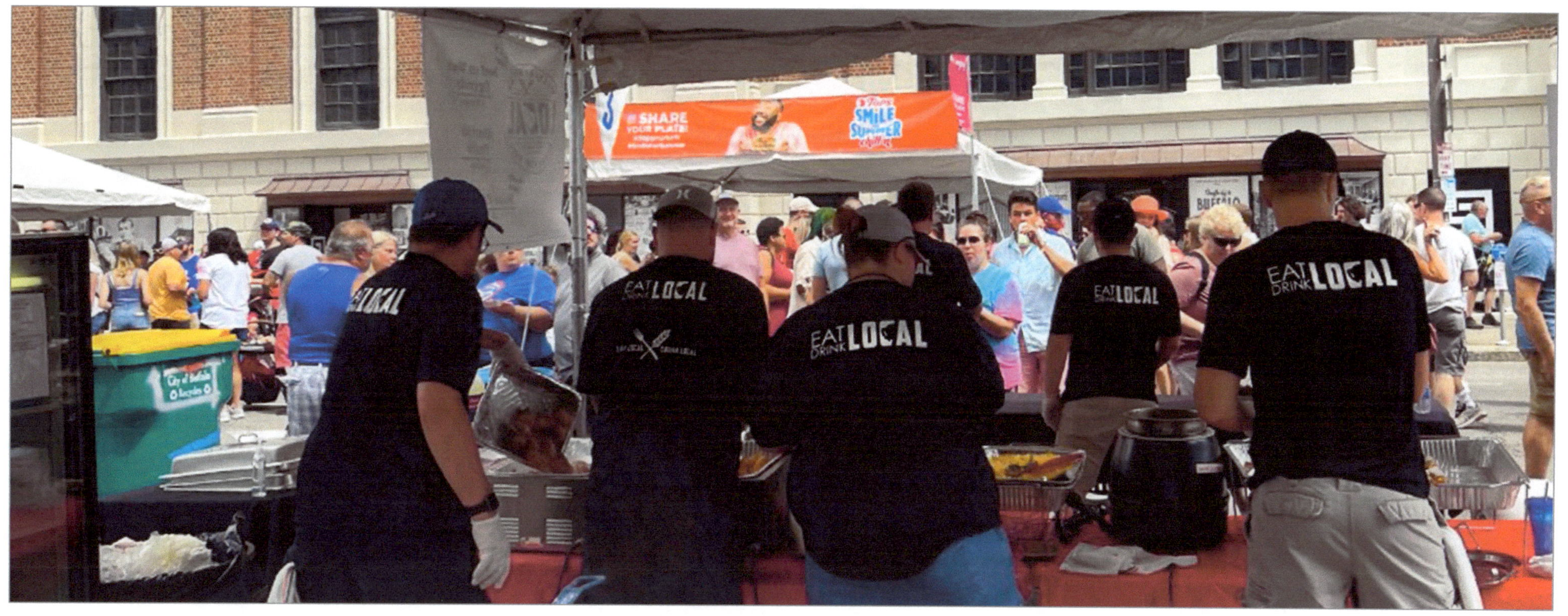

Taking it to the streets

On weekends in Western New York, we flood the streets–not with water but with smiling people. Whether it's an ethnic, food, music, or arts festival, these flowing rivers of our citizenry showcase our neighborhood and the best of our cuisine, talent, and wares.

The Taste of Buffalo *(Above)*
Now in its 40th year, The Taste of Buffalo is the nation's largest two-day food festival. It takes place along Delaware Avenue and Niagara Square in downtown Buffalo. The Taste is a not-for-profit organization with more than 1,000 volunteers helping to put on the annual event. Approximately $543,000 has been raised at the festival for local charities including scholarships awarded annually to local high school seniors pursuing a culinary or hospitality-related degree.

Allentown Art Festival *(Opposite)*
The Allentown Art Festival takes place in Buffalo's Allentown Historic Preservation District. Tens of thousands of art patrons visit the festival to enjoy the beauty of Buffalo's weather during the second weekend in June, the charm and uniqueness of the Allentown area, and the quality of the art and crafts presented by the over 400 juried exhibitors.

Since its modest beginnings in 1958, the Allentown Art Festival has become not only Buffalo's urban rite, but also a symbol for the enduring character of this re-emerging rust belt region. It has earned an important place in Buffalo's cultural and social life and a national reputation for excellence.

Featured here is the black and white photography of Cheryl Gorski and a mime that wouldn't tell us her name.

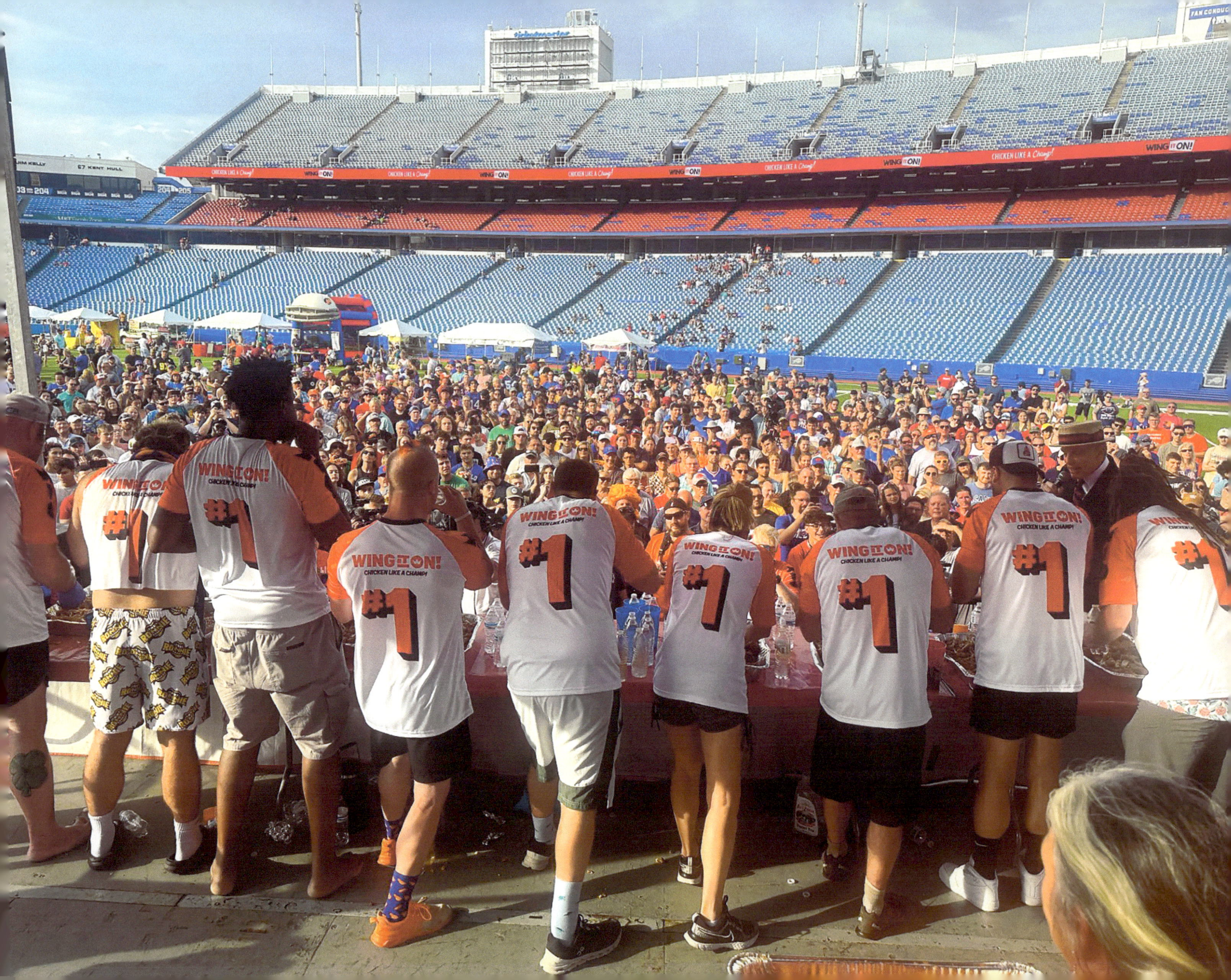
JIM KELLY
67 KENT HULL
WING IT ON!
CHICKEN LIKE A CHAMP
#1

The National Buffalo Chicken Wing Festival

It's hard to imagine a nicer way to enjoy a beautiful Labor Day weekend afternoon than at Highmark Stadium eating our homegrown international culinary phenomenon. While the rest of the world eats "Buffalo wings," here in our city we eat "chicken wings" because we know that a buffalo is a furry, wingless mammal. The festival, first held in 2002, serves more than half a million wings to as many as 70,000 attendees from all 50 states and 34 countries and features more than 30 local, regional, national, and international eateries serving more than 120 styles of chicken wings.

Realizing that we needed to create one, our community rallied with me to create what is now one of the most recognized food festivals in the country. That was 22 years ago, and since then we have had over 1.2 million attendees that have eaten approximately 5.7 million wings weighing more than 215 tons. We have had over 150 participating restaurants and raised over $440,000 for local charities. We have survived a pandemic, inflation and have found a new location in Highmark Stadium, "Home of the Buffalo Bills".

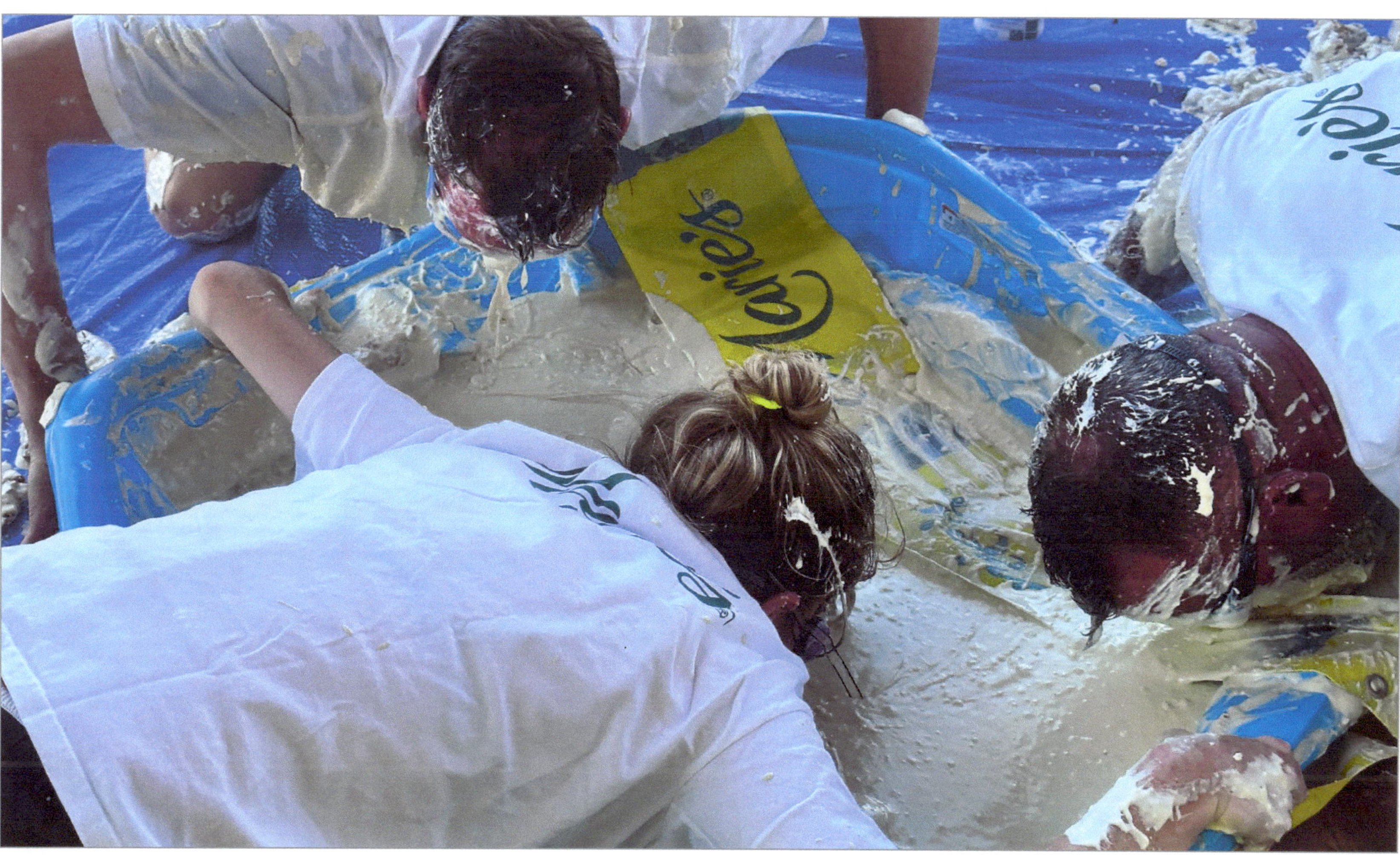

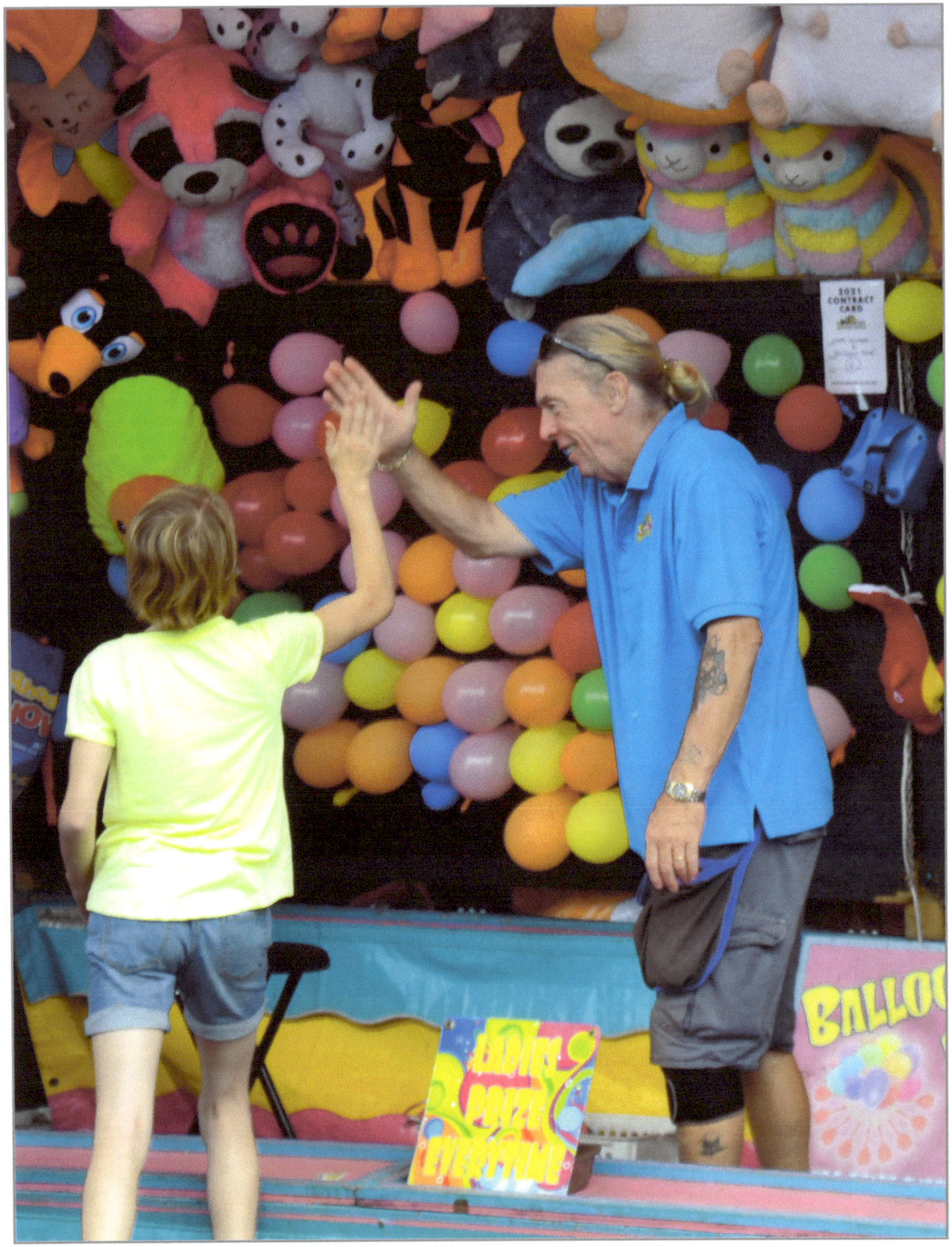

Erie County Fair

The Erie County Fair and Exposition is held in Hamburg every August. This is the third- largest county fair in the country, with an average attendance hovering around one million people.

From racing pigs, Chinese acrobats, and tractor pulls, to championship livestock, multiple concert stages, and a long list of everything possible to deep fry, the fair has something to amuse and delight the whole family.

Led by its first president, Dr. Cyrenius Chapin (more commonly known for his contribution in the War of 1812), the Agricultural Society was established in 1819. Then called the Niagara County Horticultural Society, it held its first fair in 1820 on what is now the site of HarborPlace and Canalside. One year later, Niagara County split into Erie and Niagara Counties, and so did the agricultural society. What began as a one-day event held in the fall has grown to become an 12-day event held each August. It has been held every year since 1841 with the exception of 1943, which was canceled because of World War II.

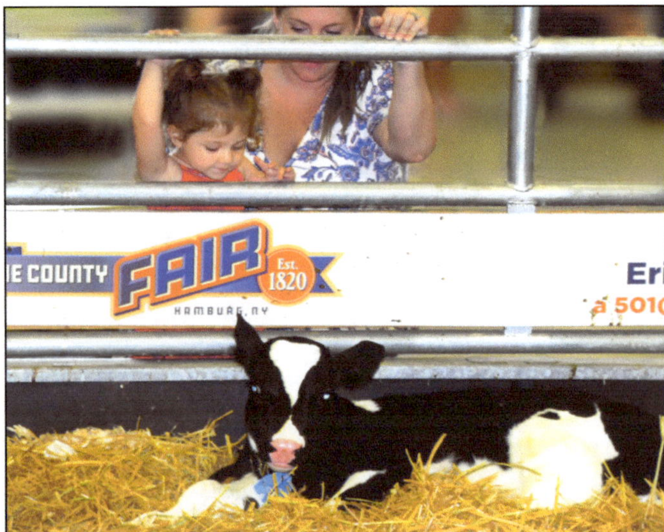

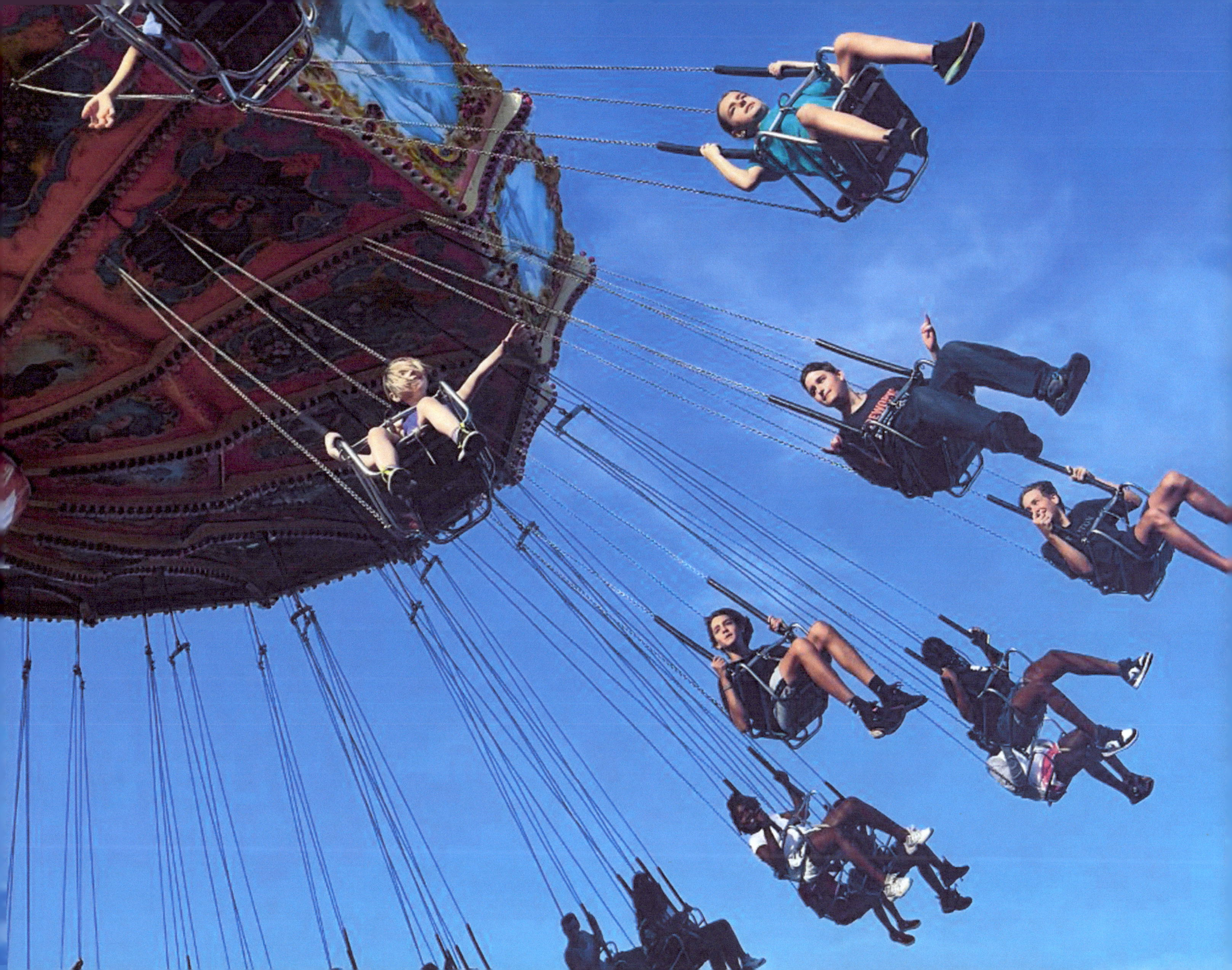

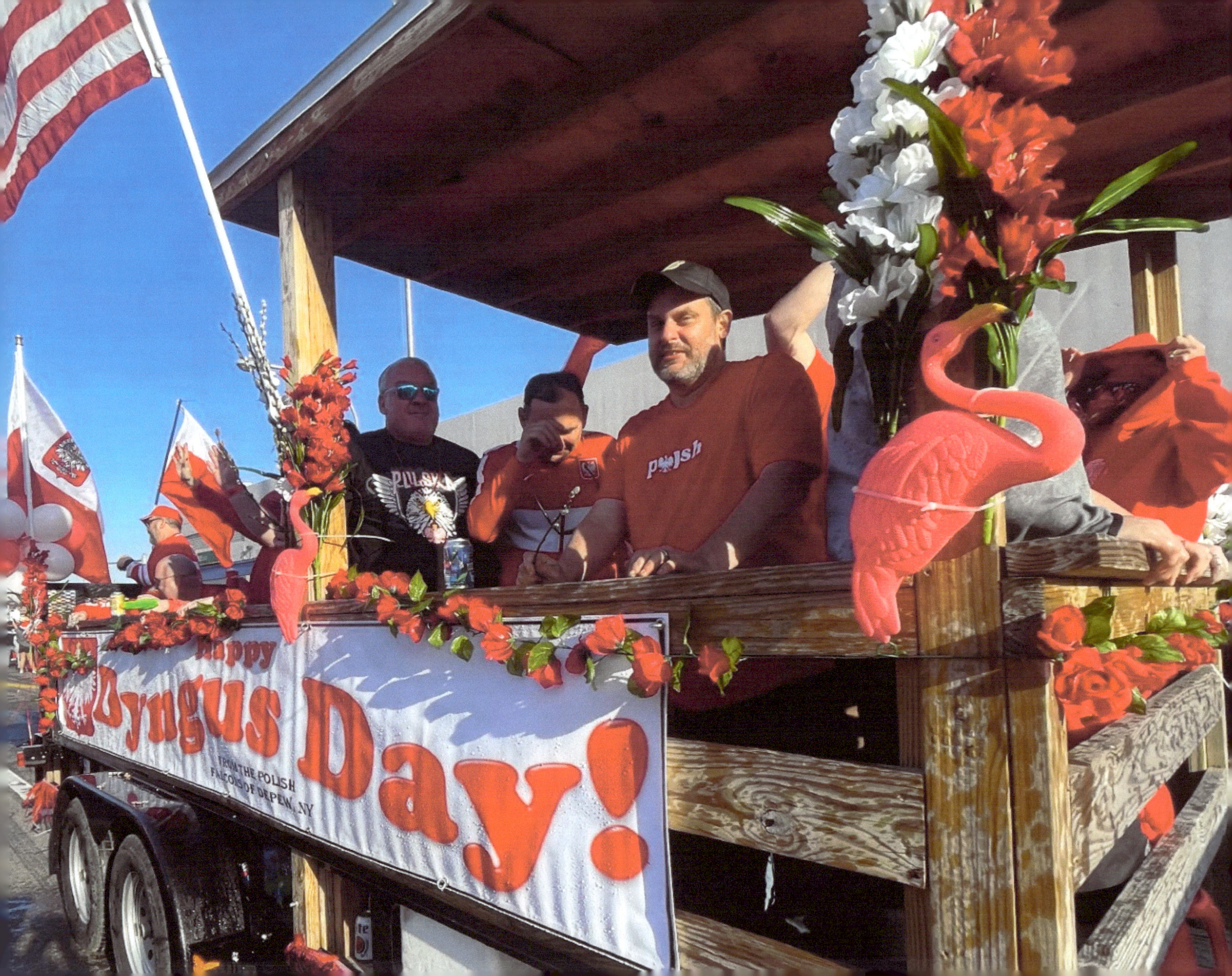
Happy
Dyngus Day!
FROM THE POLISH
FALCONS OF DEPEW, NY
POLSKA
polish

We love a parade

Other cities merely have parades. We throw linear parties with moving live music for thousands of our friends. And it doesn't take much of an excuse to throw one.

We march for African-American heritage, organized labor, our veterans, sexual orientation, carnivals, Independnce Day, a handful of ethnic festivals, and even have a parade in the middle of our county fair. Some parades have floats that throw candy to the crowd, where other parades have crowds that soak the participants with squirt guns. And after a long Buffalo winter, we have so much pent-up Irish energy that it takes two parades to get it out of our system for another year.

(Opposite:) Dyngus Day, which always falls on the Monday after Easter, is an annual post-Lenten bash that attracts tens of thousands to Buffalo's Historic Polonia District to celebrate spring, show Polish pride, splash water on and whip pussy willows at the objects of their affection and listen to the best polka bands in the nation.

What started as a rag-tag group of passionate Poles with a few flags, a couple of pickup trucks, and a band on a trailer has turned into a big splash of Polish pride surfing a sea of red and white.

(Right:) The Pride Parade marks the kickoff of the weeklong celebration of the Pride Festival. The parade showcased with colorful floats will follow Elmwood Ave, beginning at Forest Ave and ending at Allentown. The pride parade allows over 150 organizations, groups, and businesses to show their support for WNY's dynamic LGBTQ+ community.

Following the parade is a celebration of WNY's LGBTQ+ community featuring legendary performers, local eats, and fun for the whole family at Canalside.

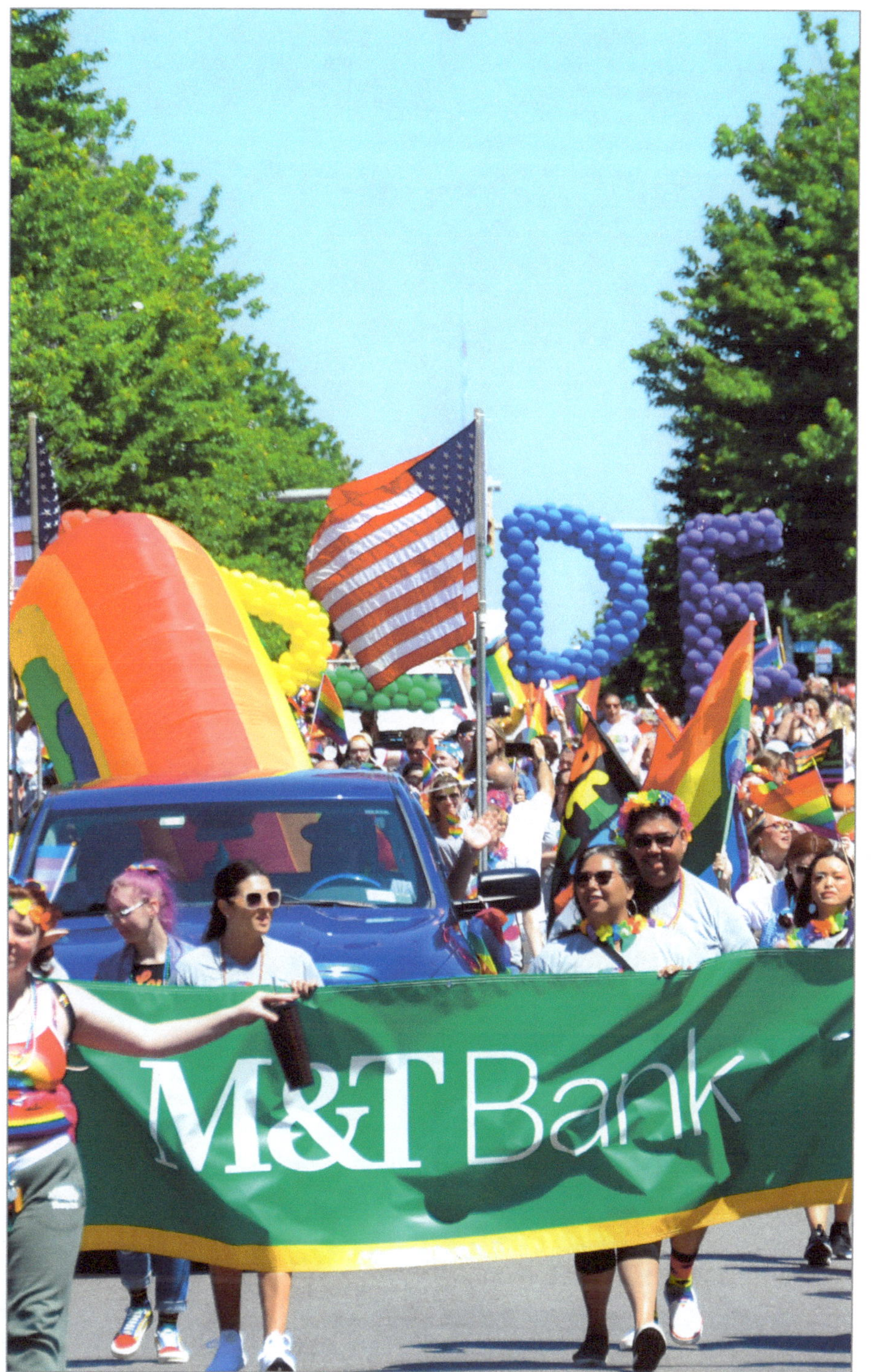

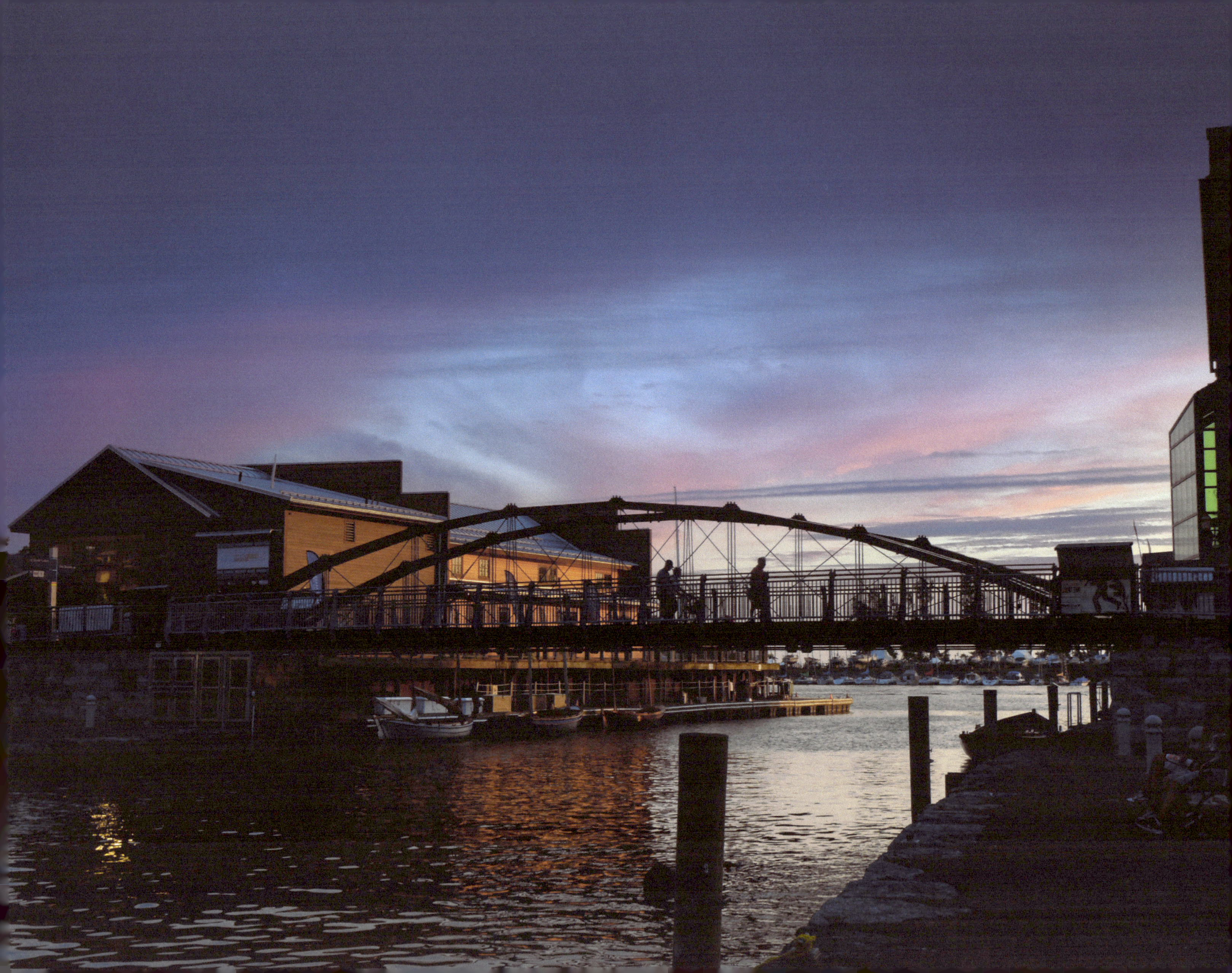

Waterfront

We live in one of the most extraordinary places on earth, on the edge of one-fifth of the earth's surface fresh water. As a city and region, we are inseparable from our water. It's an embarrassment of wealth that is our connection to our past, present, and future.

We depend on this water for our power, recreation, industry, and agriculture. It has separated us in war. It's what binds us in peace. For good and for bad, it dictates our weather.

Our waterfront is our identity to the world, reflecting our radiant beauty. When it becomes a thundering cataract, it's visited by millions. In short, our water is the glue that binds us together.

This fluid connection, however, is only a magnificent illusion. The water we gaze upon today isn't the same one we'll see tomorrow. While seemingly abundant and permanent, our glue is constantly racing away at the staggering rate of 750,000 gallons per minute.

This is a chapter to capture this moment and celebrate its journey.

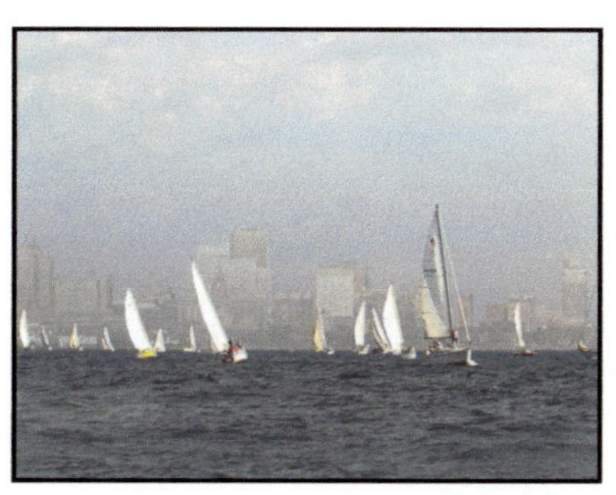

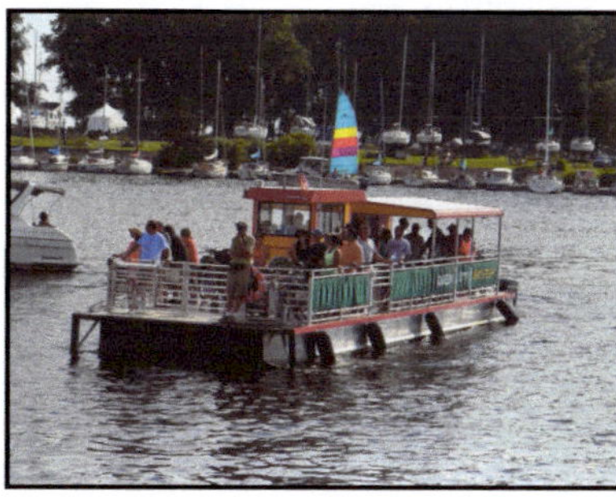

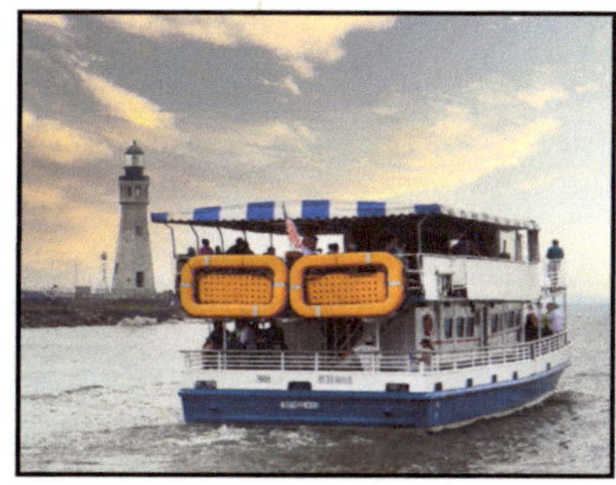

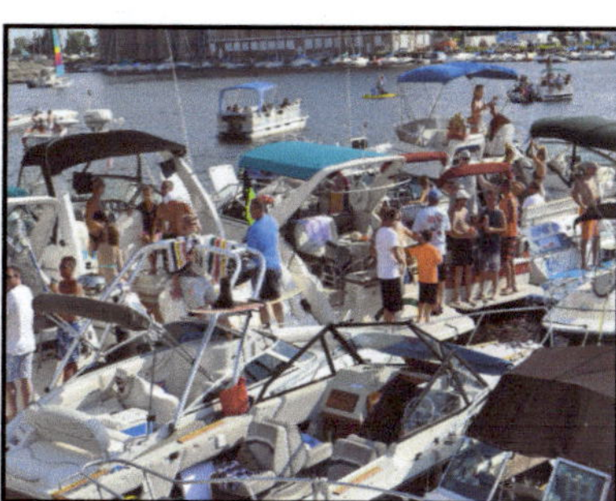

(Opposite): Sunset on the whipple-truss bridge that crosses the Commercial Slip from The Buffalo and Erie County Naval & Military Park to Canalside.

(Left to right:)
- *The Buffalo Harbor Sailing Club, the largest sailing club on the Great Lakes has been running its race programs on Tuesday and Wednesday evenings since 1977.*
- *Queen City Bike Ferry is a link between Buffalo's inner and outer harbor.for bicyclists and pedestrians will run daily from Memorial Day through Labor Day.*
- *Miss Buffalo Cruises, Buffalo's original two hour tour where you float along the waterways of Buffalo with family and friends.*
- *With one boat, you'll have a great time. When you connect dozens of them at Canalside, you have a floating party.*

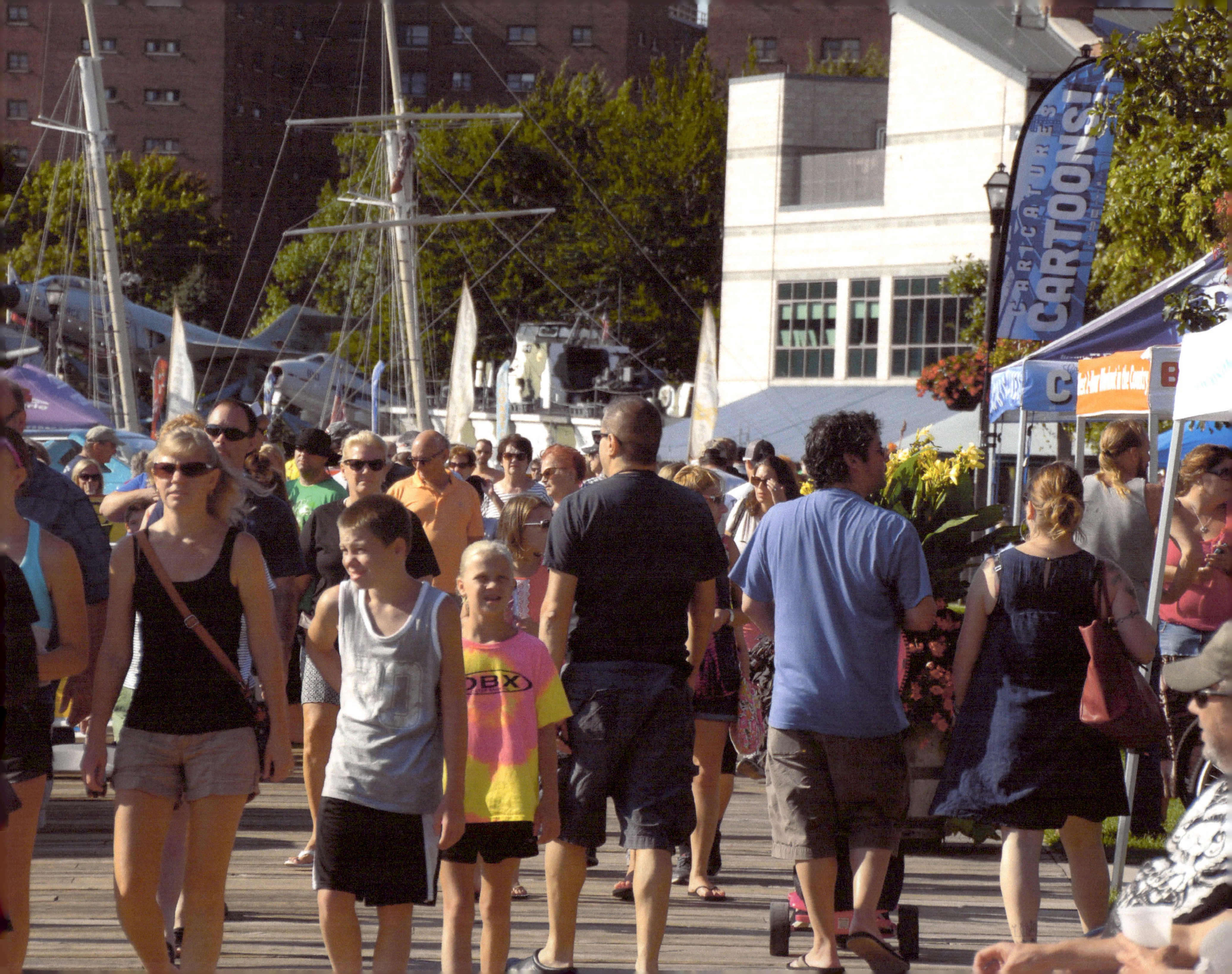
CARICATURES
CARTOONS!
OBX

Canalside

Situated on 21 historic acres of Buffalo's inner harbor, Canalside is a resugent regional destination and entertainment district. It has fast become the go-to place for residents and tourists alike, with more than 1,000 yearly events and nearly 1 million annual visitors and growing.

With roots dating back to 1825, Canalside takes its name from its storied past when the Erie Canal Harbor was the western terminus of the Erie Canal and was veritably the gateway to the West. Today, it is the gateway to Buffalo's future, blending its historic underpinnings with a considerable upswing in private and public development.

As poignant reminders of its glorious past, there are many original elements at Canalside, including the refurbished "Commercial Slip," "Central Wharf," "Whipple Truss" footbridge, cobblestone streets, and the excavated foundations of several canal-era buildings. Re-watered canals serve as a family playground with paddleboats in summer, roller skating in fall, and ice skating in winter.

Whether coming for an event or to hang out for fun, Canalside has a packed calendar of options for kids and families, fitness enthusiasts, music lovers, history buffs, festival goers, and more.

Explore the waterfront with a Blue Bike, water bike, or kayak rental. Step back in time on the Spirit of Buffalo, a History Tour Boat ride, or a Canalside walking tour. Shop at the Saturday Artisan Market, play in the giant sandbox, take an art class, or watch a movie.

Eat, drink, and be merry with a bite from The Dish or a brew from the Beer and Wine Garden.

You can get your blood pumping with outdoor fitness classes, such as Zumba, Power Yoga, Exercise Like the Animals, and Tai Chi, or simply relax on the big, colorful Adirondack chairs and, read a book and enjoy the sunset.

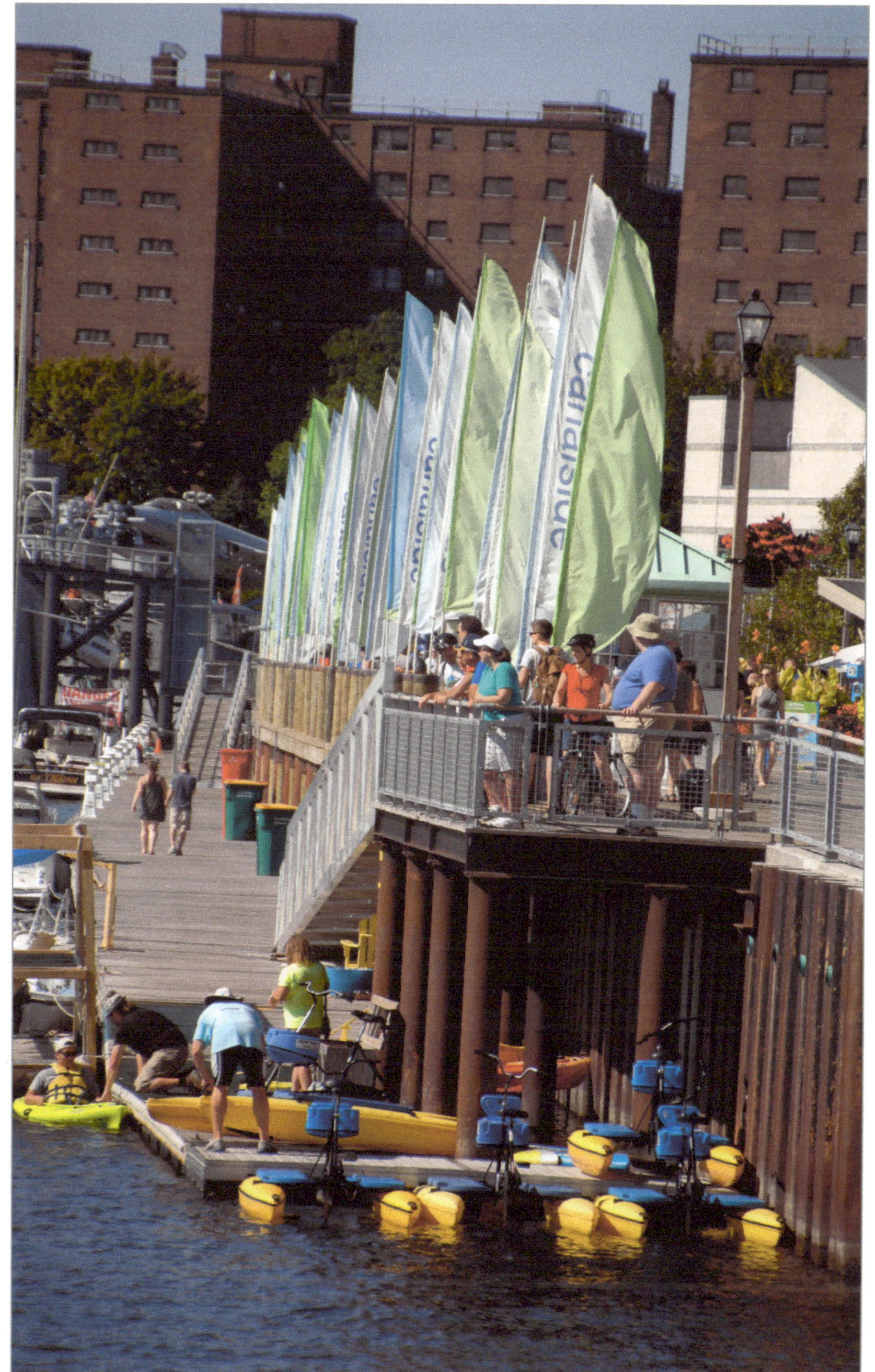

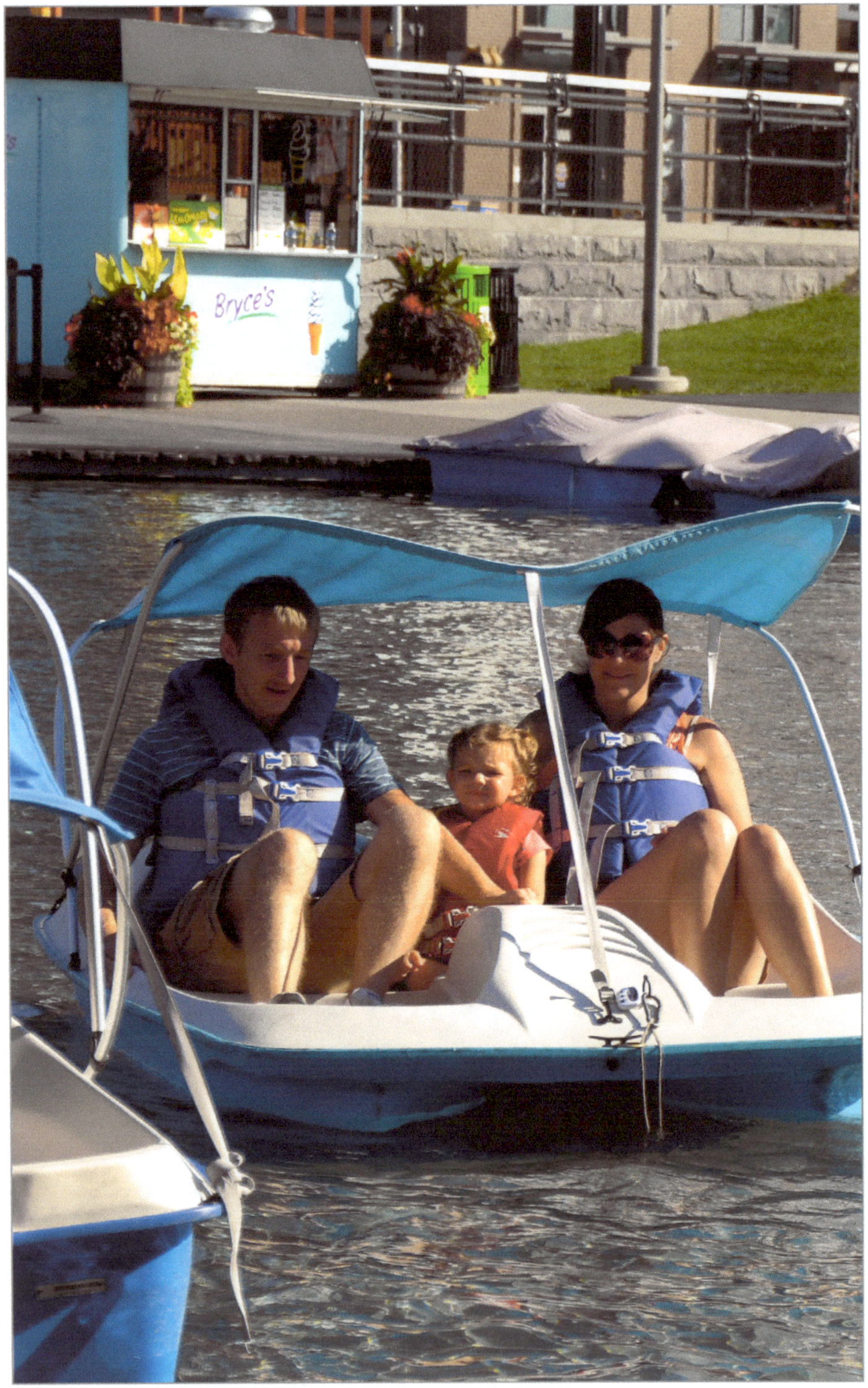

Re-watered Canal

Canalside is a magical place for young and formerly young kids filled with dozens of ways to capture their imaginations. It's buzzing with tons of children's programming, history tours, and outdoor activities.

(Left:) You can paddle your way through Buffalo's history, where shallow canals have been restored to how they were in 1825. Adult pedal boats and children's paddle boats, manufactured right here in Western New York, are available for hourly rental.

(Opposite:) When the temperatures dip below freezing, Canalside, Buffalo's beloved summertime waterfront destination, magically transforms. At the Historic Replica Canals, where paddleboats once cruised, now becomes a winter wonderland on New York State's largest outdoor ice skating rink. During Buffalo's fourth season, this becomes the domain of ice skating, ice biking (invented here in Buffalo), curling, and ice bumper cars on its 33,000 square feet of ice.

Ice Bumper Cars (Below:)
The newest way to enjoy the ice is to slip, slide, and smash your ice bumper car with your friends and family.

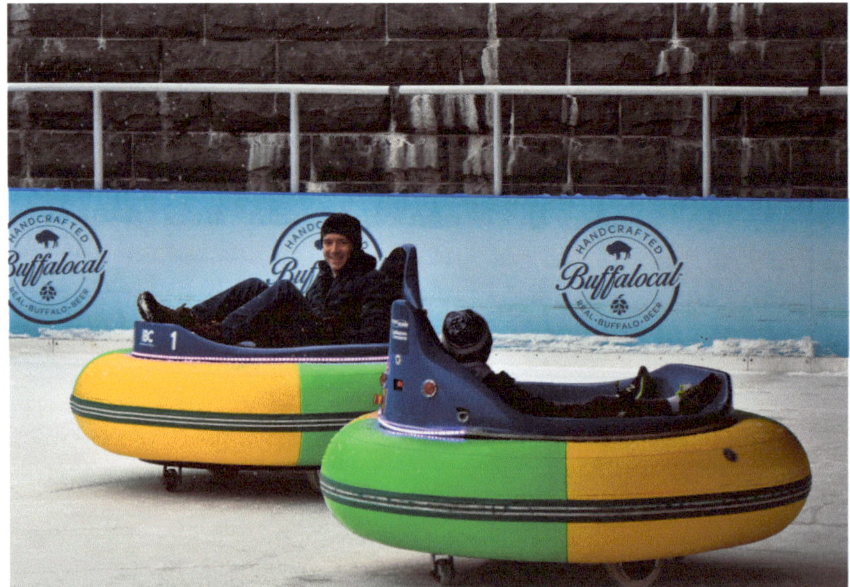

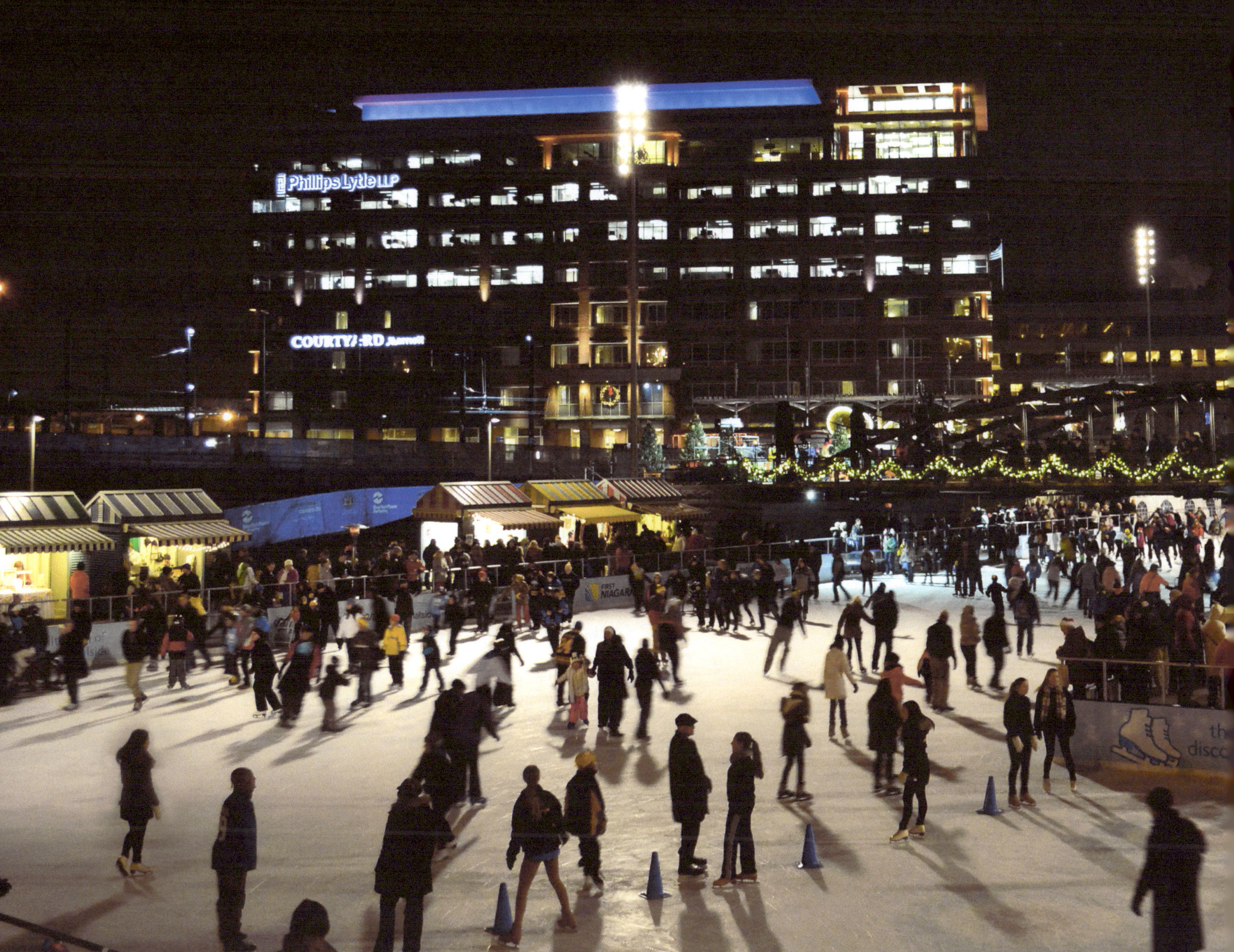
Phillips Lytle LLP
COURTYARD

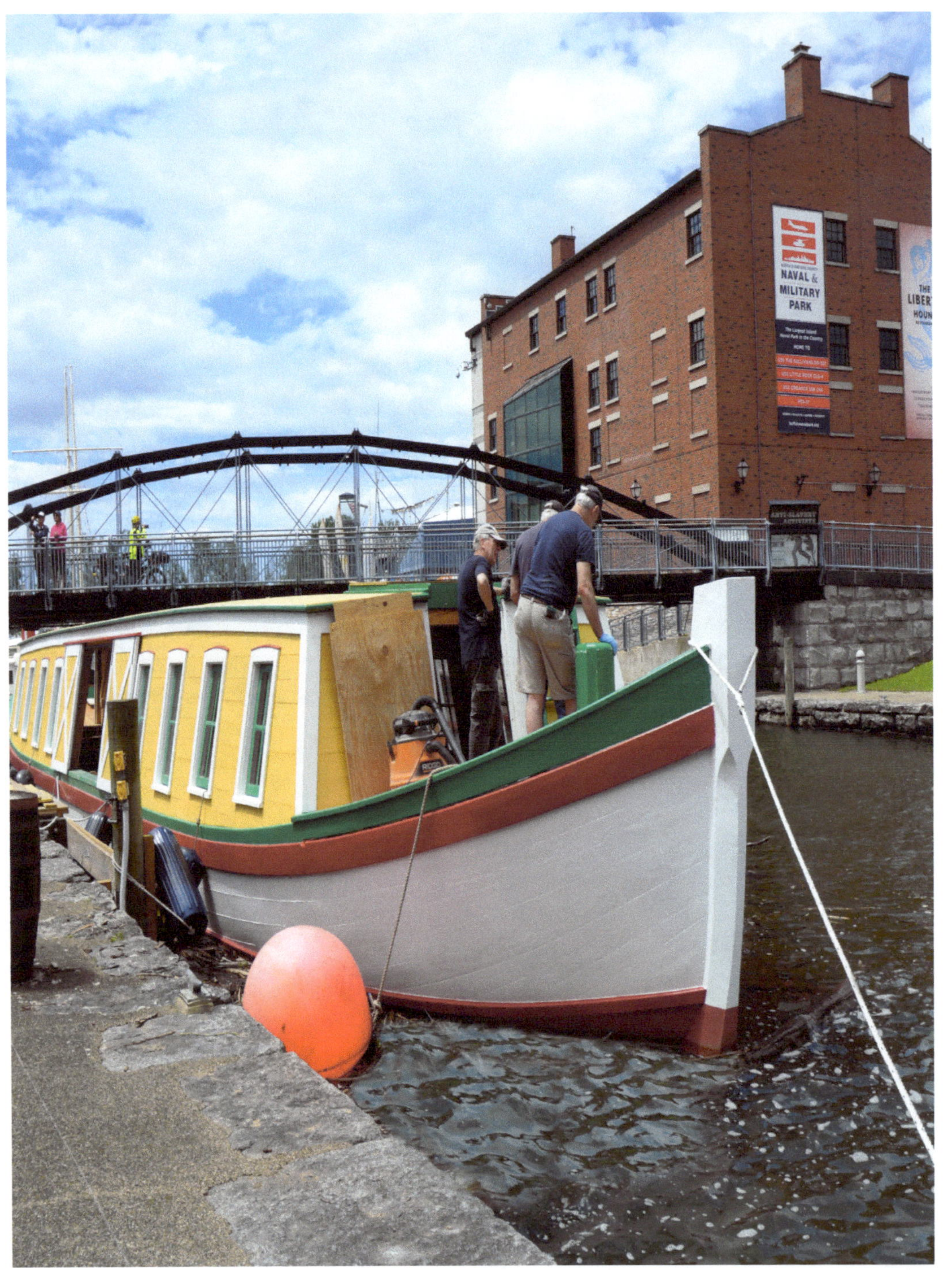

The Seneca Chief

(Left)

The Seneca Chief is a traditional, full-sized replica of the Erie Canal Boat, which originally opened the Erie Canal in 1825. It was built by the Buffalo Maritime Center inside the Longshed at Canalside on Buffalo's waterfront from October 2020 to June 2024.

This project was designed to engage the community through hands-on experiences and historical exploration. It was made possible by hundreds of volunteers.

The Seneca Chief will embark on its Bicentennial Voyage from Buffalo to New York Harbor, in 2025 commemorating Gov. DeWitt Clinton's inaugural journey.

Buffalo Heritage Carousel

(Opposite:)

The historic century-old De Angelis Menagerie Carousel's 34 hand-carved animals was built in 1924 at the Herschell-Spillman factory in North Tonawanda but then went into storage for 80 years. Its sights and sounds can now be enjoyed by children for generations to come.

The solar-powered carousel is located near Clinton's Dish inside a glass-enclosed roundhouse. It's a grand celebration of Buffalo's industrial history and our ongoing work to revive and transform Buffalo's Waterfront.

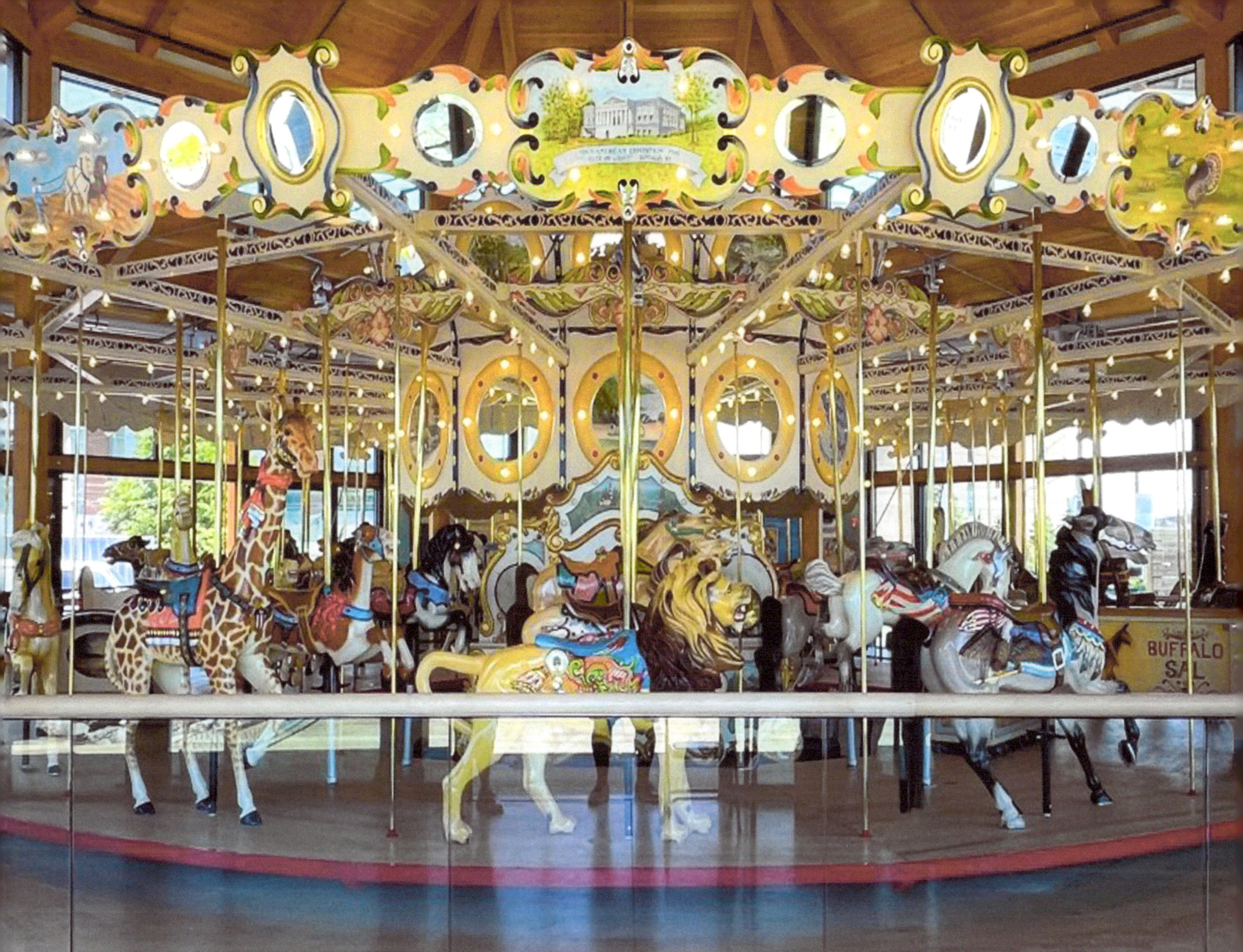
BUFFALO
SAL

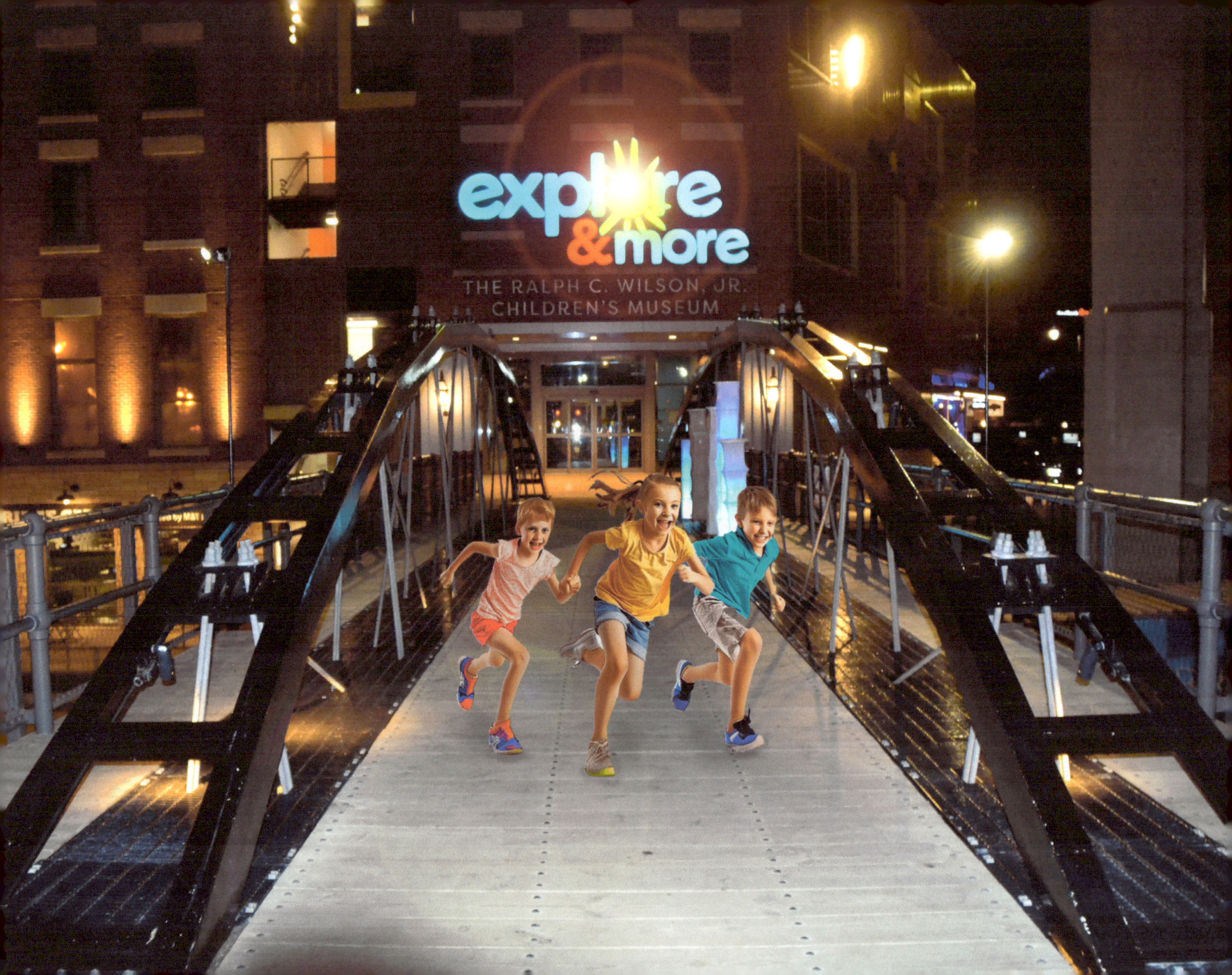
explore
&more
THE RALPH C. WILSON, JR.
CHILDREN'S MUSEUM

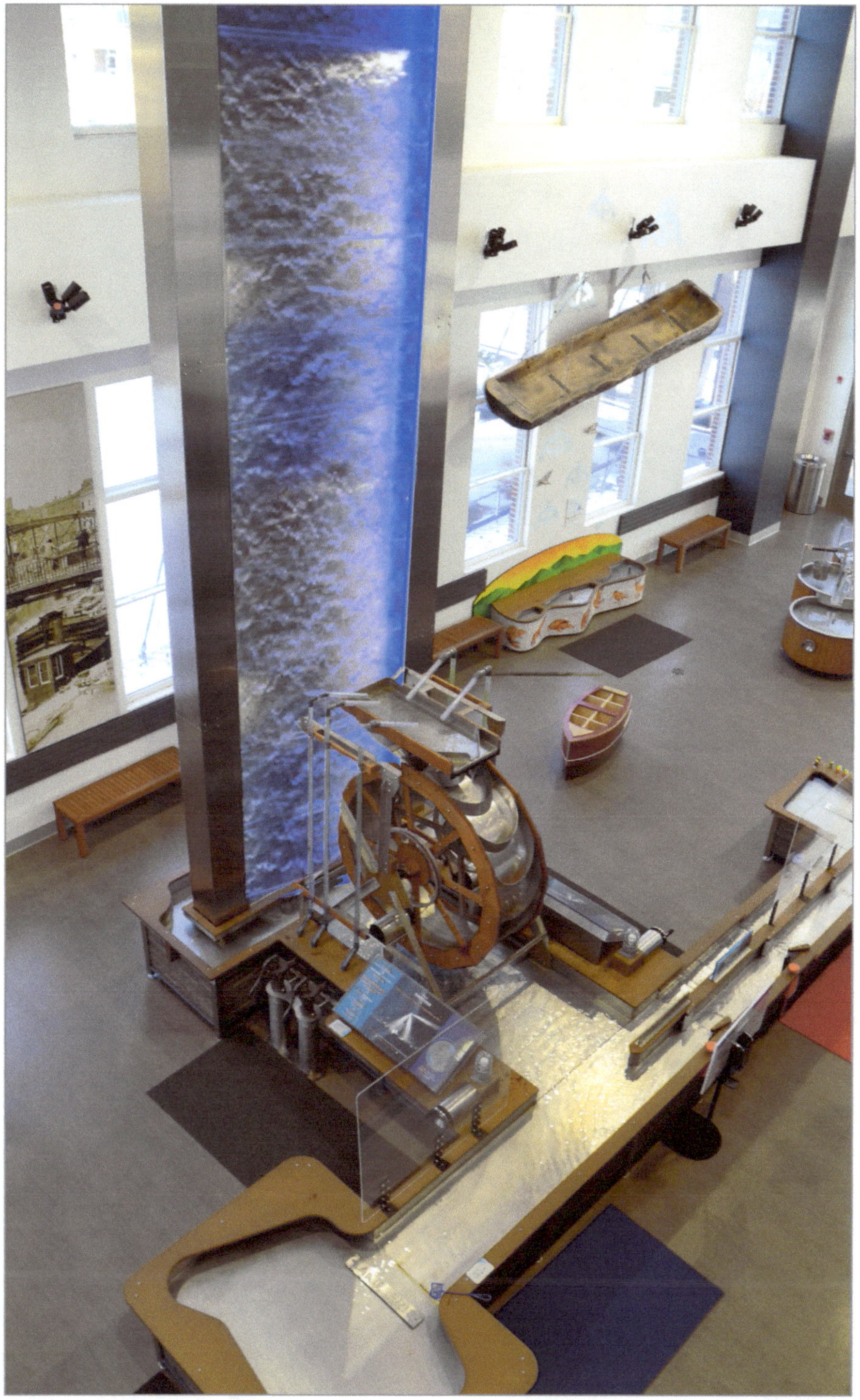

Where fun and learning play together

Explore & More / Ralph C. Wilson, Jr. Children's Museum is a 43,000 sq. ft, world-class children's museum celebrating child-led play's power.

Tucked between Canalside's replica canals and bridges, the museum has become a year-round must-see destination for anyone with children. There are four floors of fun with seven different play zones to explore, featuring thoughtfully crafted exhibits. They are designed to help children develop a deeper sense of our world, our community, and their place in it.

Learning seamlessly happens here in a fun and engaging way for children and adults alike. The museum amplifies our sense of place by showcasing Buffalo's history, waterways, sports teams, diversity, and invention contributions. Children can also learn how to grow plants, cook meals, and be creative in the art studio.

Explore & More is a place where learning feels like playing, where "Do not touch" becomes "Try it out." And where there's always a reason to come back for more.

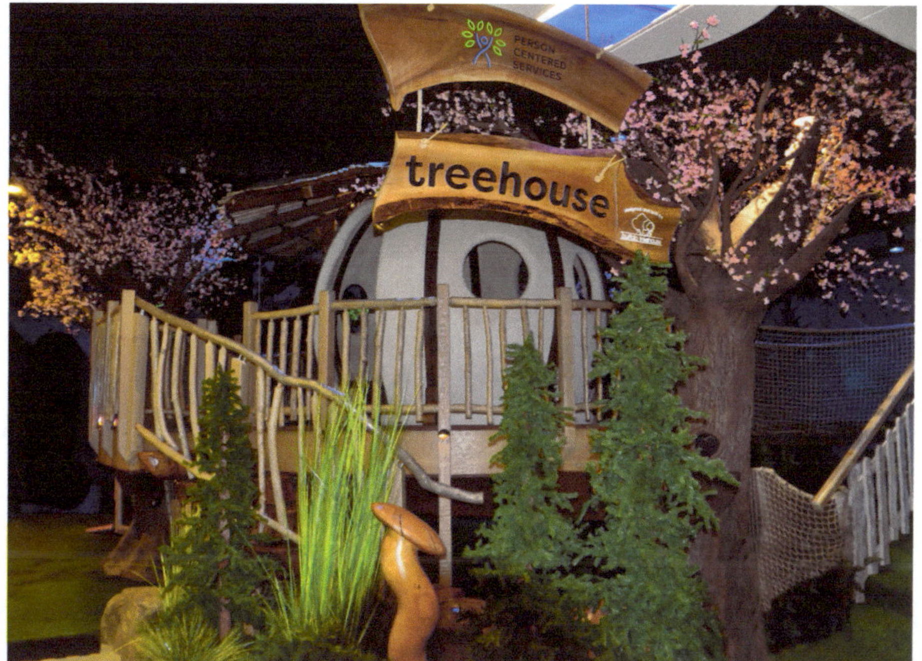

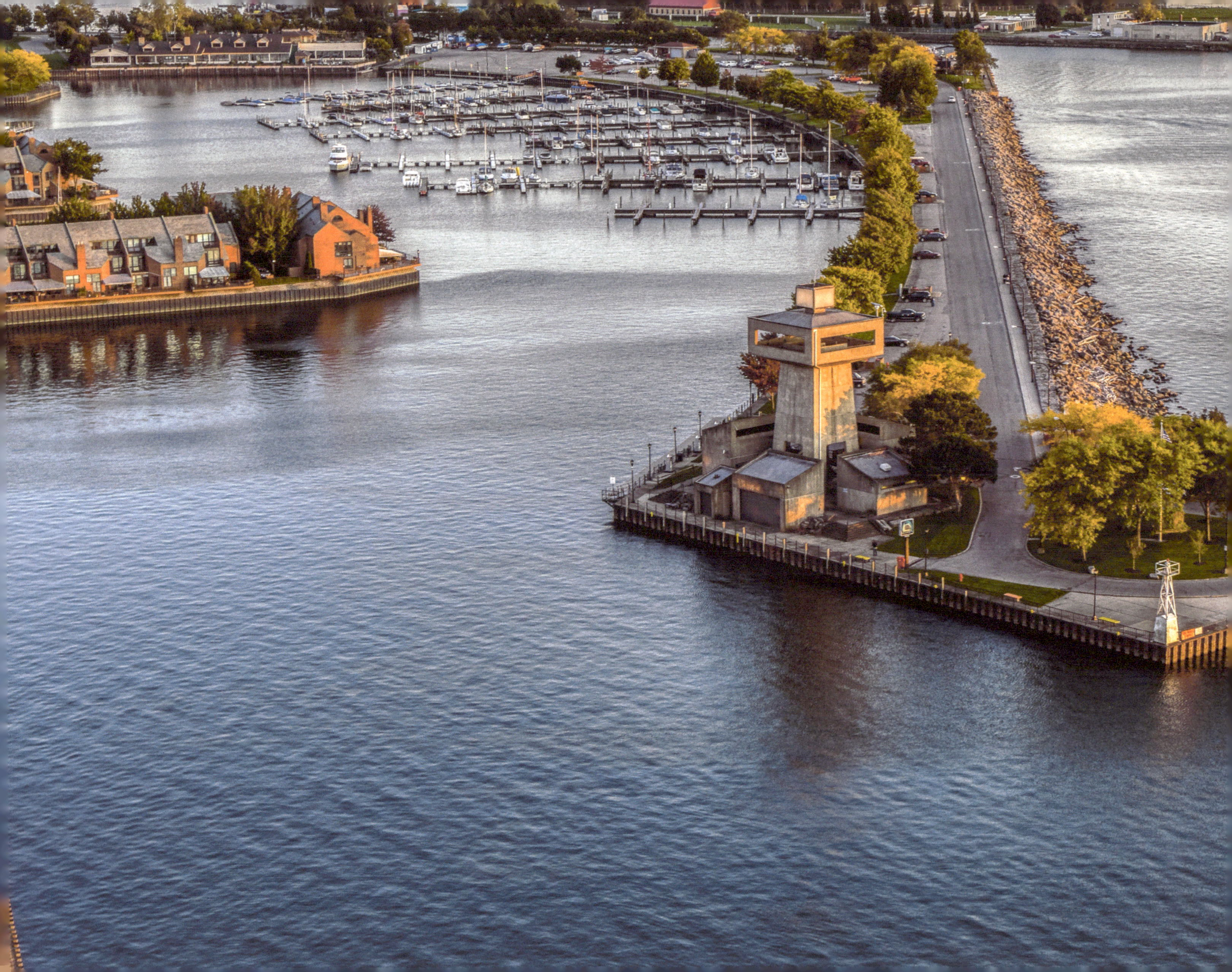

Erie Basin Harbor

It's easy to forget that the Erie Basin Marina, one of the most popular places on the Buffalo waterfront, was once just a breakwater and commercial slip at the mouth of the Buffalo River at Lake Erie designed to lessen the impact of storm surges.

Previously just a breakwater not even connected to the mainland, in 1970-1973, a major lakefront improvement project constructed the road, walkways, marina, tower, and buildings. Hidden to all but birds, airline pilots, and people viewing it from the City Hall observation deck is the fact that the marina was designed in the shape of a buffalo.

Today, Erie Basin Marina is so much more than a giant parking lot for boats. It is actually a neighborhood, complete with offices, condos, and restaurants.

Visitors come to watch sailboats skim gracefully past the historic lighthouse while being surrounded by fabulous, professionally groomed gardens. They can build an appetite as they scale the 83 steps of the Outlook Tower for the city's best panoramic views and then enjoy comfort food, ice cream, and occasionally good Karaoke at The Hatch restaurant. Many just come for their daily stroll or to sit and observe the amazing sunsets that glimmer across the lake.

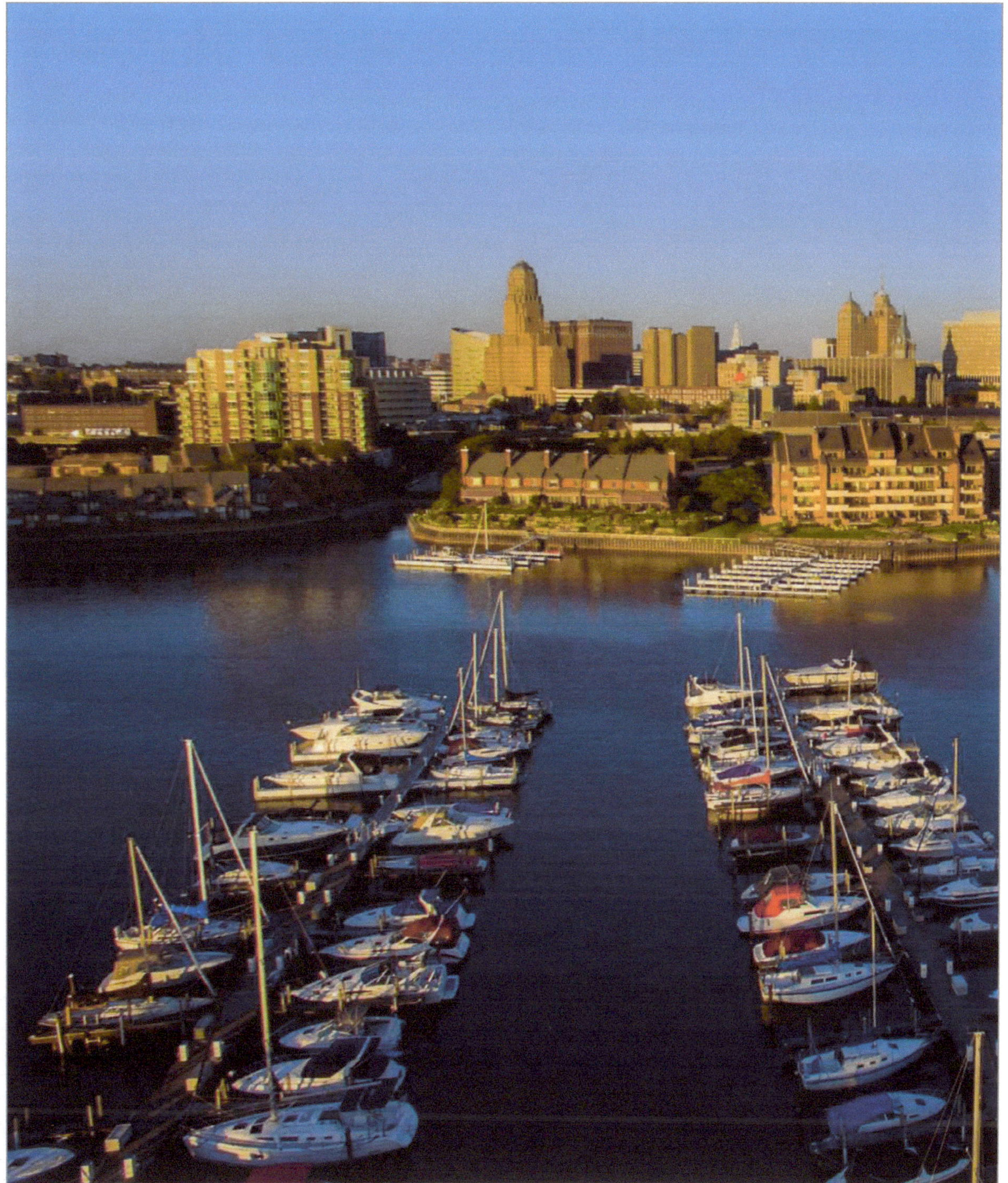

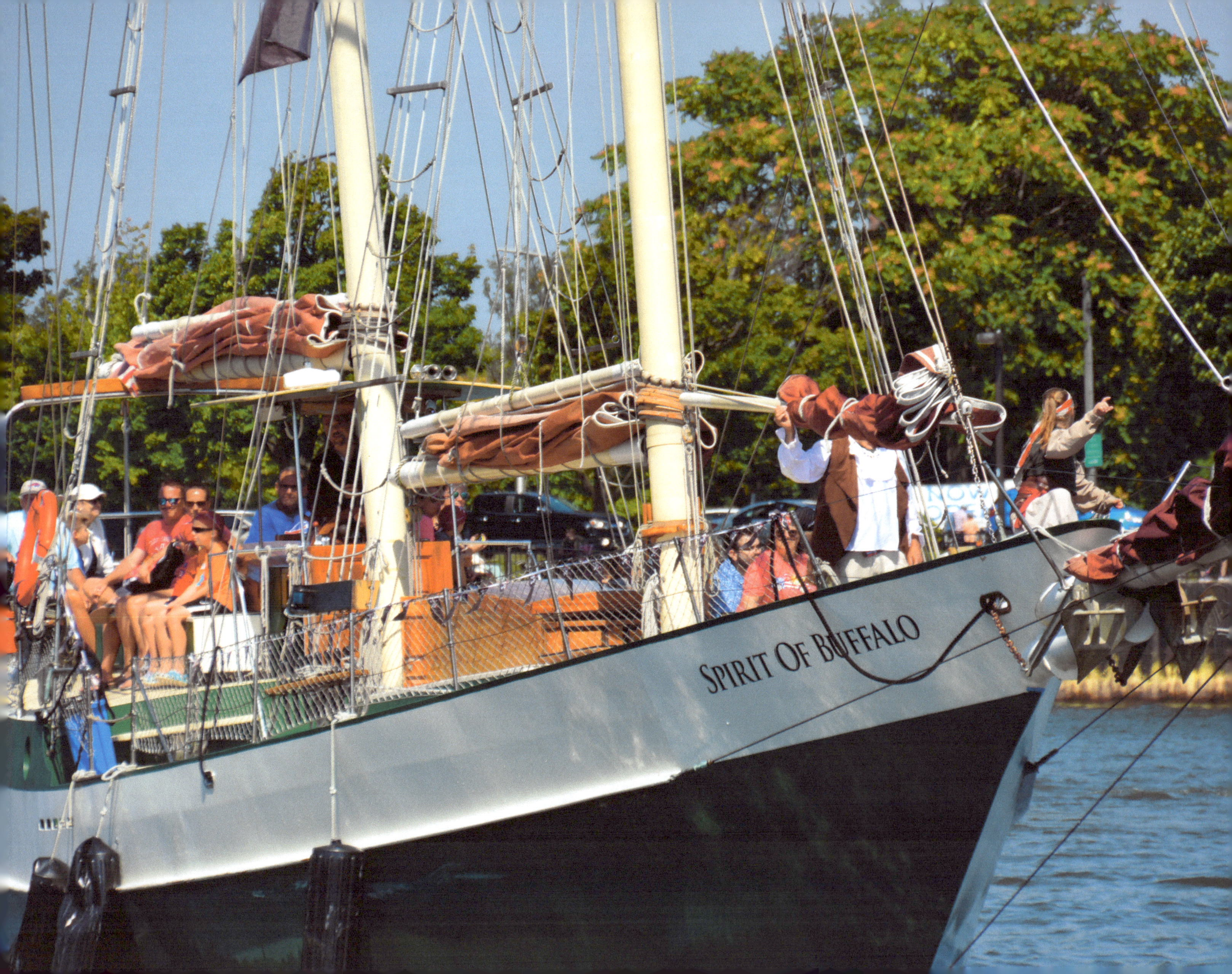
SPIRIT OF BUFFALO

On the water

There is no better view of our amazing waterfront than being on the water. Whether it is on the Maid of the Mist seeing a natural wonder of the world from the bottom up or touring our river and lakes on the Miss Buffalo, Grand Lady, Spirit of Buffalo, and Moondance Cat, Western New York never looks better than when you are surrounded by water with the sun in your face and the wind in your hair.

Moondance Cat *(Right)*
Now enjoying more than 35 years in operation, Moondance Cat is a 65-passenger elite sailing Catamaran whose parallel hulls are joined by a "party" deck that supports a full bar and plenty of room for mingling.

Spirit of Buffalo *(Opposite:)*
Enjoy the skyline and the colorful sunsets over Lake Erie as you sail back in time aboard the Spirit of Buffalo. You'll truly discover the feel of traditional sailing on this classic 73-foot topsail schooner. You'll be invited to join the crew and hoist its distinctive red sails, or you can sit back, relax, and see the city in a new way.

Westside Rowing Club *(below:)*
The West Side Rowing Club is a non-profit organization whose purpose is the advancement of the physical, mental, and moral well-being of the youth of the city and surrounding communities by education, training, instruction, and participation in the art of rowing and other athletic pursuits.

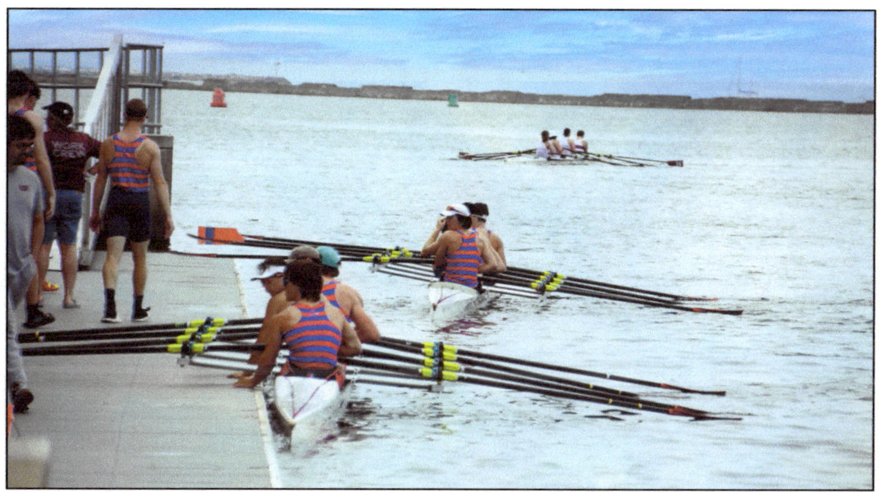

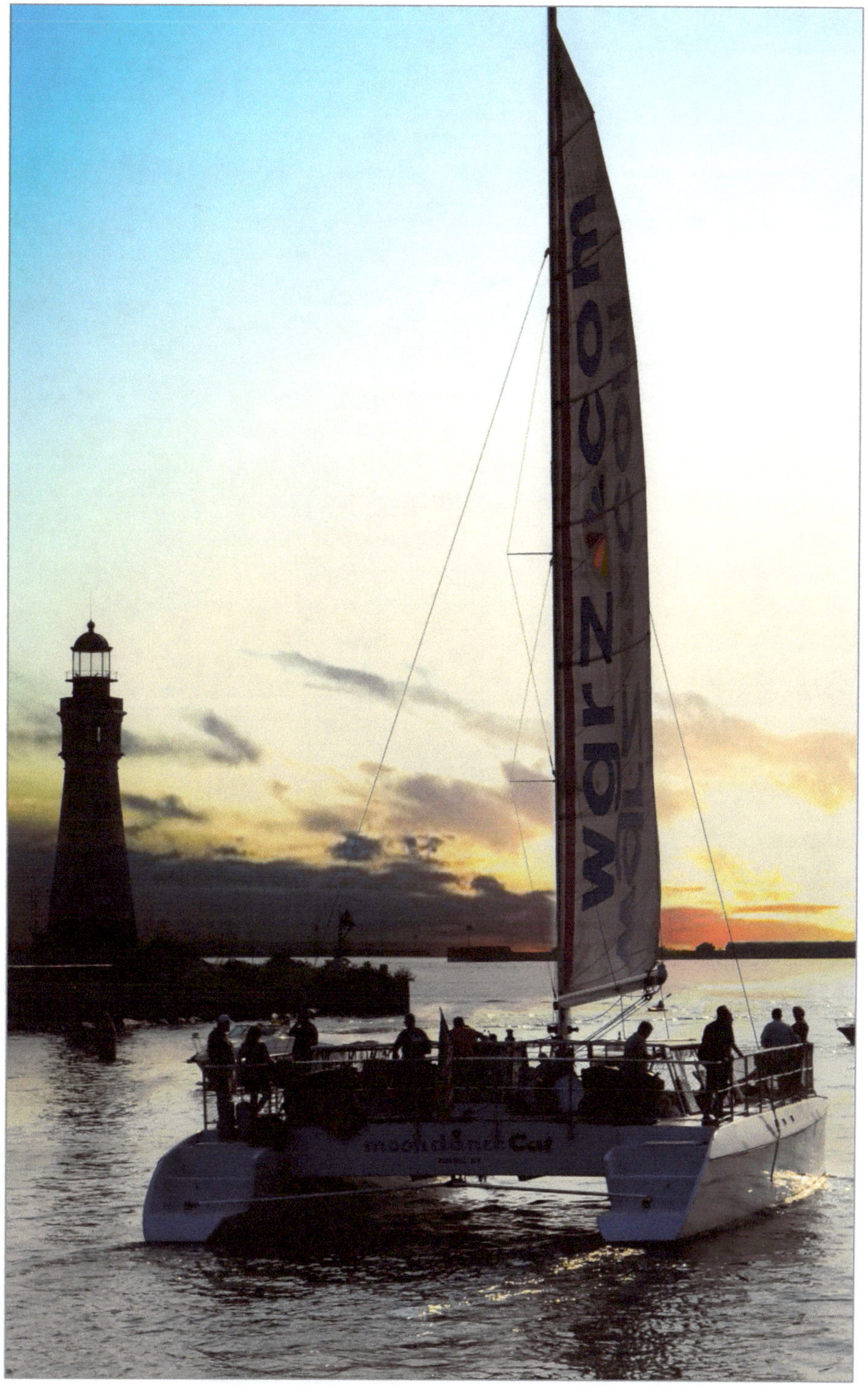

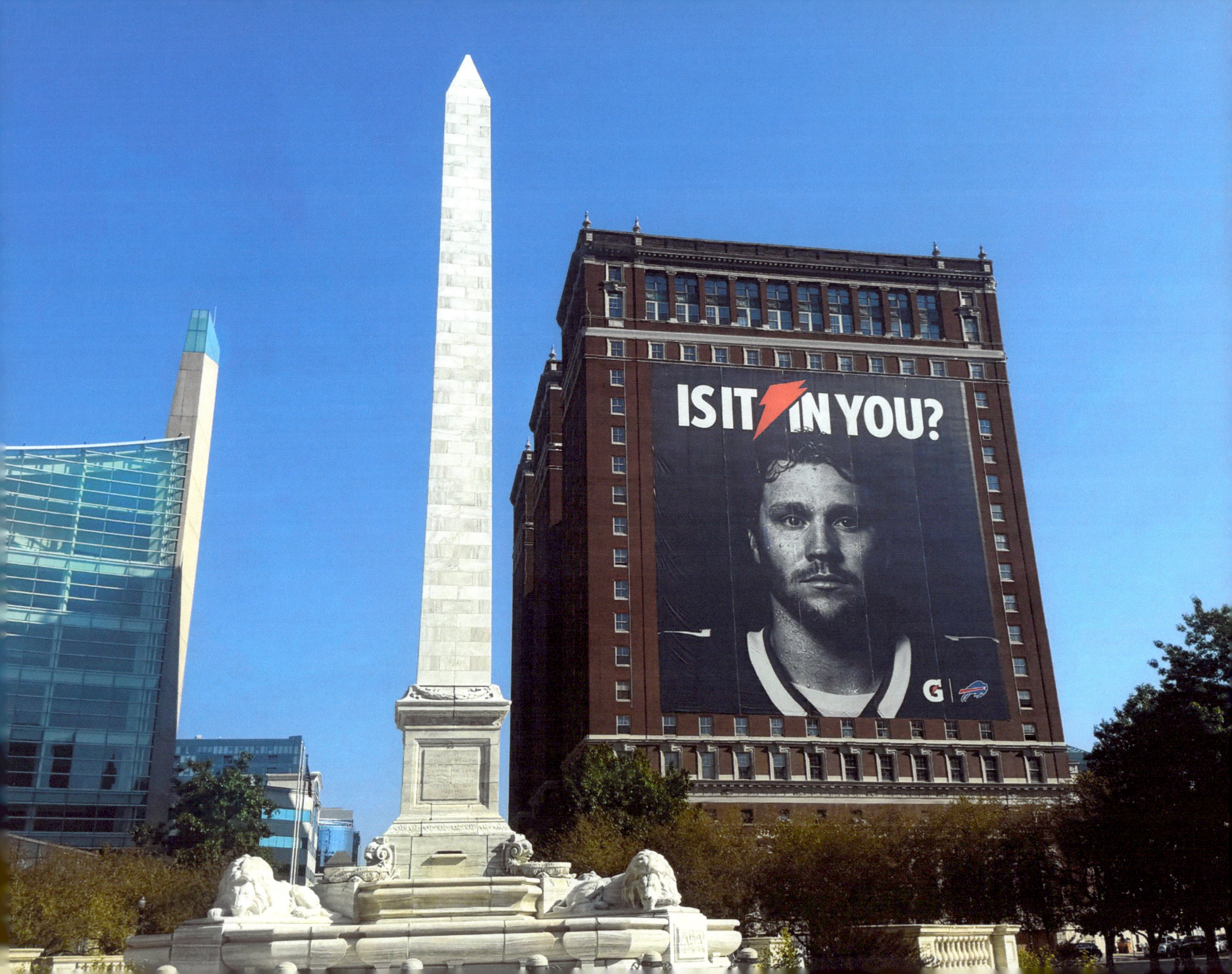
IS IT IN YOU?
G

A Beer Town With a Sports Problem

"Top shelf, where momma hides the cookies."

– John Richard "Rick" Jeanneret
The late play-by-play announcer for the Buffalo Sabres

If sports is your religion, then Buffalo is your church.

It's hard to overestimate Western New Yorkers' passion for their sports. We're home to The Buffalo Bills, New York's only major league football team (the other two play in New Jersey), the Buffalo Sabres, and several minor sports teams, including the Buffalo Bisons, Buffalo Bandits indoor lacrosse, and FC Buffalo soccer. The Buffalo Niagara region also offers various college and university athletic programs.

Our fan loyalty is legendary. As a city not known for our fair weather, we're also not known for having fair weather fans. Despite many crushing and sometimes controversial defeats such as "Wide Right," "No Goal," and the "Music City Miracle," our resilient spirit has never allowed it to define us as fans. Our capacity crowds consistently show up in full colors (sometimes half-naked), and always leave a little bit hoarse from cheering on our teams. Some of us even include being the 12th man on our résumés.

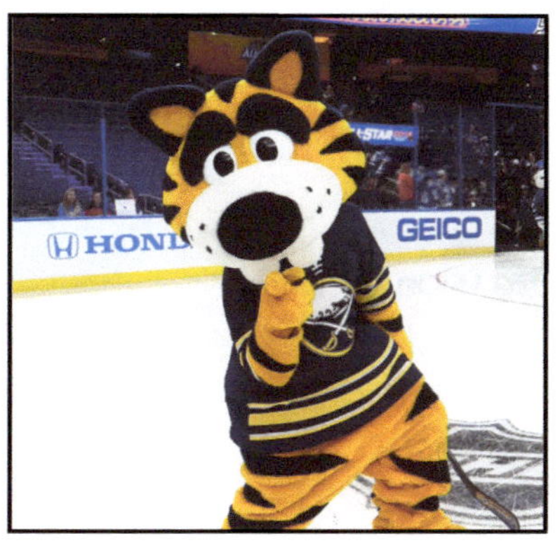

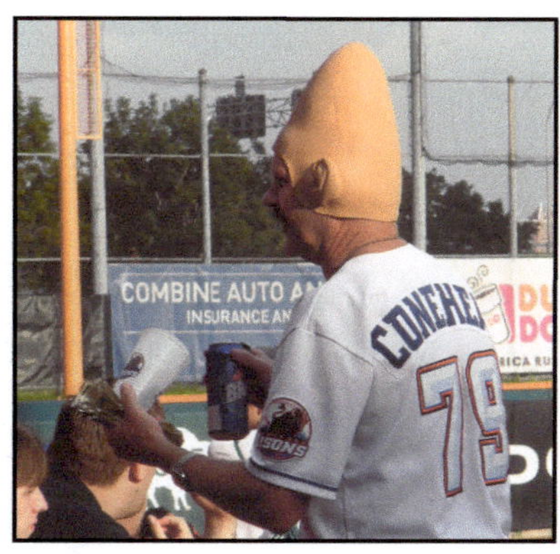

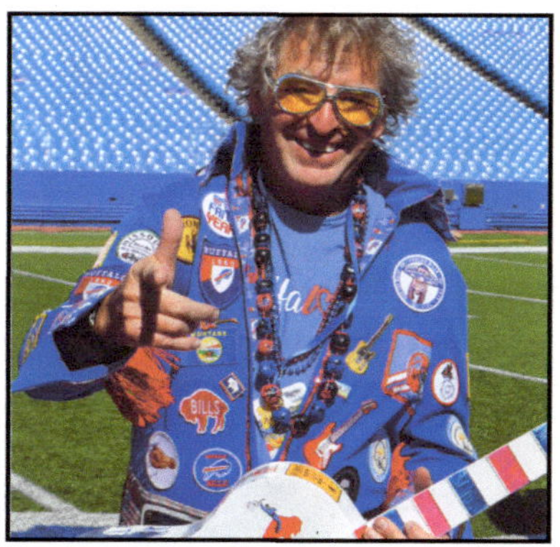

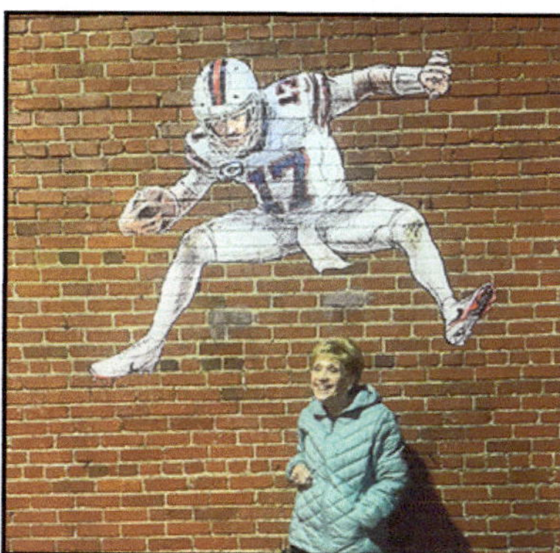

Opposite: Buffalo Statler, all decked out in a giant banners saluting quarterback Josh Allen.
(Left to right:) - Sabretooth is the mascot of the Buffalo Sabres.
- Tom Girot, better known as Conehead, has been wandering the stands of Buffalo sporting events serving ice-cold beer since 1972.
- John "Bills Elvis" Lang has been a season ticket holder since 1992. Lang became Bills Elvis when he made a bet with a friend that he could get on national television by dressing up and painting an old guitar.
- A mural of a leaping Josh Allen by Editorial Cartoonist Adam Zyglis adorns a wall on Parkside Avenue.

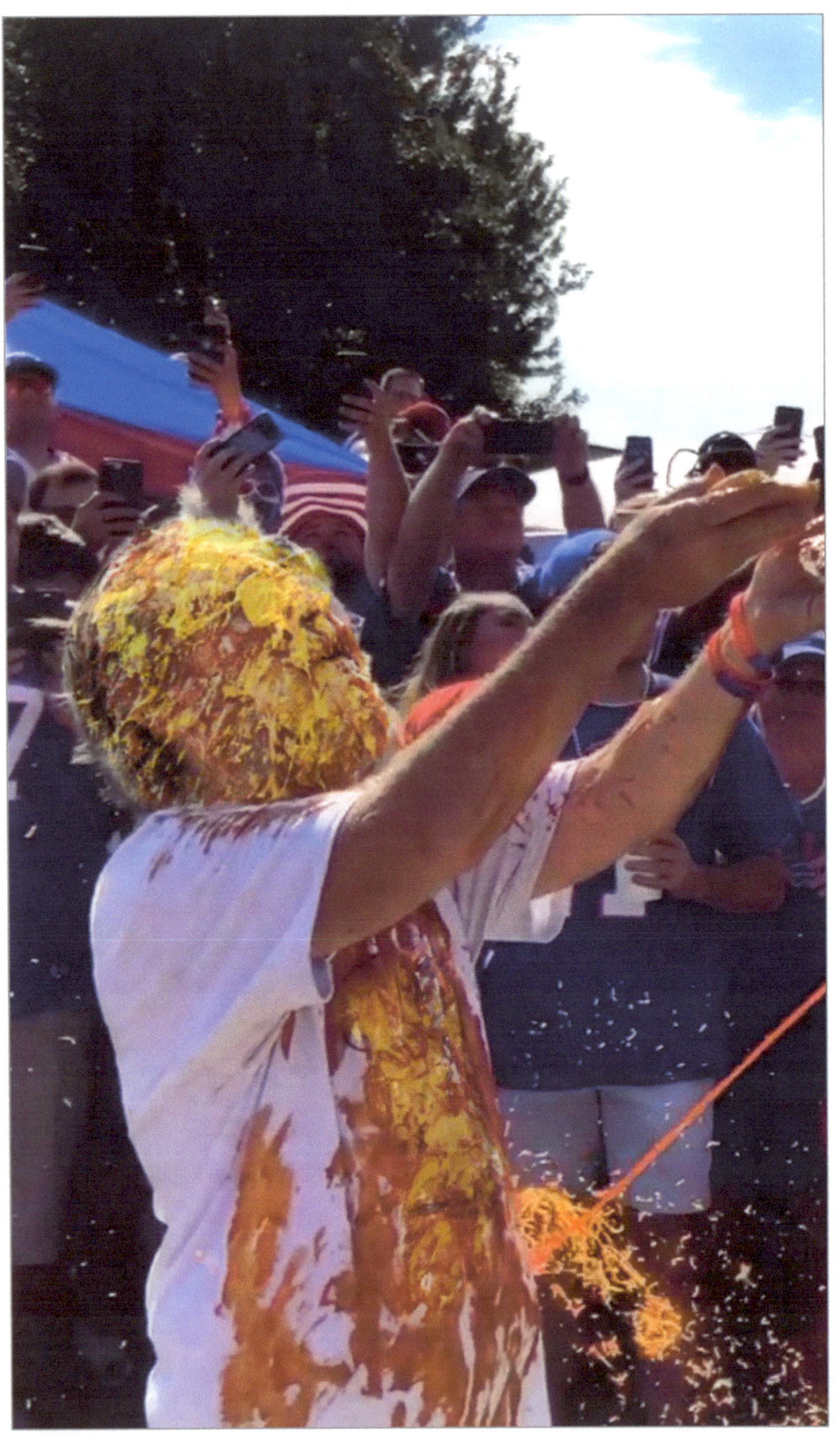

Bills Mafia.
Go big, or Go Home

Devoted NFL fans show their love in lots of ways that don't make sense out of context. For example, Green Bay Packers fans wear foam blocks of cheese on their heads. However, the Bills Mafia takes things further than most. For the past few years, safety-challenged Bills tailgaters have ended their pre-game debauchery by leaping from the top of a Porta Pottie. The target for these well-lubricated paratroopers is a plastic folding table.

It's over-the-top performance art that would make the WWF proud.

Seventy thousand plus hardcore fans, all decked out in their Bills clothing, show up like clockwork each gameday. Through thick and thin, we celebrate our team. We celebrate our food. And sometimes, we get a tiny bit carried away and celebrate our condiments.

The infamous pre-game ketchup ceremony is in the shadow of Highmark Stadium at a private parking area aptly named the Hammer Lot. The high priest of this frenzied entertainment ritual is superfan Ken Johnson, a.k.a Pinto Ron.

Best known for being the willing recipient of fountains of condiments before each game, his rusty red Ford Pinto serves as ground zero for much of the tailgate shenanigans. He's also known for the free food he cooks in totally unorthodox ways: omelets and pancakes on an old shovel, bacon on a sawblade, chicken wings in an army helmet, and hot dogs and hamburgers on a toolbox converted into a makeshift grill.

Fortunately, there is also a less outrageous side of Bills tailgating featuring a wide variety of unique foods that greatly enhance the total game-day experience without requiring a complete change of clothes and a shower.

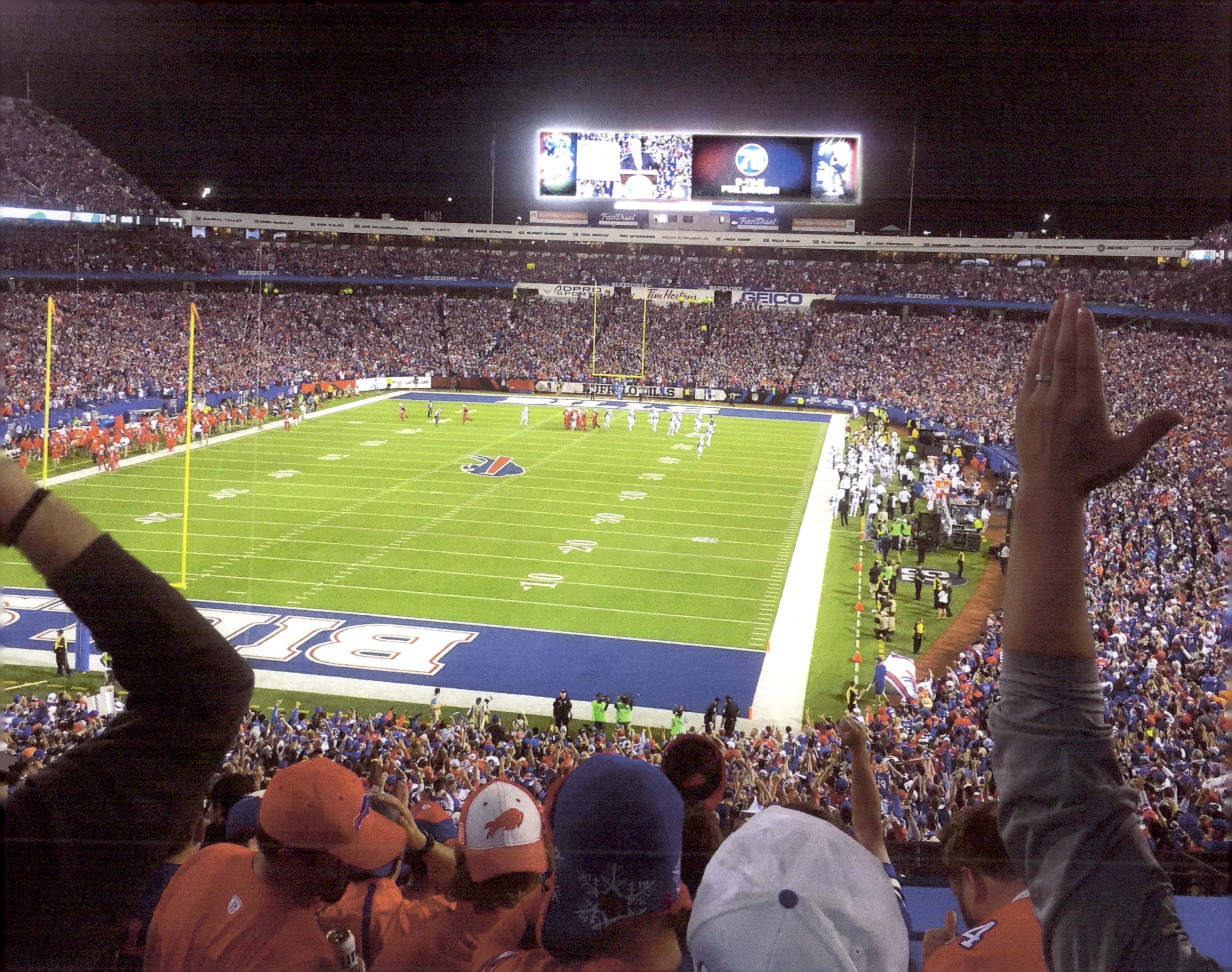
FanDuel
FanDuel
Tim Hortons
GEICO

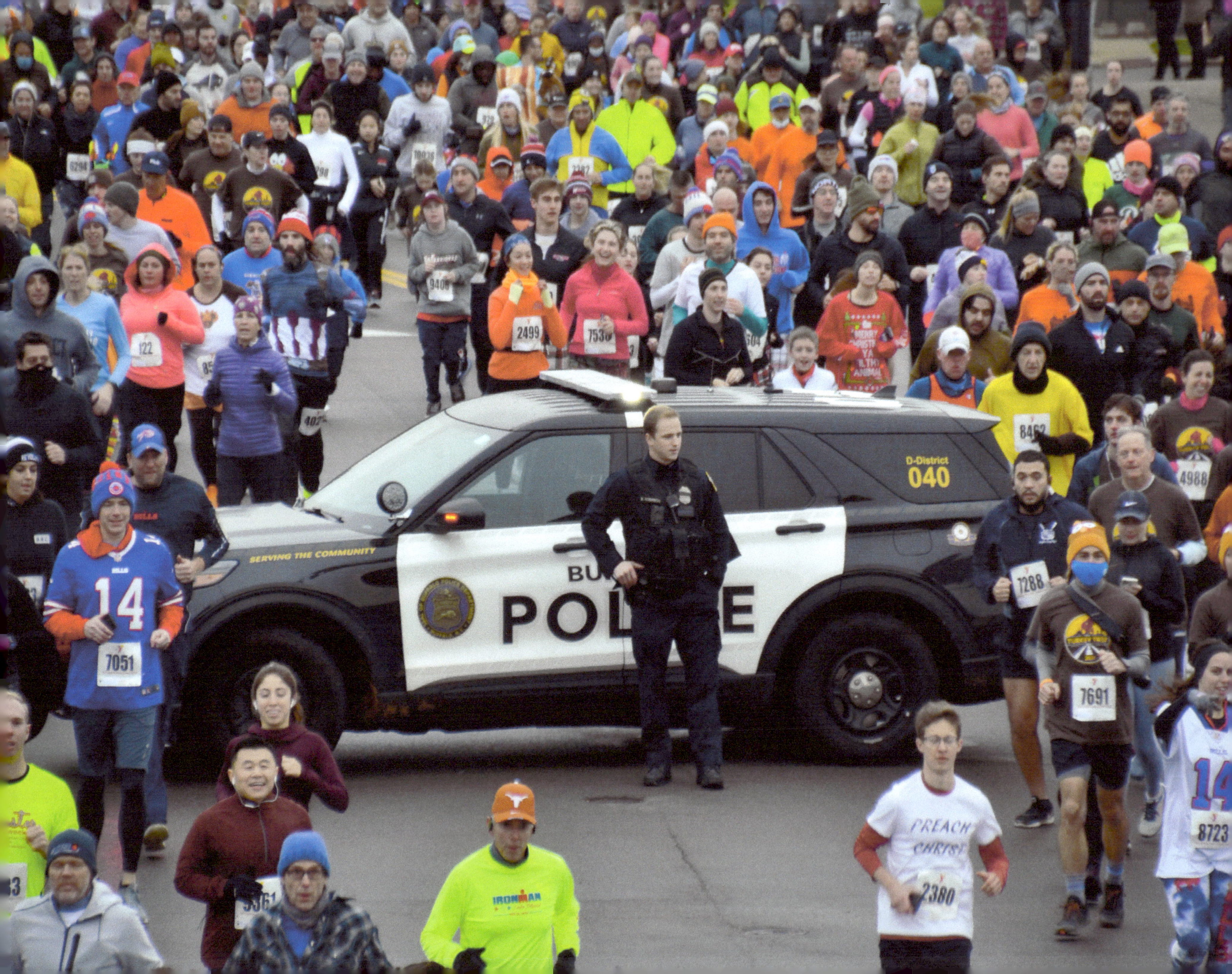
D-District
040
SERVING THE COMMUNITY
PREACH
CHRIST
IRONMAN
14
7051
2499
122
9408
7288
7691
2380
8723
4988

Making A Difference

There's a reason Buffalo has been nicknamed "The City of Good Neighbors." – we really are good neighbors, and find hundreds of ways to prove it. From pushing out cars stuck in a snowdrift, running, walking, or hosting a food drive,

Western New Yorkers have a proud history of getting involved and volunteering in mass with our region's non-profit organizations. Whether it's to improve the dignity and quality of life, overcome barriers, alleviate homelessness, create life-changing wishes for children with critical illnesses, preserve, restore, and enhance our parks for future generations, or provide nutritious food to our Western New York neighbors in need, an army of volunteers is ready to roll up their sleeves or tighten their shoelaces to get it done.

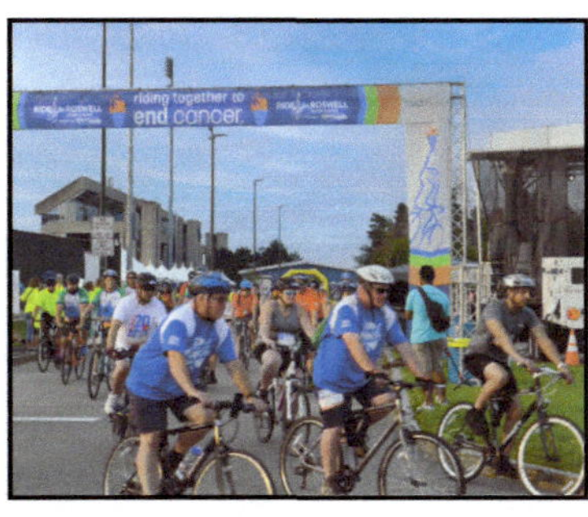

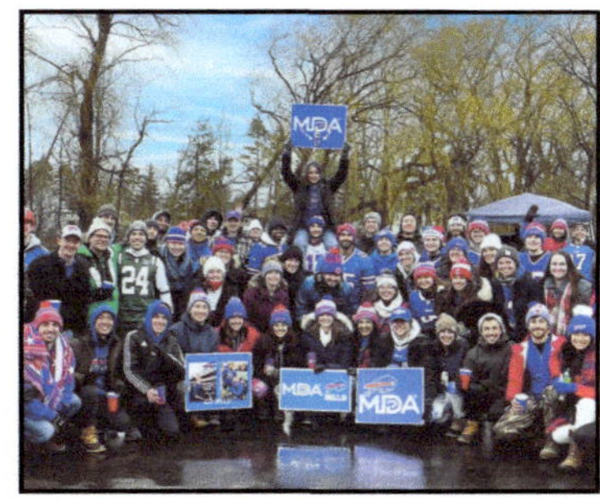

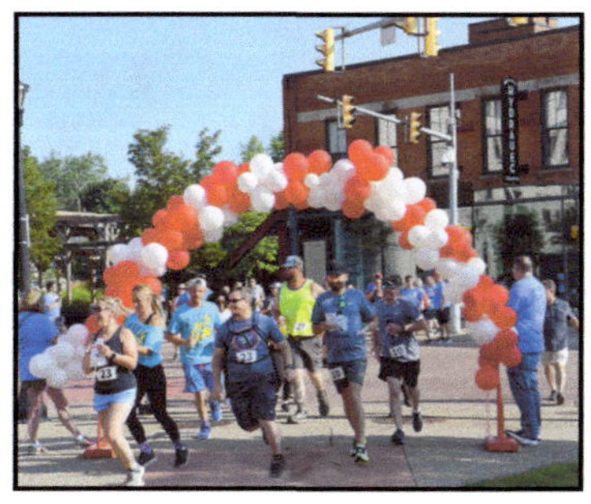

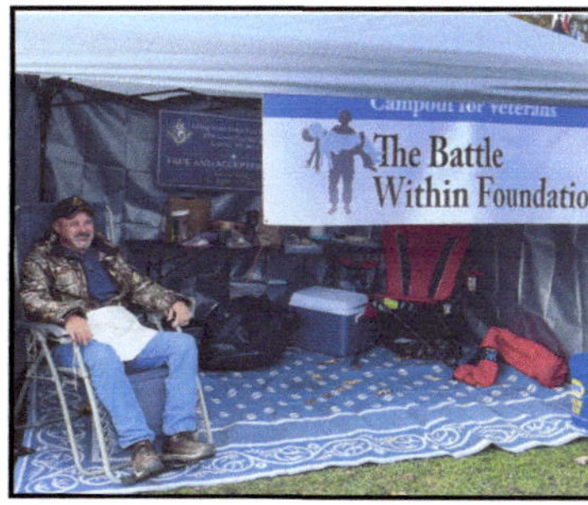

(Left to right:

- Ride for Roswell is one of the nation's largest charity cycling events, bringing a community of people together to celebrate cancer survivors, pay tribute to those we've lost, and share in the passion that connects us all: finding cures for cancer. In 2023, 8,022 riders helped raise $5.6 million.

- Each year, University at Buffalo Medical students organize a tailgate fundraiser for the Muscular Dystrophy Association (MDA) to help accelerate research and advance care.

- The Salvation Army's Most Amazing Race sends teams of two all around the Buffalo area to complete ten physical and mental challenges to raise money for their many programs and services.

- Held at Colden Veterans Memorial Park, Mike Willibey, a disabled US Navy veteran, embarks annually on a 44-hour outdoor camping marathon to raise awareness and money for PTSD and homeless veterans.

(Opposite:)

With a field of 14,000, the YMCA Turkey Trot is a beloved Thanksgiving Day tradition filled with community spirit and goodwill. Proceeds raised through this event help fund the YMCA's vital work to empower youth, ensure health equity, and support our community's most vulnerable.

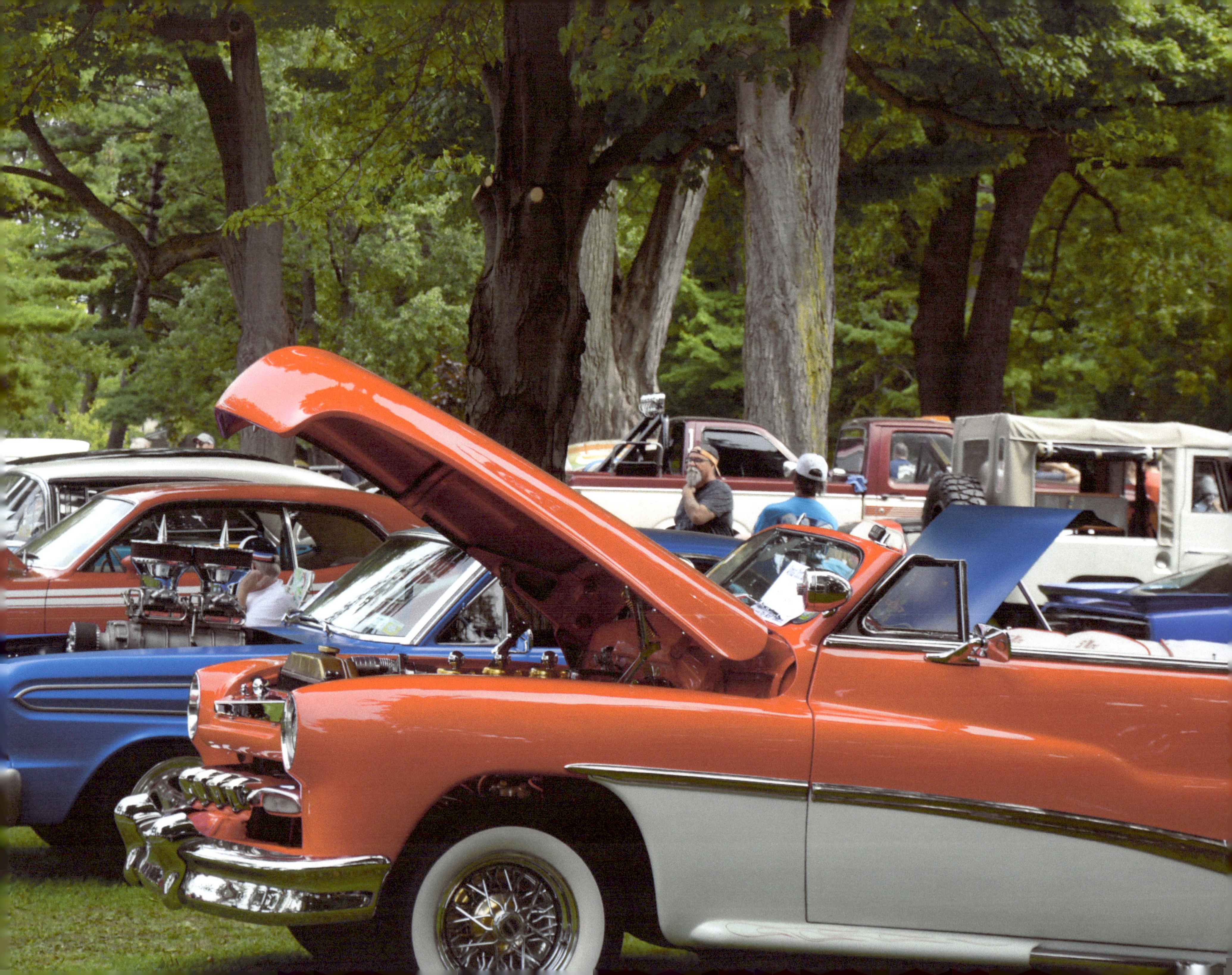

Work Hard / Play Hard

"All work and no play makes Jack a dull boy" Fortunately, Jack doesn't live here.

Some claim Buffalo is a predominately blue-collar city. We can let statistical wienies battle it out over our Demographic segmentation profiles. Still, from plumbers to CEOs, we all possess a blue-collar attitude as a city – we work hard and play hard. And we take great pride in the passion we do both.

While "play" is easily defined, there are very few places on earth where you have so many ways to achieve it.

Here in Western New York, we enjoy some of the best skiing, fishing, golfing, and boating in the Northeast. Whether served on a table between four walls or through a window over four wheels, we've got great eats. And there are equally great brews to wash it down.

Because we have four actual seasons, we can get sand in our shoes, jump in a giant pile of leaves, and make snow angels, all in the same year. There's a multitude of places and events to connect with hundreds of your friends and "not yet friends" to enjoy a cold one while watching the game. And solitude is always within reach in our fabulous parks.

Most of all, this is a city with a pulse that can make your smile grow wider with every beat. We live amid sixty canoes piled on a pole, a cemetery with a life-size black marble couch and loveseat, the world's largest six-pack, a brain museum, tailgating with Pinto Kenny, a little girl with a shark's head, and a guy who perpetually blows bubbles out his street corner window.

Western New York is a joyous place to live, work, and play.

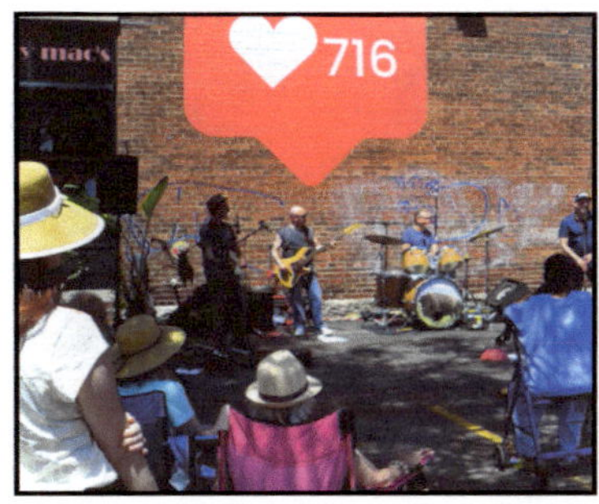

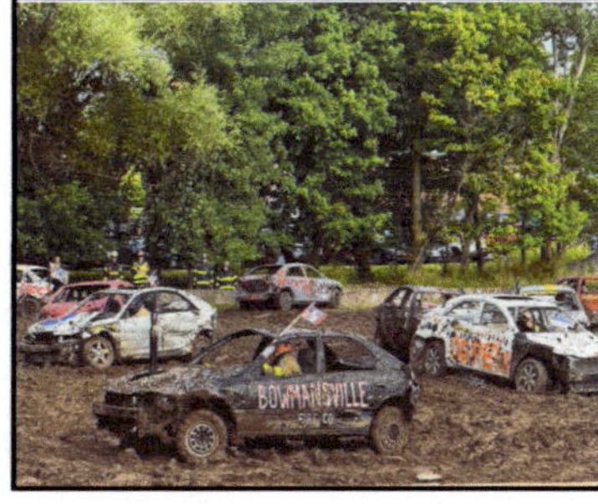
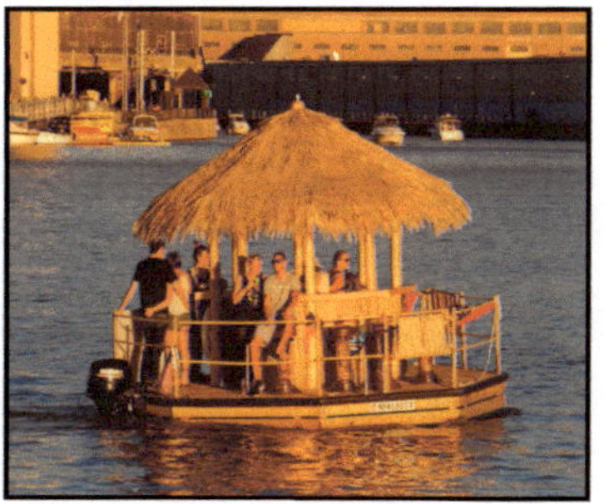
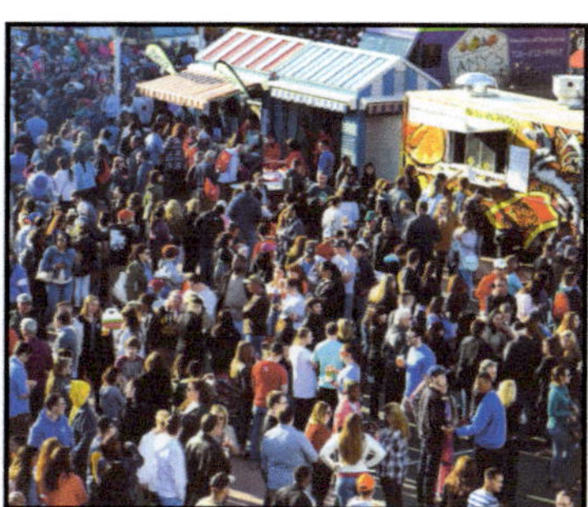

(Opposite:) The Olcott Beach Car Show has grown into one of the largest outdoor car events in Western New York.
(Left to right:) - A band entertains a parking lot full of fellow revelers at Porchfest.
- Demolition Derby in Clarence at the Annual CCVFC Benevolent Association's Labor Day Fair.
- Taking a relaxing tour around Buffalo's Inner Harbor with 20 of your friends on a Hawaiian-style Tiki Hut.
- Dozens of food trucks gather to celebrate a night of food, live music, and fun at Larkin Square.

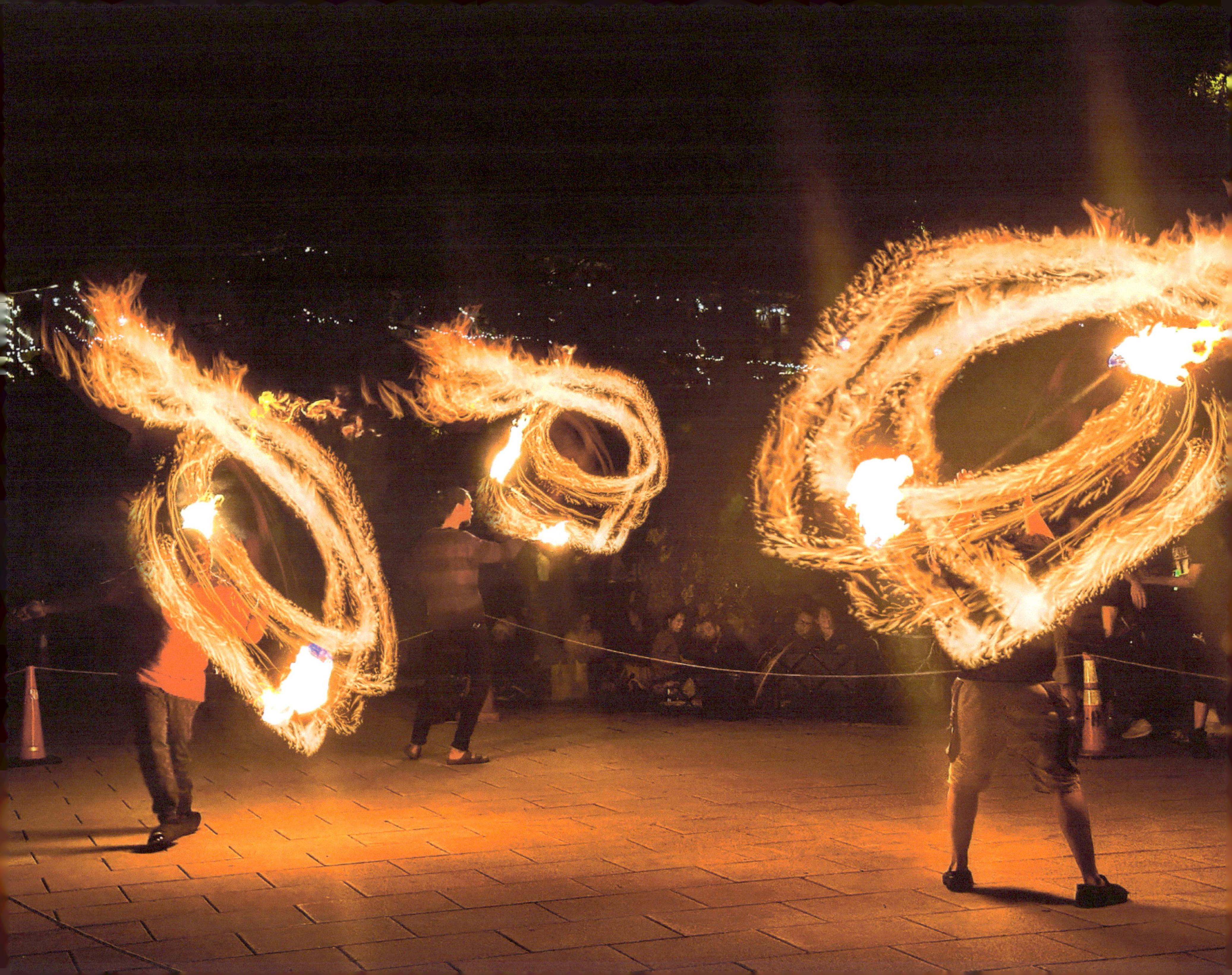

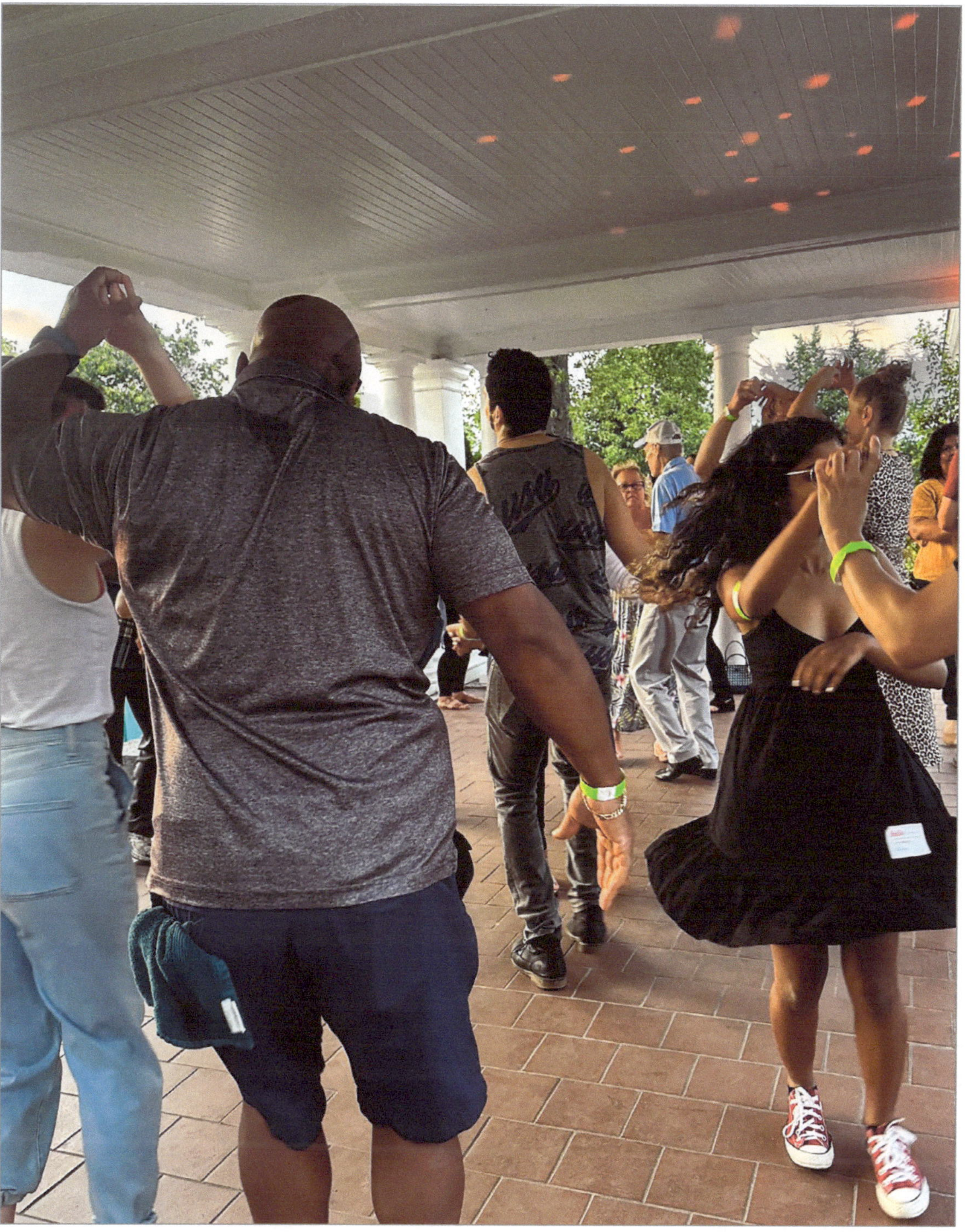

GETTING OUT AND LETTING LOOSE

Buffalo's parks are a wonderful place for solitude, but they are also a clarion call to get off the couch and shake what you just ate back in place.

1.1-Mile Hoyt Lake Loop is considered an easy route that takes an average of 20 min to complete. This area is popular for birding, road biking, and running, so you'll likely encounter other people while exploring.

1.8-Mile Delaware Park Ring Road is a popular trail for biking, running, and walking. The road is open year-round and is beautiful to visit anytime. Dogs are welcome but must be on a leash.

Salsa in the Park *(Left:)*
Salsa in the Park is asummer dance party at The Rose Gardens Pavilion at Marcy Casino in Delaware Park on the 1st and 3rd Mondays, June through August.

This summerlong salsa dance series kicks off with a beginner's dance lesson, followed by an open social dancing to Salsa, Timba (Cuban Salsa), Bachata, Merengue, Cha Cha Cha, and Kizomba.

Beginners, singles, groups of friends, and families are welcome to participate and encouraged to join in on the fun.

Buffalo Flow Jam *(Opposite:)*
Buffalo Flow Jam is a beautiful community of artists that put on a free event with talented fire spinners and LED light performances with the accompaniment of a local band or DJ, vendors, and food trucks.

On Monday nights in the summer, head to Hoyt Lake at Delaware Park for Flow Jam, a night of sonic and visual arts.

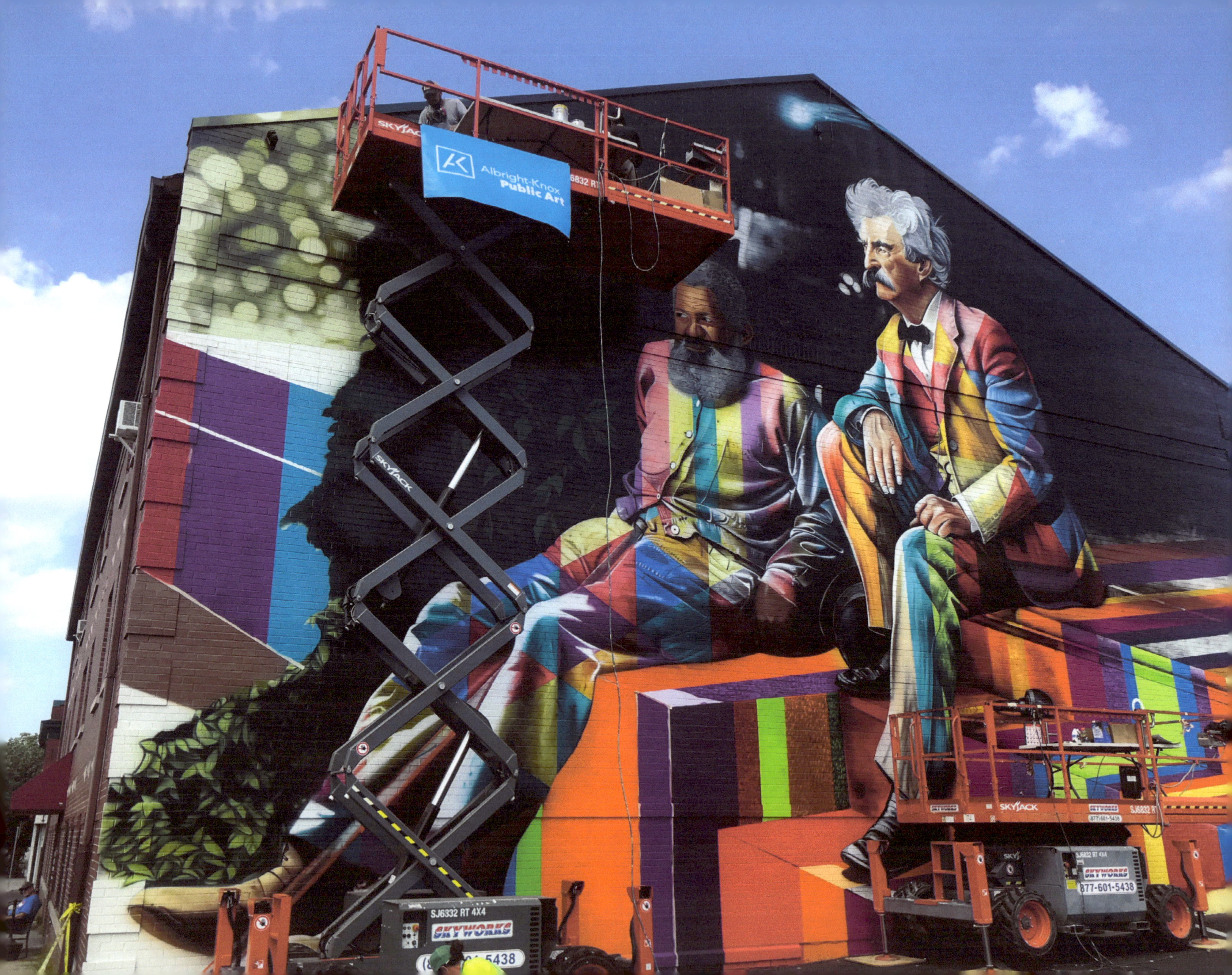
Albright-Knox
Public Art
SKYJACK
SJ6332 RT 4X4
SKYWORKS
877-601-5438

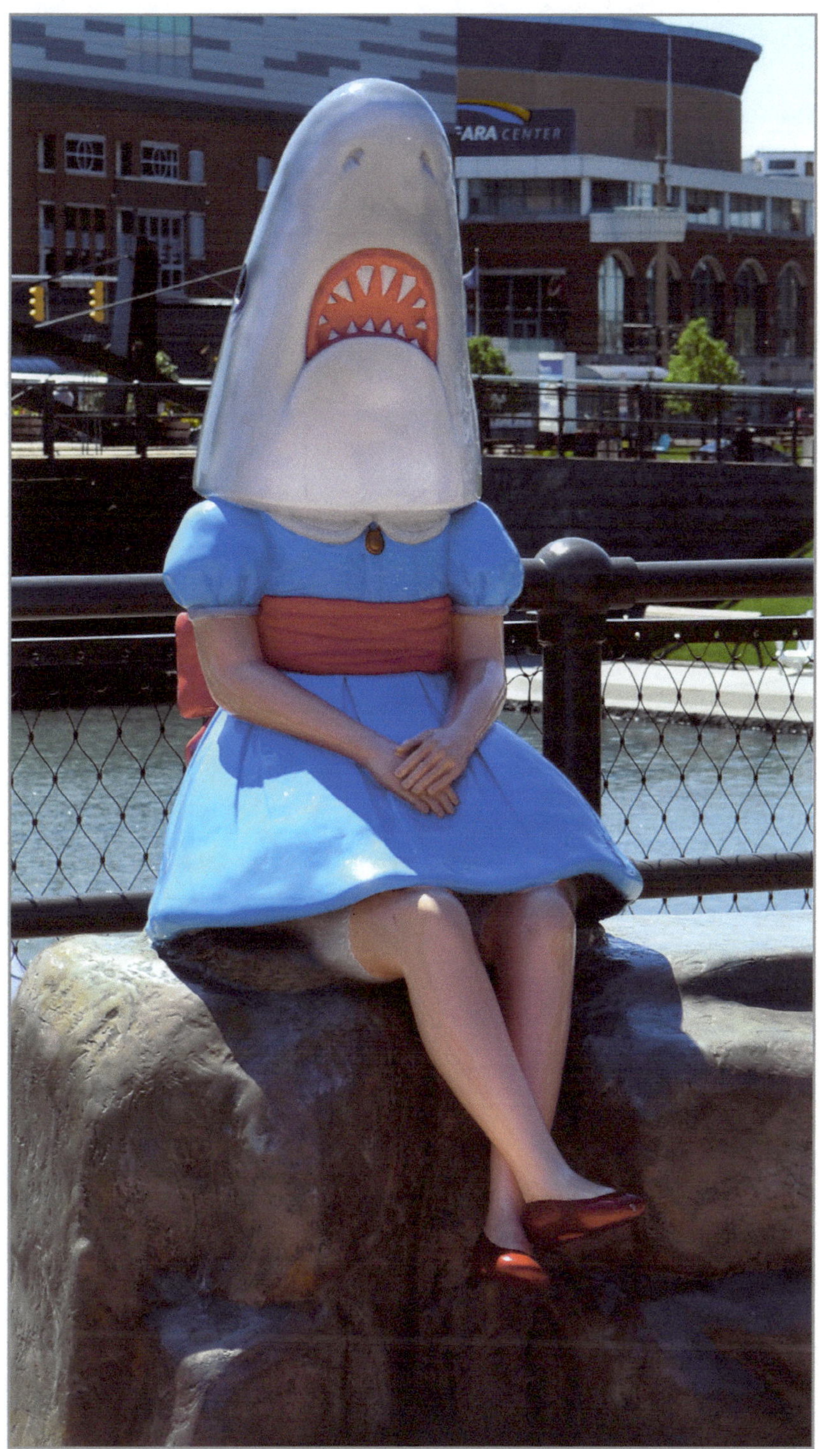

The joy of art is everywhere

While we have more than our fair share of galleries, large and small, our exuberance for art can't be held in by walls. Hand-painted murals decorate our urban walls; sculptures and statuary dot our street corners and line our expressways; and our airport and transit stations are alive with creative work.

***Untitled, 2019**, 1188 Hertel Avenue (Opposite:)*
Brazilian muralist Kobra often connects his work to the history of the community. Research led him to a 1903 photograph of Mark Twain and John Lewis that captured the unlikely pair sitting on the steps of a vine-covered porch in Elmira. The two, born the same year and buried next to each other, developed a lifelong friendship after Lewis saved Twain's sister-in-law and niece. This friendship impacted Twain's understanding of race and inequity. Kobra believes the mural alludes to the issue of racism, which existed then and now.

Eduardo Kobra, nicknamed Kobra, is a street artist who officially began his career in 1987 at 11 years old, in his hometown of São Paulo. Since then, he has painted over 3,000 murals on five continents, utilizing his trademark bright colors and bold lines while staying true to a kaleidoscope theme throughout his art.

***Shark Girl** (Left:)*
Located on a bridge at Canalside, Shark Girl patiently sits in her best dress, hands folded and legs daintily crossed. This lonely half-shark, half-girl waits for a companion to join her on her boulder. It's an irresistible invitation to initiate a friendship and perhaps have your picture taken with her.

Evolving in 2003, Shark Girl began as one of Casey Riordan Millard's sketchbook drawings before she became a character of her own. Shark Girl emerged from the artist's irrational fear of sharks in swimming pools as a child and symbolized a desire for normalcy. Her blue dress and bloomers arose from her admiration of Kate Greenaway, an artist from the Victorian Era. Shark Girl spent a few years posing for photos on the Ohio River before making her way to Buffalo in August 2014. The sculpture was refurbished in 2015 and placed in Canalside, where she instantly became a tourist sensation.

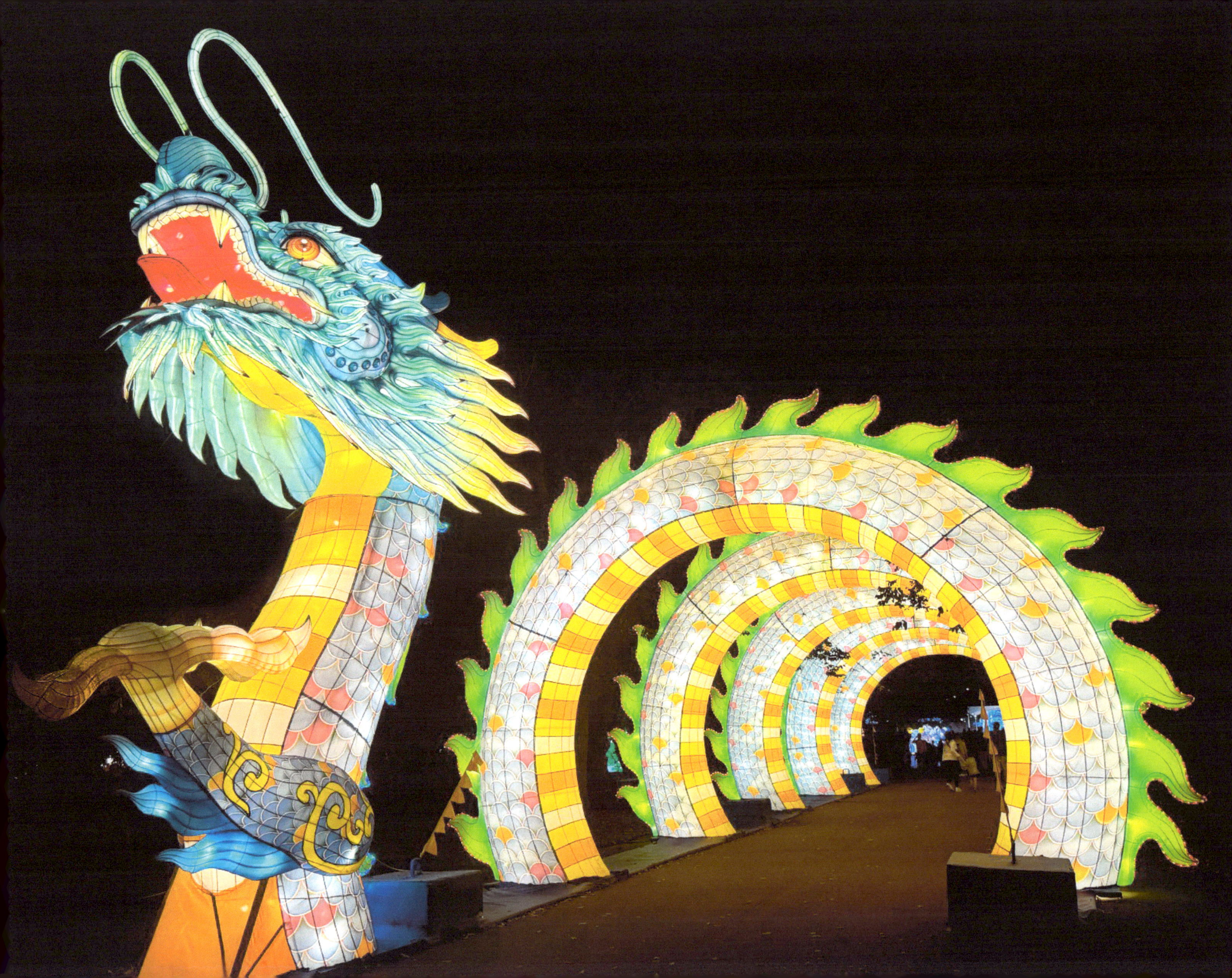

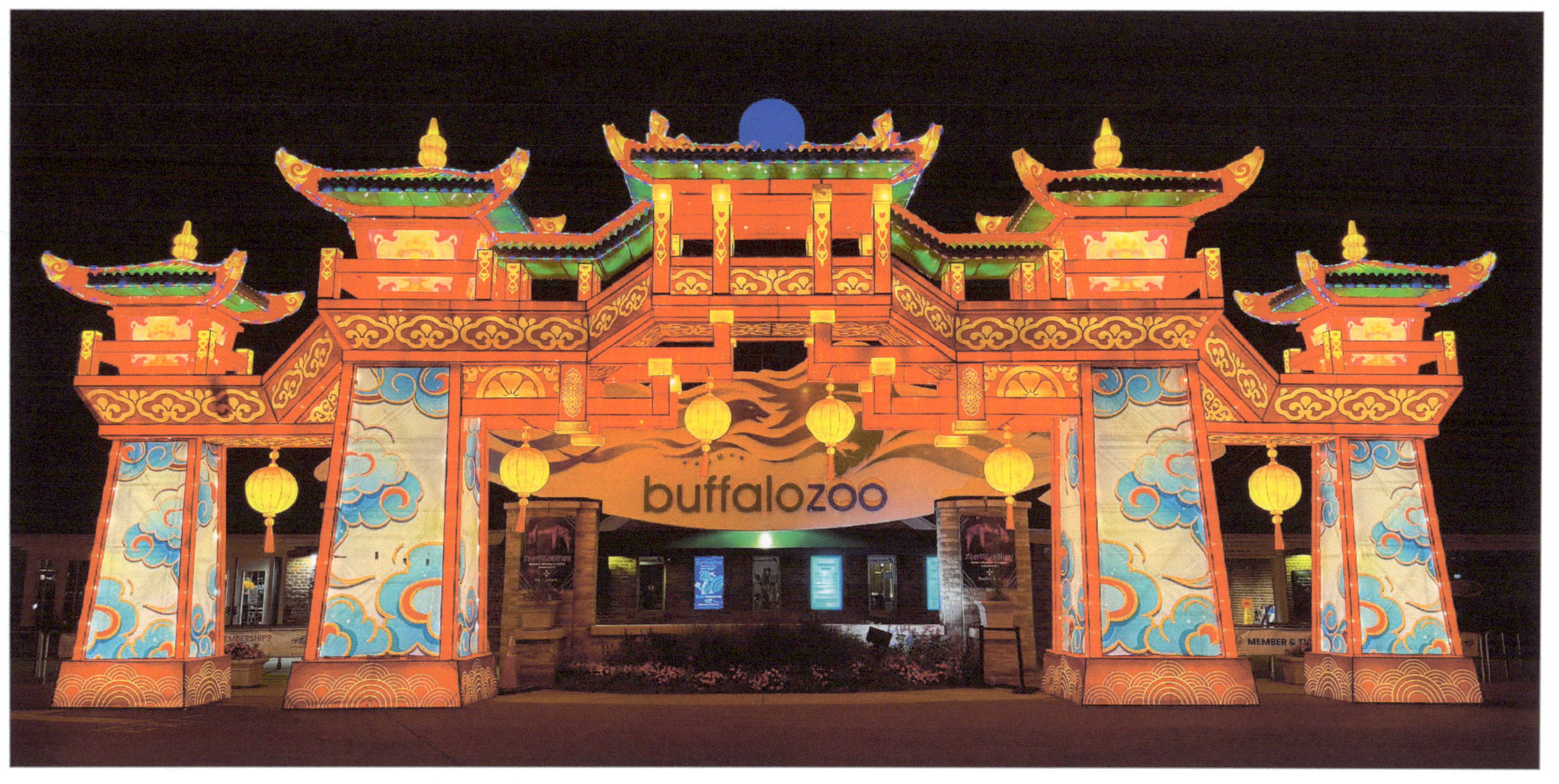

When the sun goes down, we light up

When the sun goes down and the animals are in bed for the night, the Buffalo Zoo lights up with Zoomagination: The Festival of Lanterns and Lights. This must-see summer attraction allowed visitors to immerse themselves in the 40 larger-than-life displays of beautiful florals, curious creatures from under the sea, and breathtaking landmarks worldwide. This festival celebrates the Asian culture and includes cultural performances at the Zoo's newly built performance stage.

This summer festival is the perfect spot for a night out— on top of exploring the gorgeous lanterns; visitors are invited to indulge in Asian-inspired cuisine, relax in the Beer Garden, and shop for artisan-made goods all night long.

Presented by Five Star Bank, Zoomagination has been named the most popular WNY event.

Where Buffalo Graze

Our hometown is the birthplace of many of the foods we love and ground zero for culinary treasures like Cheerios, Sahlen's Hot Dogs, Weber's Mustard, Galbani Cheese, and Bison Chip Dip. We're hooked on regional classics like chicken wings, char-grilled Ted's hot dogs, beef on weck, fish fry, and anything else that pairs well with an ice-cold brew and a football game.

Five-Points Bakery & Toast Cafe *(Right:)*
Owners Kevin & Melissa Gardener have elevated the simple elegance of toast to a whole new level. Opened a decade ago, their breads are made from 100% whole grain, local, organic ingredients from nearby farmers, and a giant helping of community.

Lloyd *(Opposite:)*
In the summer of 2010, Lloyd hit the Buffalo streets, developing the first of a growing food truck scene and proving that great food is not the sole domain of brick-and-mortar restaurants. Today, there are enough fantastic local food trucks to create their own traffic jam.

Red Top *(Below:)*
This is one of the whimsical artworks surrounding a local gem of a hotdog stand called Red Top. It's a nostalgic step back in time with a great view of Lake Erie's shoreline.

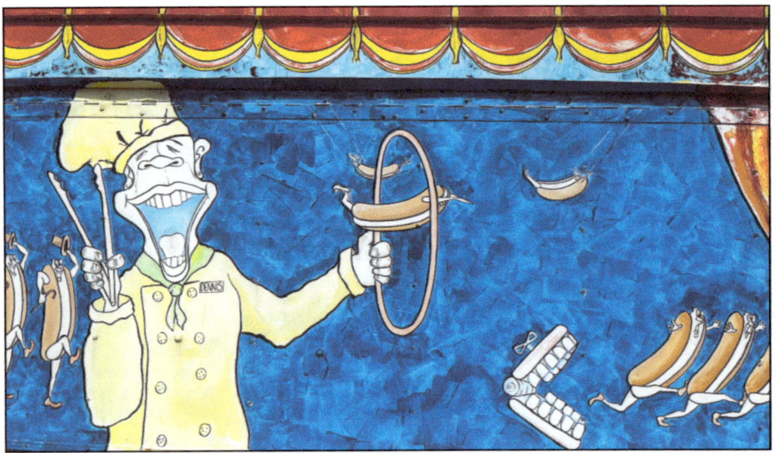

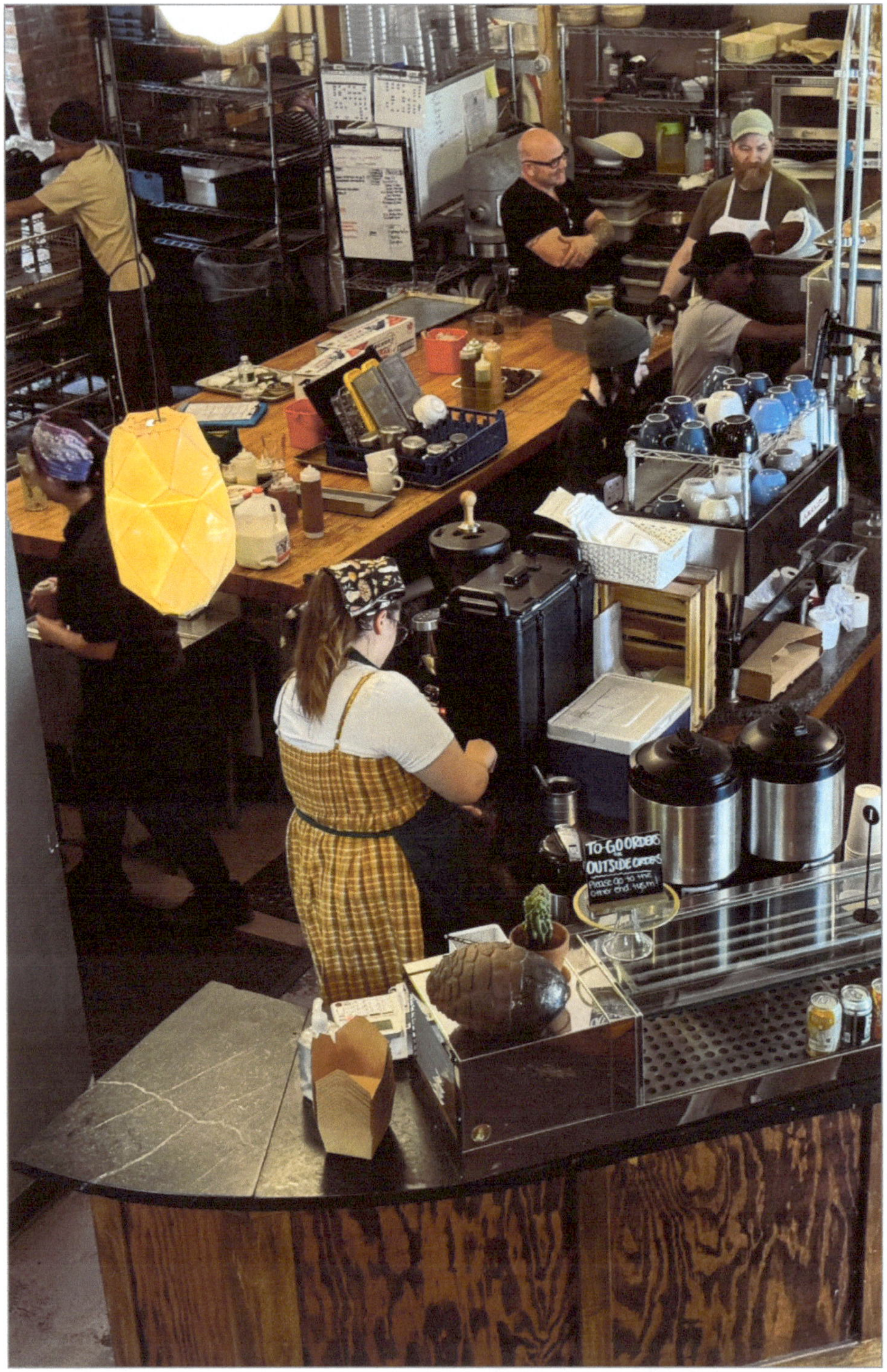

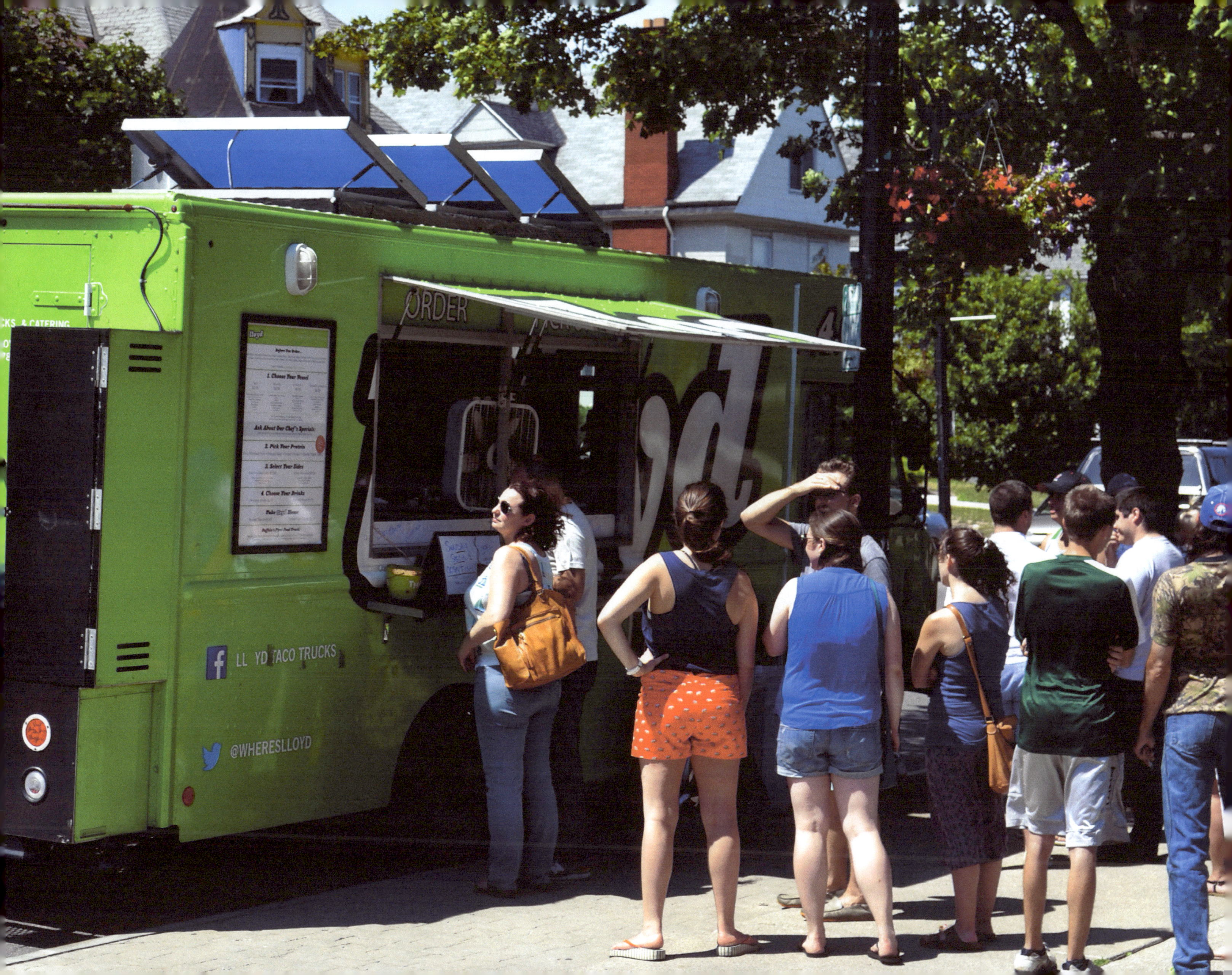
ØRDER
LL YD TACO TRUCKS
@WHERESLLOYD

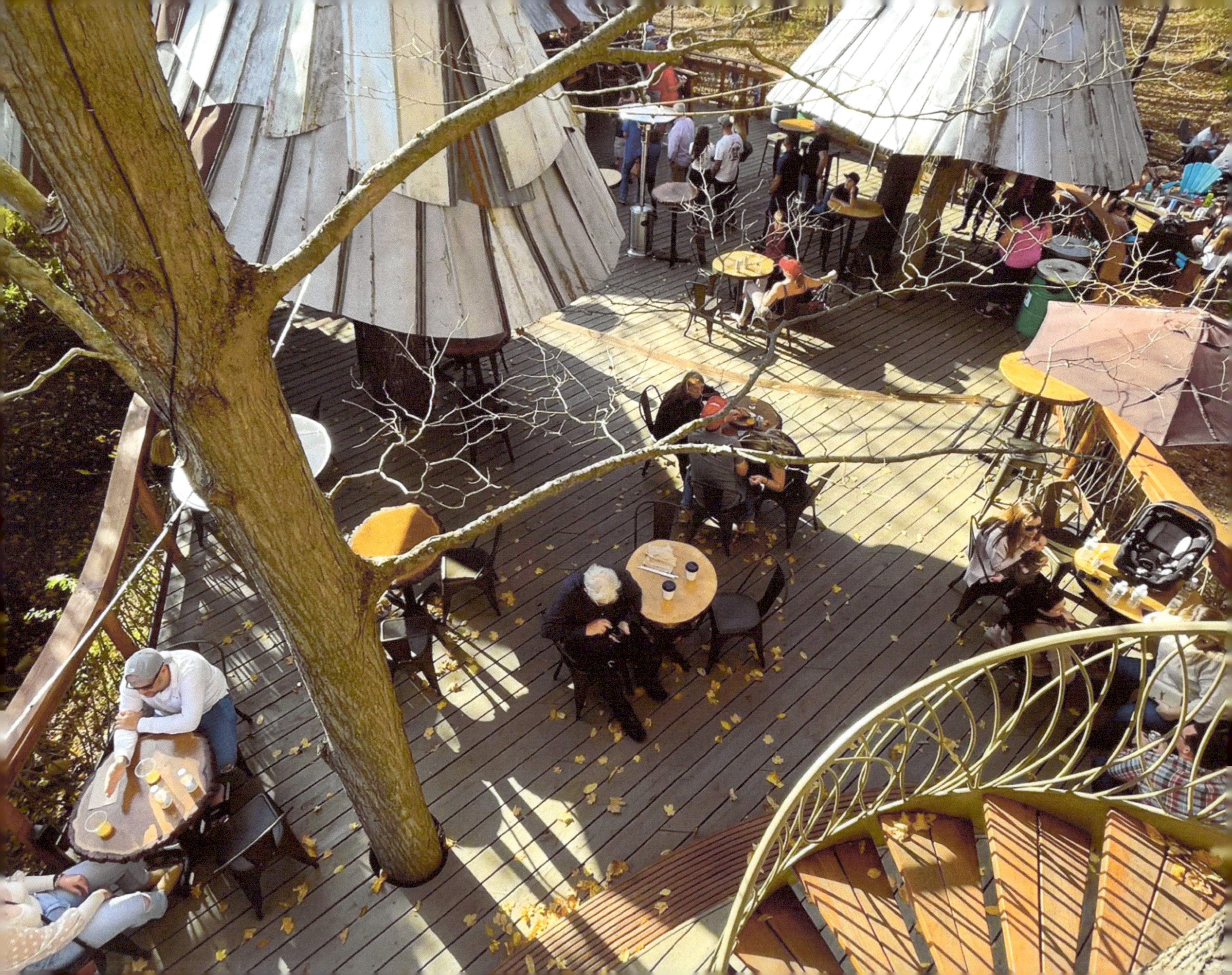

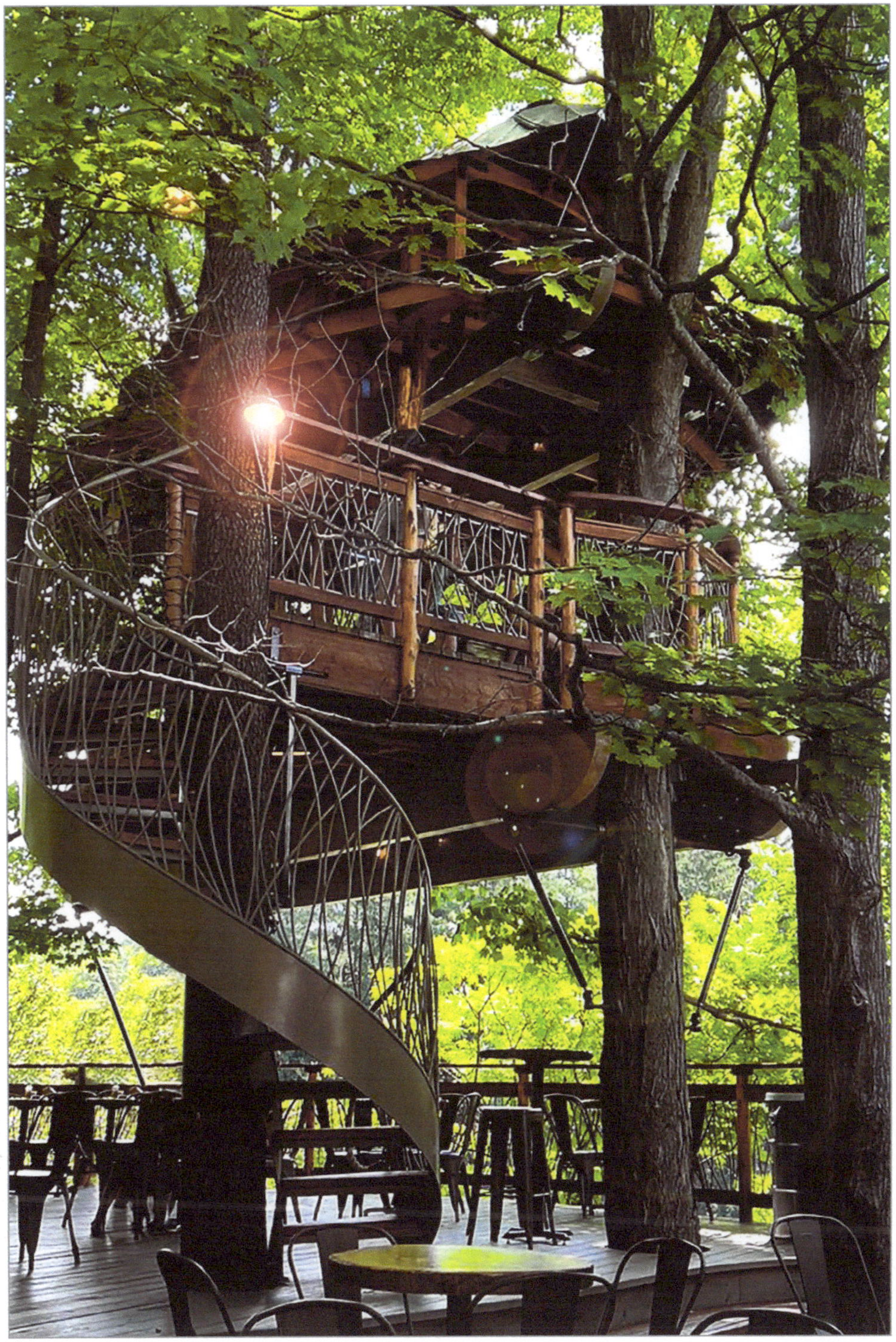

The Blueberry Treehouse Farm Café

The Blueberry Treehouse Farm Café in West Falls is an ecotourism destination that serves as a natural outdoor playground for kids and adults, an event center, an intimate music venue, a healing retreat, a café, and a community resource that supports all things local.

The Treehouse Café, a 3,000+ square foot outdoor bar and hosting area nestled in the woods and overlooking our organic U-pick blueberry fields. There are firepits all around and lights strung throughout the branches and within the treehouse creation. There's also a children's play space, music stage, nature trails,

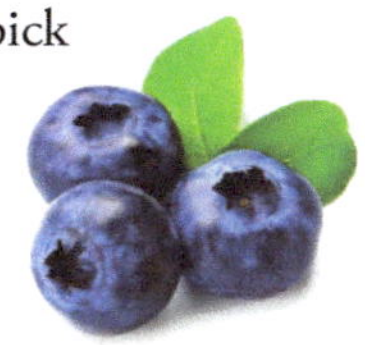

BTF hosts a huge variety of family-friendly events throughout the season, including a Bluesberry Festival this August with the West Falls Center for the Arts. Live music, including small acoustic sets, plays thrice weekly from July through August.

Whether you enjoy the food and drinks, the benefits of forest bathing, the unique treehouse architecture, this family-friendly, fun, and picturesque event space is sure to enchant.

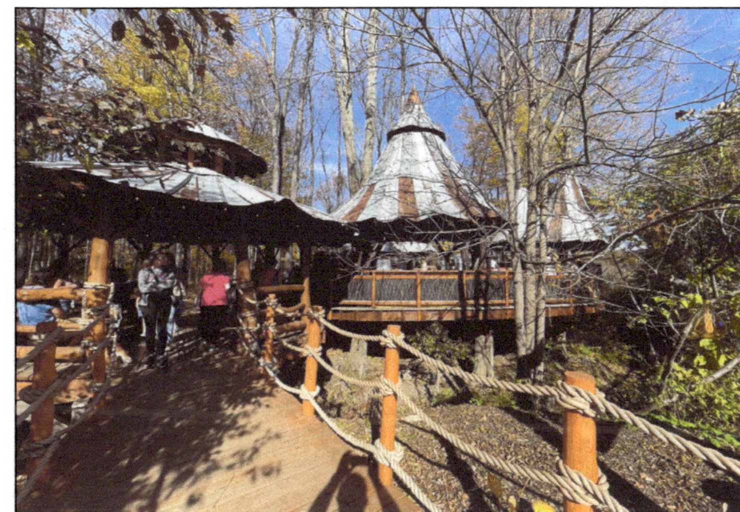

Retail Therapy

Western New York has seemingly endless ways to enjoy the shopping experience, from large malls and quaint antique shops to Elmwood boutiques and cultural gift shops. It feels good to put your money where your heart is.

Now more than ever, it is essential for us to stand together and support each other – which means that each of us has to do our part to keep local businesses open and our neighbors safe and employed.

Vidler on the Roof *(Right:)*
With over 75,000 items spread over two floors in four connected buildings, Vidler's in East Aurora is arguably the largest 5 & 10 in the world. Owned and operated by the Vidler family since its opening in 1930, this isn't just shopping; it's an adventure. It's easy to wander their squeaky wooden floors, intoxicated by the overflowing abundance of nostalgia and unique products for hours.

Broadway Market *(Opposite:)*
Since 1888, the Broadway Market has celebrated our city's food, people, and enduring legacy. The sounds and smells of this old-world public market are provided by family-owned businesses that have passed from generation to generation and are responsible for some of Buffalo's best-loved foods.

Although it's open year-round, the Broadway Market is best known as a holiday tradition. For many, it is an annual pre-Easter pilgrimage to wade through the crowds to buy their pierogi, a butter lamb, pussy willows and any confection imaginable dipped in chocolate at Strawberry Island.

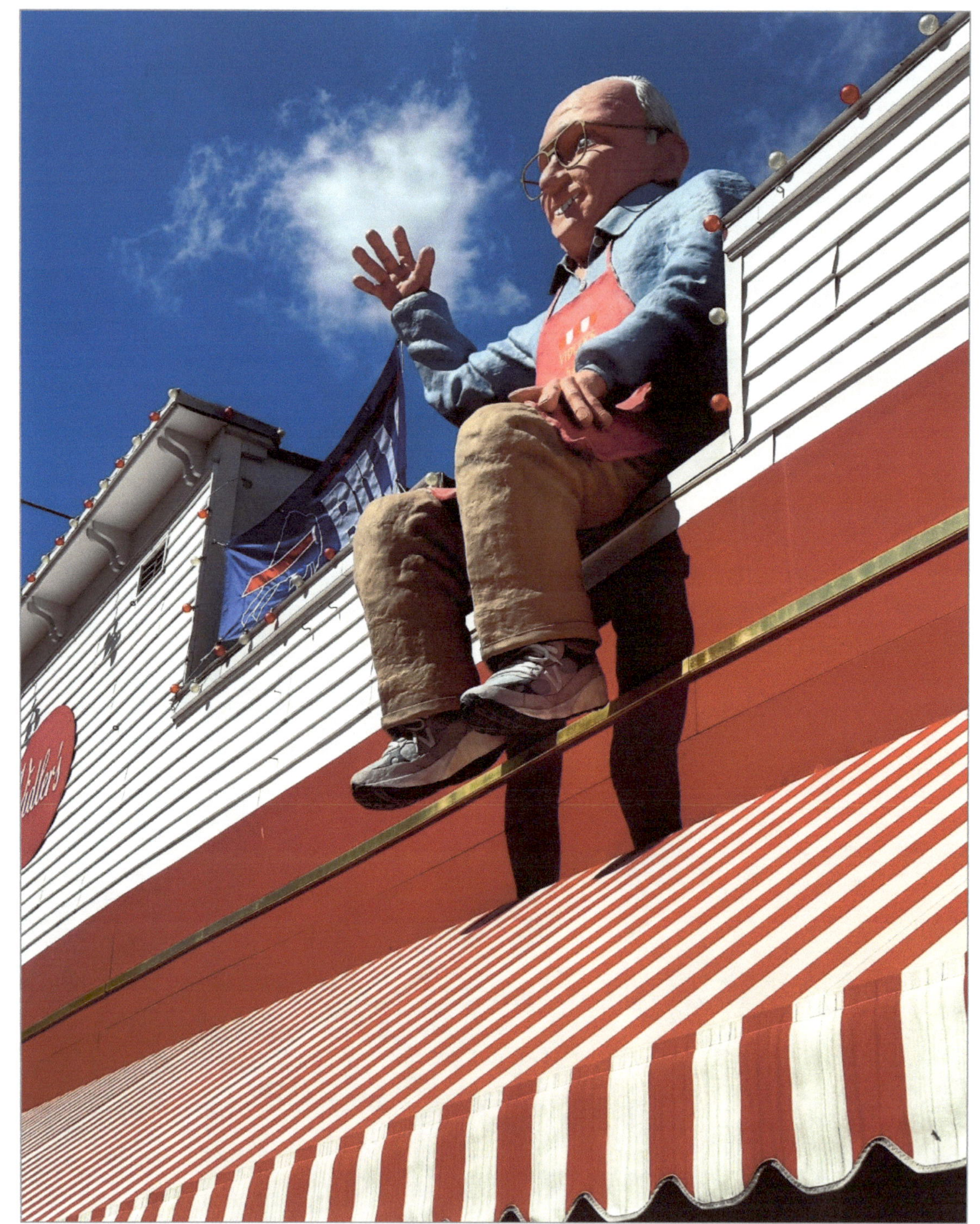

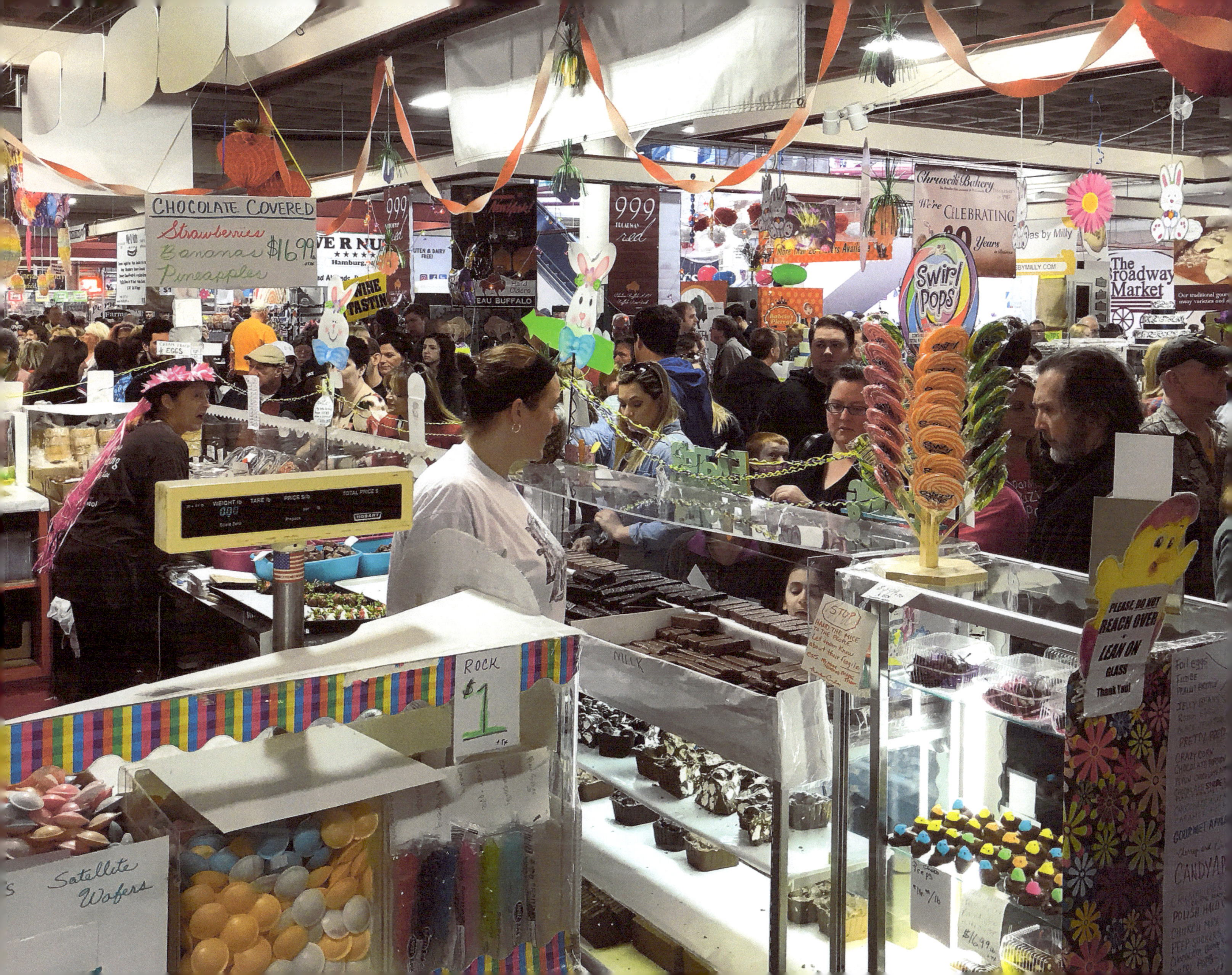
CHOCOLATE COVERED
Strawberries
Bananas $16.99
Pineapples
999
999 Broadway red
Chrusciki Bakery
We're Celebrating
Years
Swirl Pops
The Broadway Market
ROCK
$1
Satellite Wafers
PLEASE DO NOT REACH OVER
LEAN ON GLASS
Thank You!
CANDY AP

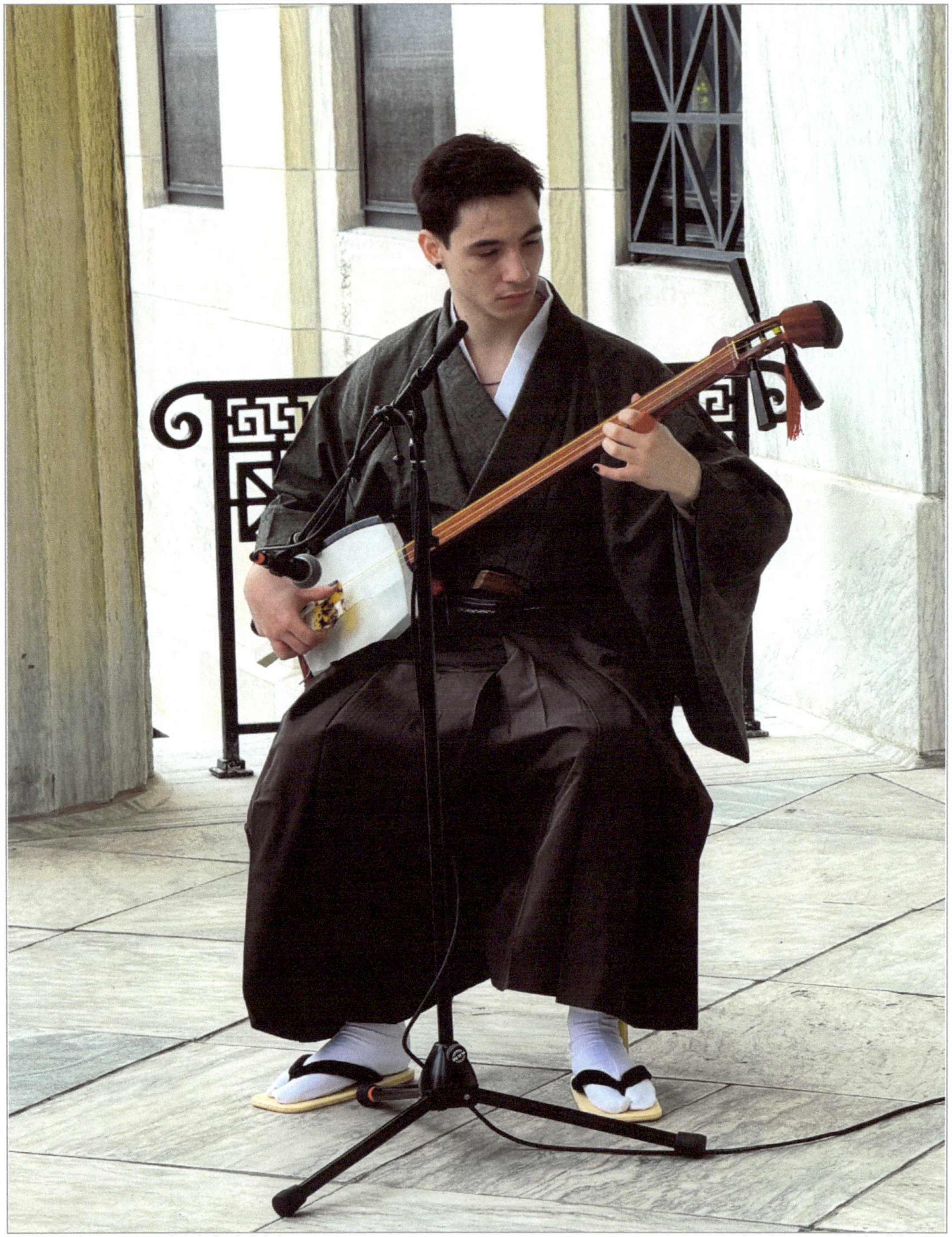

There's always something to do.

(Left:) The Japanese Garden in Delaware Park was established through a special sister-city initiative between Kanazawa, Japan and Buffalo. For over a decade the garden has been home to the Buffalo Cherry Blossom Festival, which seeks to celebrate the blossoming of the 40 Cherry Blossom trees in the garden. Visitors to the Festival are treated to music, displays, and activities that build awareness of Japanese culture.

(Below:) Creative Mornings Buffalo is a breakfast lecture series that celebrates the power of the creative community. Its concept is elegantly simple: breakfast and a short talk, one Friday morning a month. Each event is free of charge and open to anyone because anchored to their core is the belief that because everyone is creative, everyone is welcome. Attendees gather in cities around the world to enjoy friendly face-to-face connections and a months worth of encouragement. And by 10 a.m., they're all on their way to work.

(Opposite:) Giant foam party at Ralph Wilson Park Conservancy Kick Off the Summer festivities.

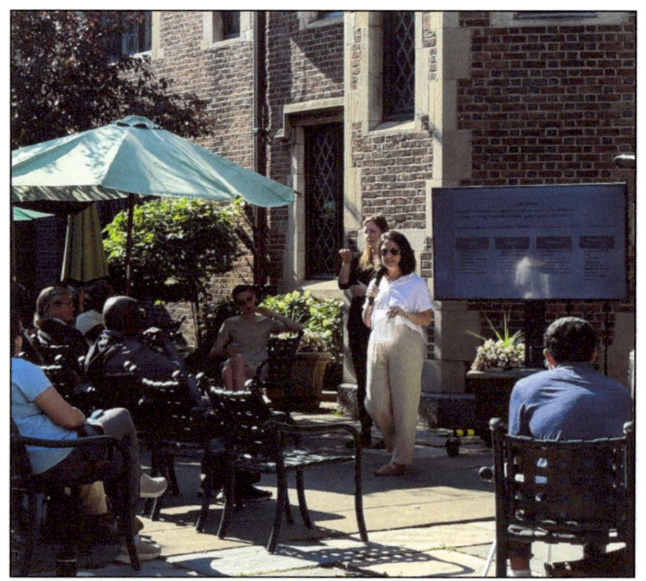

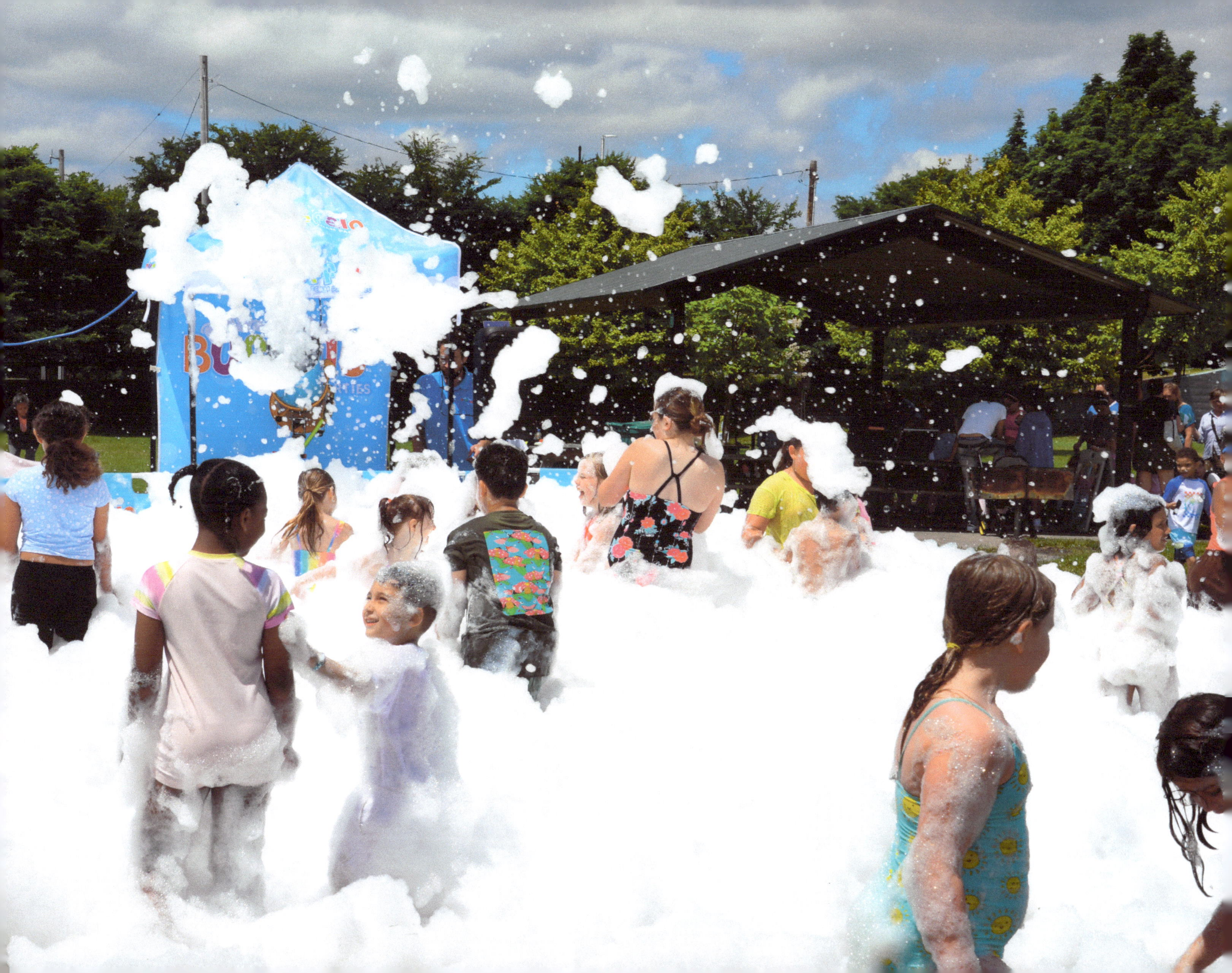

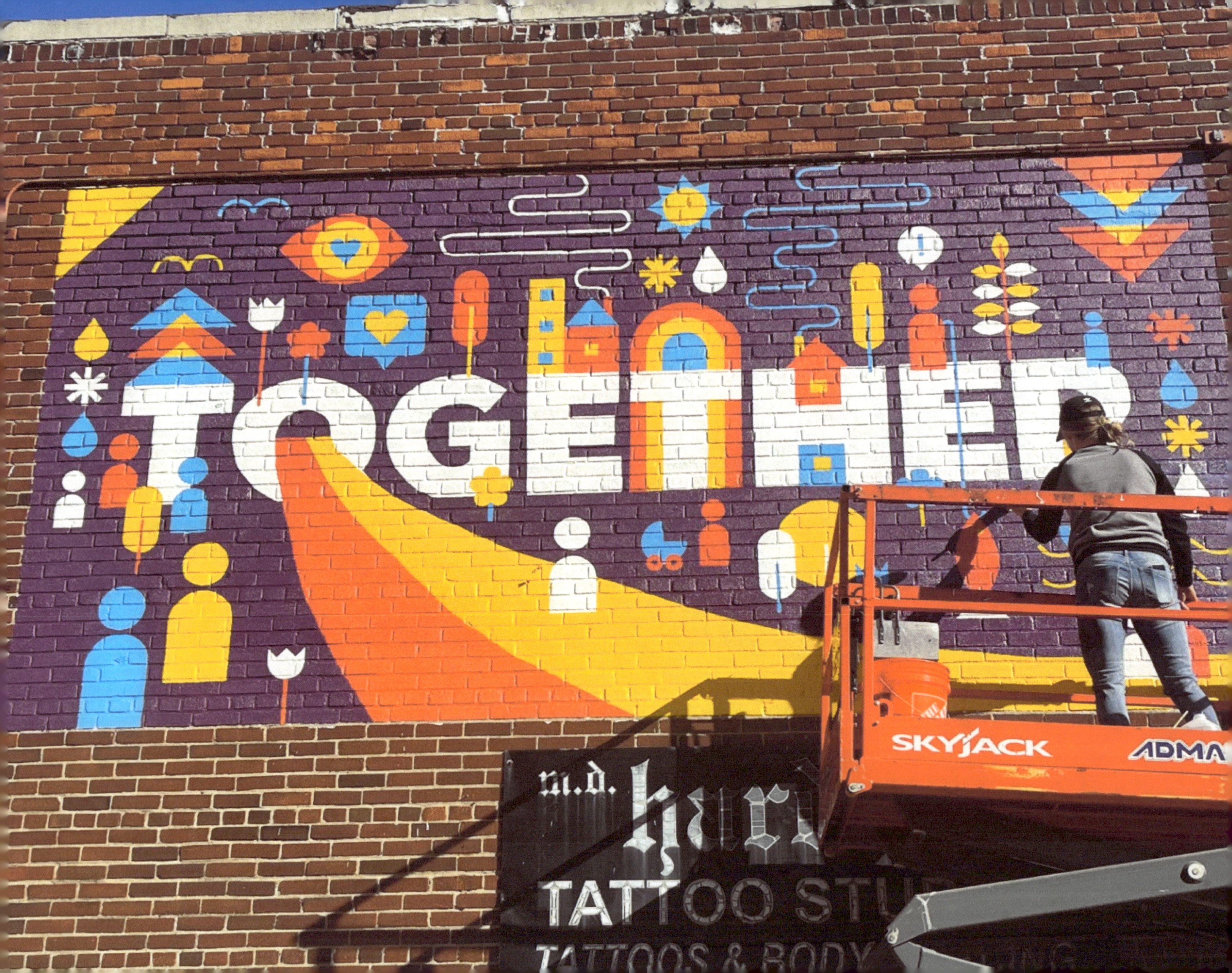

TOGETHER
m.d.
TATTOO
SKYJACK

A Brilliant Future

"We imagine a vital, vibrant City of Buffalo that is a world leader in research, design, innovation, and entrepreneurship supporting a flourishing small business ecosystem that thrives on collaboration and community connections in an environment that fosters sustainability, health, and well-being."

– Matt Enstice, President & CEO
Buffalo Niagara Medical Campus

While as a city and a region we still have a ways to go, there is a noticeable sea change taking place here. There's a noticeable new spring in our walk and twinkle in our eye knowing that our trajectory is changing toward the positive.

The signs are everywhere. Our skyline is quickly morphing as construction cranes dot the horizon. High technology manufacturing is sprouting up where "rust belt" steel plants once stood. The Buffalo Niagara Medical Campus is now home to the UB Medical School and John R. Oishei Children's Hospital. 43 North has been an amazing catalyst for entrepreneurial innovation, and Roswell Park is making new discoveries about cancer every day and using these discoveries to set the global standards for how to treat it.

Our youth is beginning to return or deciding not to leave at all. And the Waterfront is bustling at a rate few thought was possible.

Our foot is firmly on the gas pedal and there is a palpable excitement about what is around the next corner. Once again we're "Talkin' Proud" because there truly is so much to love.

(Opposite:) Casey Kelly Perez is the artist behind the mural. It is located at 902 Elmwood Avenue,

About the Author

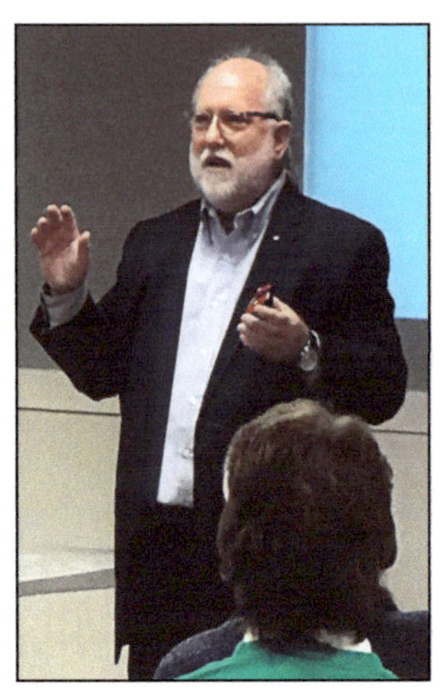

Mark Donnelly, PhD., is an artist, educator, community activist, Freemason, a proud husband and father, and a man seldom separated from his camera.

As one of WNY's most enthusiastic cheerleaders, Dr. Donnelly is the author of several books on our great city's history, waterfront, architecture, and weather. He's also written novelty cookbooks and a series of children's books.

As one of the regions premier photographers, his work has appeared in dozens of exhibitions and galleries, including the Albright-Knox Art Gallery, ZGM Fine Arts, Burchfield-Penney Art Center, Rodman Hall Arts Centre, and the Art Gallery of Hamilton.

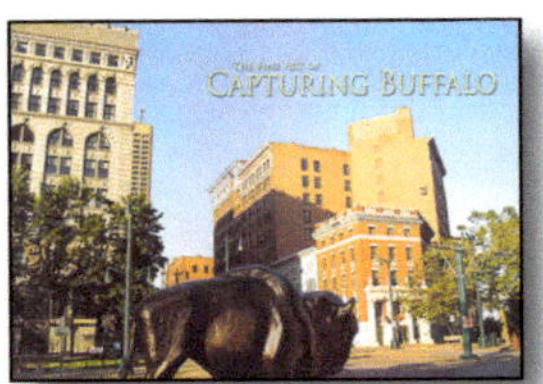

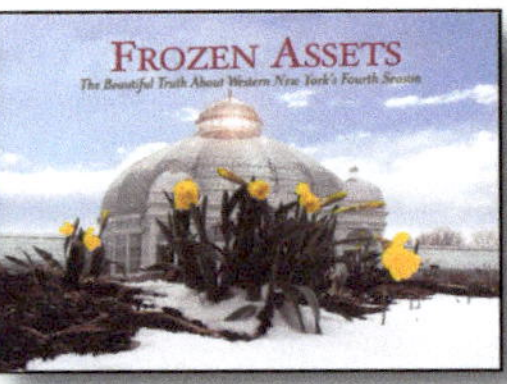

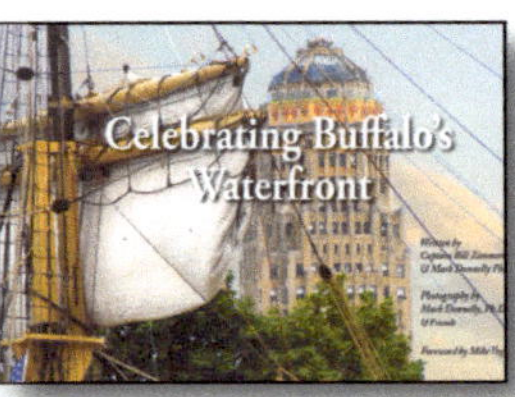

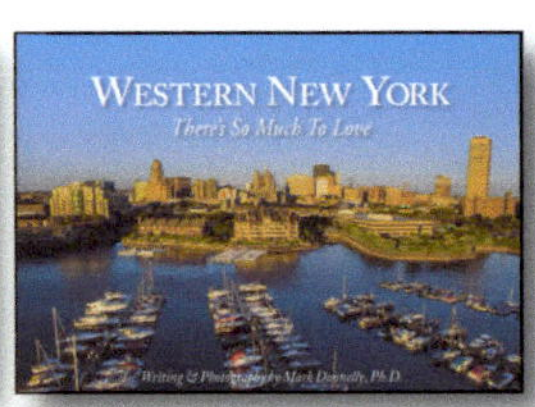

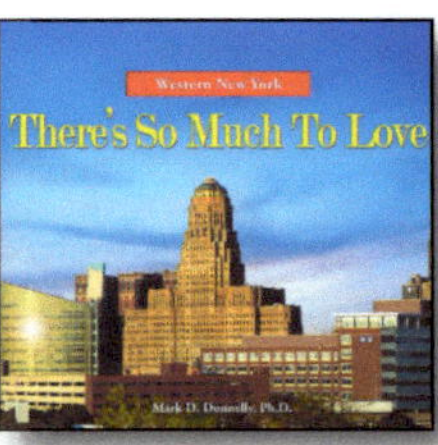

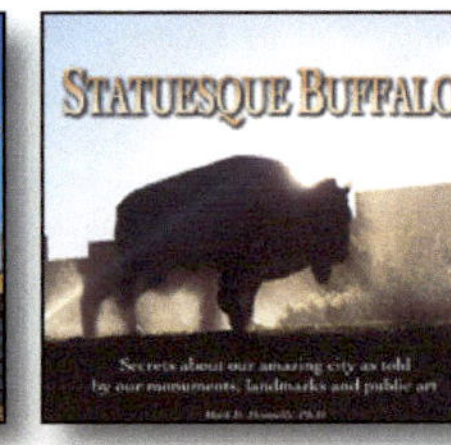

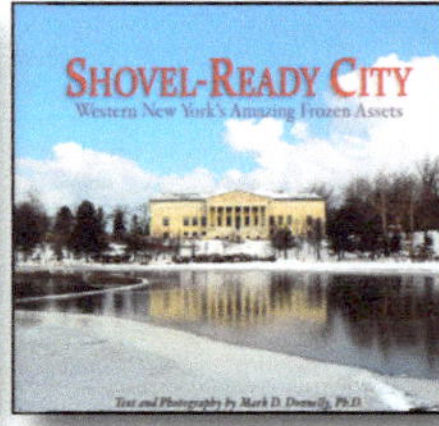

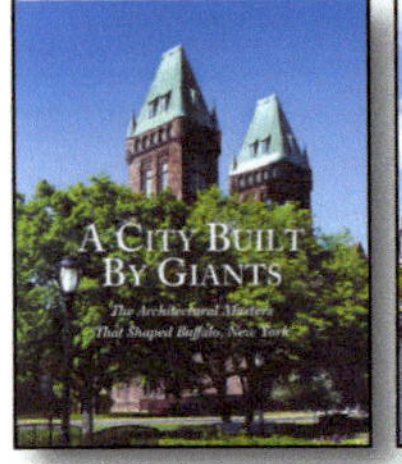

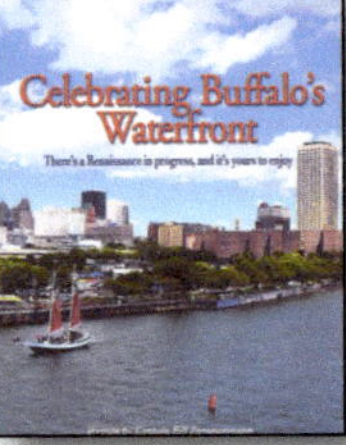

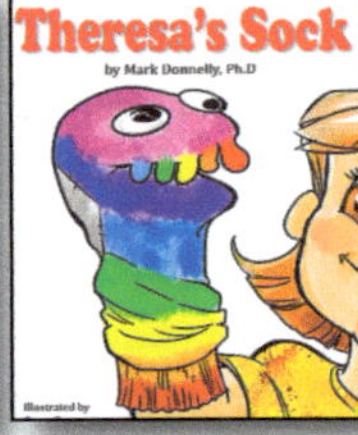

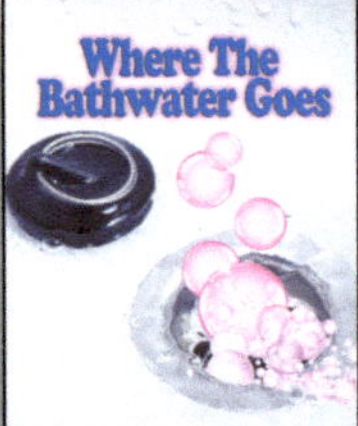

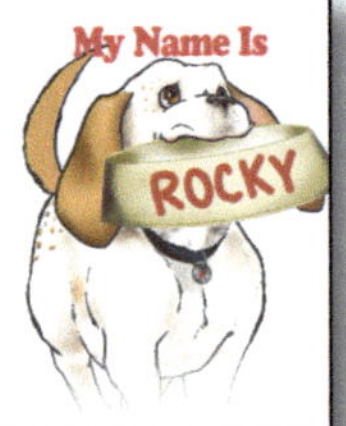

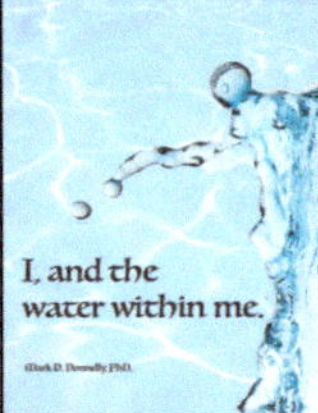

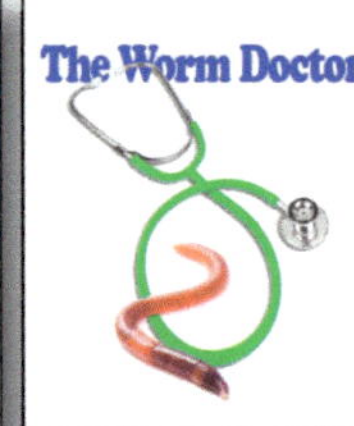

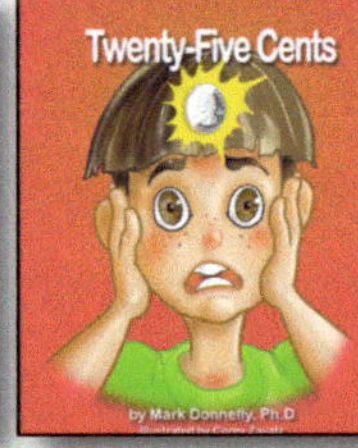

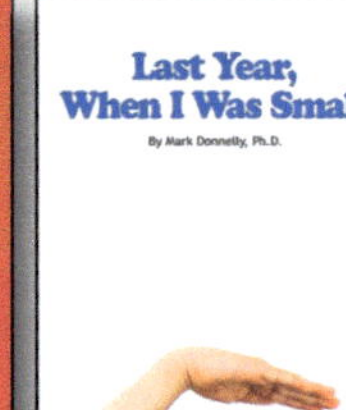

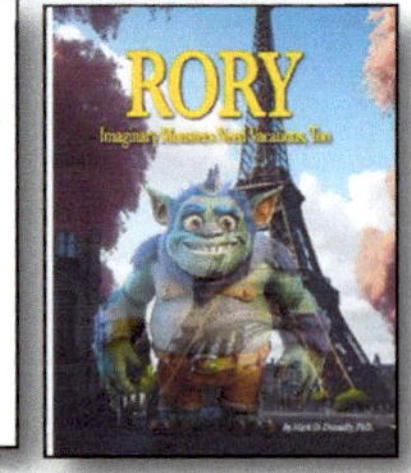

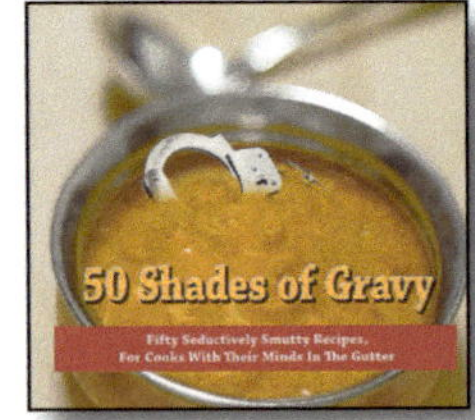

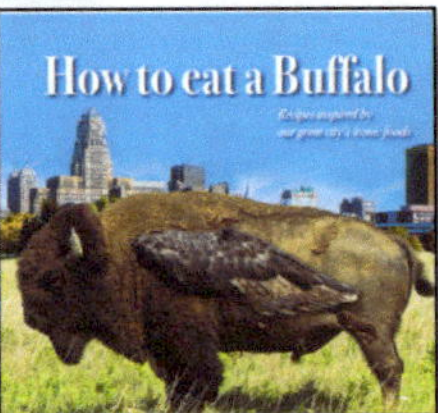

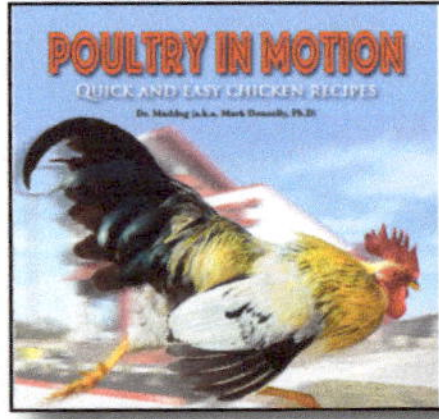

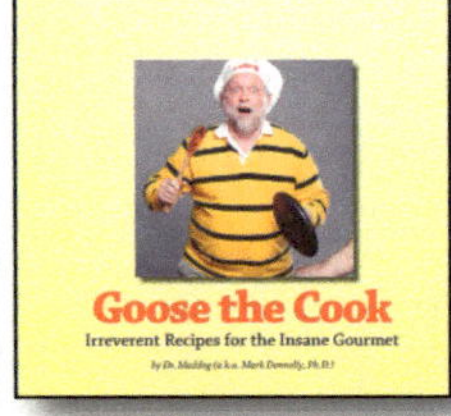

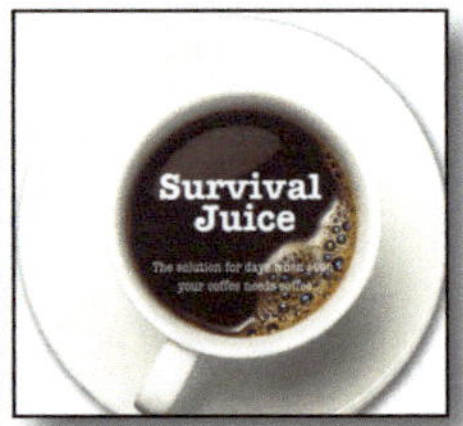

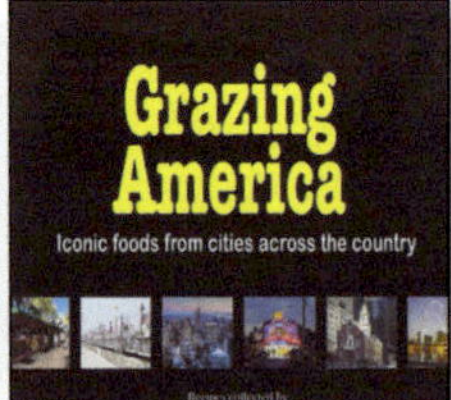

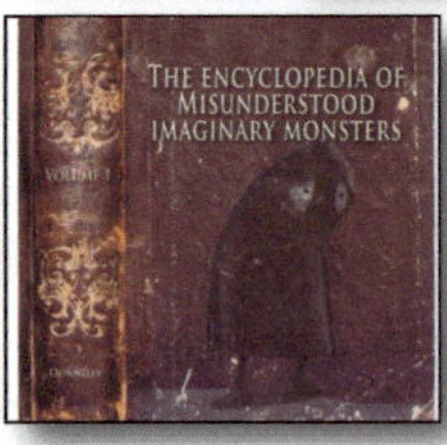

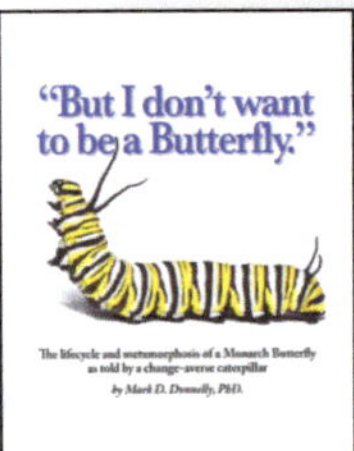

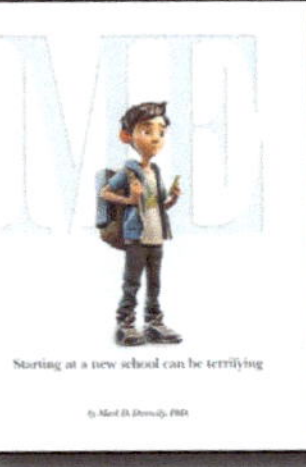

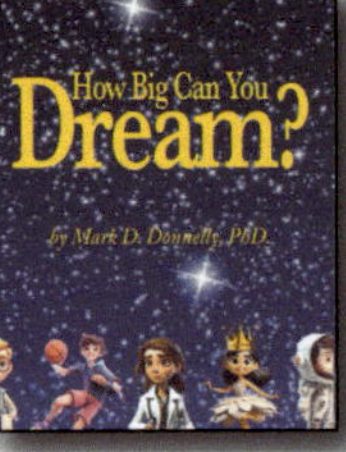

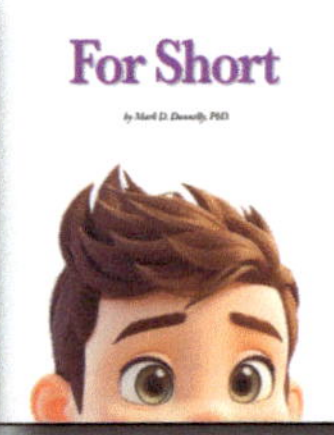

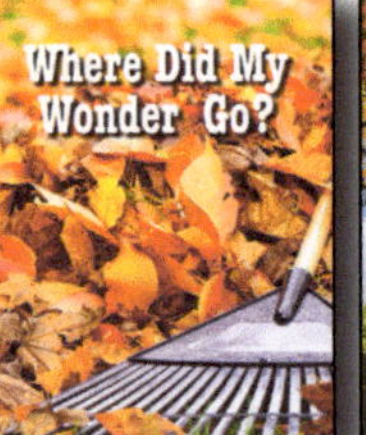

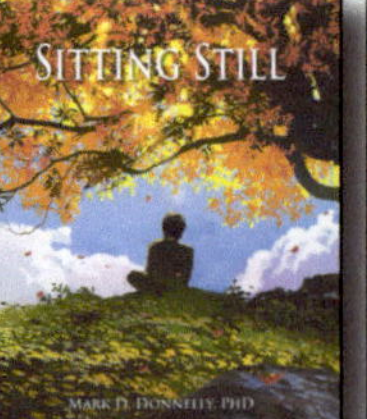

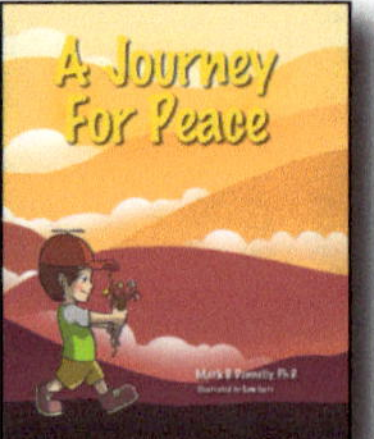

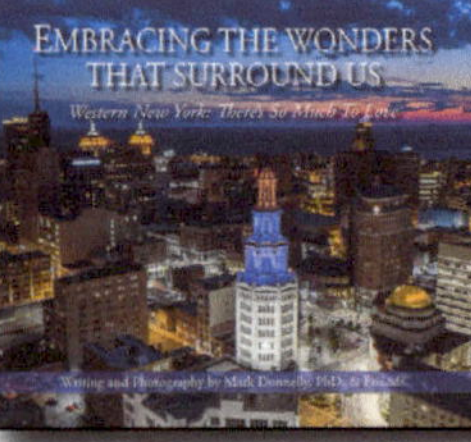

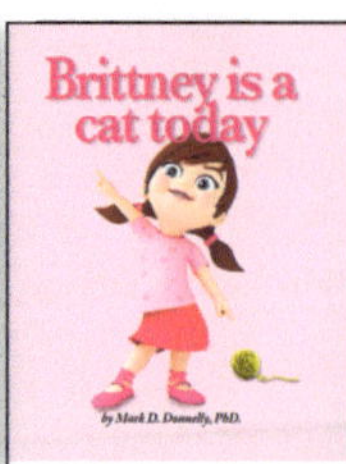

www.ingramcontent.com/pod-product-compliance
Lightning Source LLC
LaVergne TN
LVHW072327100826
845147LV00004B/658

9781956688436